Roamer Round The World

Roamer Round The World

Bob (Cap'n Bob) Burns

Compiled and edited by
Terry Burns

ROAMER
BOOKS

ISBN 978-0-9565241-0-2

Printed and bound in Great Britain by
MPG Books Group, Bodmin and King's Lynn

First published in the UK in 2010 by

ROAMER
BOOKS

Roamer Books
41 Prince Charles Close, Southwick, Brighton, East Sussex BN42 4PQ

For the family
and all the fantastic friends
who helped me as I sailed around the world

A Brotherly Introduction

Even after all these years I still find it very difficult to imagine how Bob managed to complete his circumnavigation. But then the realisation of how grimly determined he is once he has a project in his sights kicks in, and his seamanship, courage and the ability to make decisions under very difficult climatic conditions make me realise the reasons for a successful completion of his ambition.

The usual schoolboy pursuits of ball games were not Bob's preference – he would head for the sea from our home near Brighton Racecourse to immerse himself in anything remotely nautical. Certainly not a surprise then that when he left school at the first opportunity on a Friday, and by Monday had signed on as a Boy Seaman in the Royal Navy at Portsmouth at the age of 15.

Appointed somewhat glibly as Project Manager for the voyage I realised very quickly just what a job he had taken on. The planning and construction of 'Roamer' is all contained in the story and, as the days progress, all the stress and strains of his voyage paint a dramatic picture. Three times he nearly lost his life and there were other numerous occasions when the voyage came close to ending.

The Falkland Islands episode was an example of Bob berating himself for staying just one night ashore and the consequences of the damage sustained by 'Roamer' haunted Bob for many months. But he persevered and after some 27,000 miles and 28 months, I was at Falmouth shortly after his arrival and can remember quite clearly just how gaunt, tired and thin he was after quite a battering off Lands End.

As you read of Bob's voyage perhaps you, too will grasp a sense of his exploits and, like me, feel a sense of pride and relief for his welcome return.

And finally, my sincere thanks to the *Evening Argus* of Brighton, now called *The Argus*, for allowing us to show cuttings from their newspapers within this book.

Terry Burns
February 2010

Preview

Midway through the forenoon of a cold and blustery English "Summer Sunday", in late July 1985, a chunky, black, unusual looking yacht motors out of the inner Harbour of the ancient Cornish port of Penzance.

"Where are you bound?" calls the lockmaster.

"Cape Town, South Africa."

"Blimey, the best of luck to you then."

The sailor calls his thanks, and continues out into the choppy waters of Mount's Bay, then to the west a little to gain a lee under Newlyn. Here he awaits the Shipping Forecast, grunts his semi-approval of its information, and hoists some sail on each of the two unstayed wooden masts. Shutting down the engine, he heads Southwest, out into the open sea.

For two days, "Roamer", for that is the name on the bows of this chunky black schooner, sails uncomfortably over the grey waves of the Channel approaches, past the famous lighthouses, the Longships, the Wolf, the Bishop Rock. Past the Scilly Isles, making to the Southwest to clear the land.

Then, as if by magic, having escaped from the English "summer", the grey clouds clear, the wind settles in the Nor'west, and the lone sailor and his ship sail across the calm blue waters of the Bay of Biscay.

As they sail on towards Madeira and the Canary Islands, the skipper of ship becomes more relaxed, the tension of the past months of work and preparation, falling from him. He is happy to sit in the sun-filled cockpit doing very little, savouring the peace and quiet he has long sought. Happy he is that at last he has shaken off the bonds of the land and is sailing on the long-awaited voyage of self discovery, on the way to achieving his greatest ambition to sail around the World – Alone.

As he and his bonny ship as he calls her, make to the South in the sun and warm breeze, the sailor gives vent to the occasional chuckle, and even sometimes an out-loud laugh at the sheer pleasure and excitement of it all, behaviour which would surprise his small circle of family and friends could they but hear! He is not renowned for having a great sense of humour – as he thinks that here is common working chap Bob Burns, born and bred in his beloved Brighton a-sailing his own ship southwards in the mighty Atlantic.

Preface

It has been said that there is in everyone, at least one book. Maybe this will be my only one. If so, I'll be quite happy, I've enjoyed writing it, enjoyed seeing it grow over the years. For it was written as "The Project" went along. All the preliminary chapters were written before the voyage began, all the voyage chapters were written, and typed, at sea, and, with exception to the last few weeks, were completed before the end of the voyage.

It is my first book, my first venture into the printed word, save for some magazine articles, and anyone seeking flowery language, or perfect grammar may be disappointed. I will be happy if my book is described as unusual, but interesting and informative.

My aim is to tell a story, a true story, of how an ordinary chap like me dreamed up, and brought into being, a small but rather special ship, designed to allow him to carry out his ambition to do something rather special in his life, and then how he went and did it.

I hope that the book will not only entertain, as a story of a voyage round the world, but, if any reader is contemplating a similar project, that it will be an aid in avoiding the problems and pitfalls which I suffered in the creation of Roamer, and give helpful hints and encouragement for the actual carrying out of any such voyage.

I hope you will enjoy accompanying me on the voyage, enjoy the good times, thrill to the excitements, but also share the pain and depression of the bad times, the disasters.

But – If you should meet me, and ask, "Was it all worth it, Bob?" you will only get one answer.

"Oh yes. It was."

Acknowledgements

There will be no organisations or contractors on this "thank you" page. They will be found in an Appendix, and their helpfulness or otherwise, can be read in the text.

Here, I should like to record personal thanks to Friends and Family who have helped me, for free, and without seeking anything from me.

To you all, I say, Thank You.

Mum, for being my No. 1 Fan, and Roamer's first visitor.

Terry and Brenda, Terence, Mike, Sue, Sandie.

Doreen, Lisa, David, Gareth.

The family, who never said, "Don't do it".

John Ridgway, for getting me back to sea after too many years ashore, we weren't always the best of friends, but life has its ups and downs. Also for the two "Maxims". "Grit the teeth, Bob", and, "Nothing worthwhile is achieved easily".

Marie-Christine Ridgway, Lance and Ada Bell, for many kindnesses whilst at Ardmore.

Terry for being the hardworking, unpaid, project manager and for lots of transport help. And Brenda, for putting up with my various stores and belongings at "76" and for feeding me.

Eileen Clark, at Wadebridge, for cosy digs and lovely food, during "the building"

Mr. Elcock, for daring to do the "Myringoplasty" on my ear.

Mick Spurgeon, for help with the electrics, and for putting a "spark" of knowledge into me.

Roy and Carol, of "Spray", Roy for electrical advice, both for hot coffee and a warm ship, in the cold winter days.

Cliff Groves, the only "soldier" prepared to be a sailor in the cold days of the early sea trials. Remember Cliff, you were the first to "drive" her to sea.

Mike Richey of "Jester", for many helpful suggestions. (I'd have been lost without those cringle eyes, Mike.)

The Beguiristains, particularly my young friend Becky, for being good friends and neighbours. My wish is that you may get to sea again one day.

At the "Naming and Leaving party", Thanks to –

Sandie, for "doing the honours" so well.
Mum and Doreen, for the lovely grub.
Doreen, for the "Bon Voyage" cake.
"Stormalong" David, for being a good first mate.
Tom and Kathy of the "Wellington", for the "hampers".
Jack and Betty of the "Roundhill". for the "Pussers rum".
Bert and Eileen, many thanks for the "you-know-what".
Cliff, Neil, and Gazy for the Australia Pilot.
Phoenix Brewery, for the beer.

And, for various food and drink and other goodies, thanks to –
Des and Shelia, Suzy and Andy, Mick and Sue, Ronnie the Birdman, Dan and Delia, Angie, and anyone else I may have missed in the confusion. Thanks to everyone who came to see me off.

Brooke Bond Oxo, for the food parcel.
Golden Wonder, for the 144 Pot Noodles and Rice.
Damart Thermolactyl, for their very warm clothing.
L. V. Motors, for the last minute gift of their wonderful "Aerogen 50".

In the West Country:-
Ashley Woods and the crew of "Magnum", for saving me in the Scillies.
Alan and Rosie Cummins, Smokey the Boatman, and all friends at the Falmouth Marina Club.
Mrs. Boon for the woollen mittens.
Mr. Boon for the "Hair shirt".
Robin and Shirley Boon for a delicious fruit cake.

At Lambert's Bay, South Africa, Jan Hunter and the Golf Club, for saving me with beer and a braai, after 125 days at sea.

At Port Owen. What can I say about Port Owen? It's all in the book, "A great big thanks to all at Port Owen, Goodbye, Good Luck, I had to get going".

At Cape Town. Joan Fry, Bobby Cattemore, and all other friends at the Royal Cape Yacht Club.

Syd Crocker and family, Jim and Rosie.

At Hobart, Alan McCormic, Frank Bennett, and the Royal Yacht Club of Tasmania. Geoff Gore and the guys in Harbour Control.

All friends around Constitution Dock, at the "Red Lion", and at the "Telegraph". John and Jill Day, Vic Reynolds, Joan and Louisa Kley, The "Mercury" newspaper.

At Sydney. Peter and Jan Bradley, for looking after me so splendidly. The Sydney Bus Drivers.

At Canberra. Merv and Elizabeth Palmer.

At Port Stanley.
Ron and Friends at the "Globe".
Bill and Friends at the "Victory".
Des and Mrs King at the "Upland Goose".
Mike McKie, my saviour, and his friends, Thanks Guys.
Les Halliday and the Harbour Office Staff.

Bob and Rose Peart, and Darren. And, Bill Roberts, Ron the Blacksmith, Tim and Ronnie, Billy and Dennis, "old" Bill, Kenny, Taffy, Riley, Les, Micky, Ron, Yvonne, Rampo, Jill, the Bank Staff, The Post office staff, F.I.C staff, etc.

In fact all "the good people of Stanley".

At Recife. The "Thunderbirds", Terry, Glynis, Samantha and Michelle Hawkins Thanks gang, for beer and braai, on the "wrong" side of the Atlantic.

Flavio and Regina, the friendly Yacht Club staff.

Once again, Thanks Folks, and if I've missed anyone, my apologies, its been a long project.

Bob

Contents

A Brotherly Introduction 7

Preview 9

Preface 11

Acknowledgements 12

Chapter 1   Early Days 17

Chapter 2   1982 – Roamer Takes Shape 23

Chapter 3   1983 – Year of the Building 28

Chapter 4   1984 – Hull into Ship 36

Chapter 5   Afloat – Early Sea Trials 47

Chapter 6   Sea Trials 62

Chapter 7   Off to the Start – Brighton to Falmouth 77

Chapter 8   The Voyage – Falmouth to the Equator 84

Chapter 9   The Voyage – The Equator to South Africa 106

Chapter 10   South African Interlude 137

Chapter 11   Leg 2 – Cape Town to Hobart 153

Chapter 12   Australian Interlude: The Friendly Country 177

Chapter 13   Leg 3 – Hobart to Stanley 184

Chapter 14   Port Stanley – Triumph and Disaster 202

Chapter 15   Leg 4 – Port Stanley to Recife – The Painful Voyage .. 221

Chapter 16   Rest at Recife – Hot and Steamy 239

Chapter 17   Leg 5 – Recife to Falmouth 249

Afterword 282

Appendices 290

Chapter One

Early Days

Plenty of people can be met within a Yacht Club or on the jetty who will tell you "I would love to do what you're doing but ... but the mortgage, the wife, the kids, the job."

But to achieve ambitions, there can be no buts.

I'm Bob Burns and I'm going to tell you how I got my ship and how I sailed her around the world alone.

My ship is "Roamer" a 36-feet, steel, Junk-rigged schooner, which I will be describing to you in detail shortly. She and I are a team. We have known each other since she was a pile of steel plates on the floor of a workshop in Cornwall. I watched her take shape, had her built as strongly as possible, solved all the problems of getting her painted, fitted out, launched and finally turned in to one of the most seaworthy sailing ships afloat.

How is it possible that I, an ordinary working chap, has been able to get together the money for this fine ship and her equipment, and the necessary knowledge and experience to dare set out on this voyage? It is the sailor's equivalent of a mountaineer's attempt to climb Mount Everest.

For the answers we have to go back many years to find a skinny, shy boy, spending many hours on his own gazing out to sea from the hills of East Brighton. Cycling to the ports of Newhaven to the East, and Shoreham to the West, to gaze enraptured at the ships in those ports dreaming of their voyages across the seas.

Although my parents struggled hard to give me a good education, scraping together the money for my Varndean School uniform, schooling wasn't in my heart. Varndean was self-defeating, as its South facing classroom windows gave me a wonderful view of ships far out to sea!

So, at the age of fifteen, with my head packed full of ships and the sea, into the Royal Navy I went and served for nearly 12 years. I was not a great success. "A good seaman, but too much of a rebel." as one of my officers described me. But, the Navy filled out the skinny frame I had and did make a seaman of me, confirming to me that I loved the sailors life, if not the uniformed life of the Royal Navy.

Probably the best thing the Navy did for me though was to introduce me to sailing, firstly at the "Boys" training establishment at Gosport, Portsmouth, and then on the various ships in which I served. All through my Navy days I was always a member of each ship's sailing club, and sailed in many diverse places such as Bermuda, Singapore, Hong Kong, Malta and Greece. I was even sailing Coxswain to the Commander-in-Chief, Portsmouth for a year in 1963.

On leaving the Navy in 1966, I lost touch with the sea to a great extent, mainly with the need to earn a living in 'Civvy Street'. I was an aerial Rigger in the Civil Aviation Authority for 8 years, then took a big chance, threw up my Chargehand Riggers job, and started as a Roustabout on the North Sea oil rigs. At 34, I was rather old for the tough life out there but I worked hard, kept my mouth shut and my eyes open as the saying goes, and was quite a success. I took the occasional sailing holiday but wasn't really in touch with the sea until 1976.

On the rigs I worked two weeks on and then had two weeks off. I took to touring the Scottish Highlands in my Volkswagen campervan from the rig's base in Aberdeen. This routine had dual benefits, allowing me access to my second love, the mountains, and keeping me, to a large degree, from my enemy strong alcohol. I was earning good money on the rigs and it would have been easy to sit in Aberdeen and drink it all away! Luckily I refused to do it!

On one tour of the far Northwest of Scotland I came across the John Ridgway School of Adventure situated just about as far as its possible to get from "civilisation", at Ardmore which is near Cape Wrath. I made contact with JR and within a few months was an unpaid, part-time instructor at his school. Businessmen and women and children underwent outdoor activities in the rugged but beautiful environment of lochs and mountains. Courses included canoeing, rock climbing, hill walking and camping but I was mainly involved in the sailing department. There were half a dozen small dinghies, two 32ft yachts, and then the "Big Un" a 57ft Bowman Ketch which JR had bought and fitted out for work at the school, and then for a project to mark the School's 10th Anniversary, namely participation in the 1977 / 78 Whitbread Round the World Race.

In late 1976, J.R asked me to be part of his crew for the Race, an opportunity which was jumped at, of course. I worked on the Bowman quite a lot during the fitting out, preparation for the Race, and in selection and training of the crew, who were to be, in the main, the young instructors of the School. In the summer of 1977 we sailed 'Debenhams' as she was now named, to the River Hamble, and then to H.M.S. Vernon at Portsmouth ready for the start in August.

The story can be read in J.R's book 'Round The World with Ridgway' but as far as I'm concerned, I enjoyed most of the first leg to Cape Town, then an exciting second leg to Auckland, during which we went so far South on a Great Circle course, right down to 59 degrees South. How we ran into the Antarctic pack ice and had a difficult time extricating ourselves. These were the exciting parts of the adventure, the ice and the icebergs, the exhilarating sailing, but under them lay the not so exciting parts such as living aboard a small yacht with 13 other people of widely differing backgrounds and opinions. There came to be an atmosphere of bickering and bitchiness which I found very depressing. All of which led to my facing J.R in a hotel room in Auckland in 1977 and telling him that I couldn't face another 3 months of this, as specially as how he and I seemed particularly unable to get on. I was very upset about this, and believe he genuinely was too but couldn't go on with him. The Race Fleet sailed, I stayed.

New Zealand had very strict rules about would-be immigrants. I managed to by-pass them by having a very lucky break. I 'just happened' to meet the Minister of Immigration in a bar of the Great Northern Hotel late one evening. He listened sympathetically to my story, and gave me a introduction to 'his man in Wellington'. That way I eventually got all the necessary stamps on my passport for a Work Permit. Imagine that happening in Whitehall! I made my way down South, stayed with Roy Bree and his wife at their wine shop in Otorohanga, had a hotel all to myself in New Plymouth, and spent Christmas with their Maori staff in their homes.

Visiting Rotorua, Wellington, Dunedin and Christchurch, I eventually arrived at Invercargill, where I found the offices of Hunt International Oil Company. They had a rig drilling to the South of Stewart Island, and gave me a job maintaining rig equipment as it was sent in on the supply boats. I worked in the docks at Bluff, the port in the very South of New Zealand, found good digs in the New Eagle Hotel which was also a pub and had a really great time. I had an interesting job in the fresh air, was well paid and surrounded by wonderful people in a friendly country.

Nice as this was, I couldn't hide from myself the hurt that having worked with Ridgway for two years, worked long and hard to get the yacht, and most of the crew ready for the Race, here I was just four months after the start, completely out of it. Worst of all was the fact that I had lost my chance of rounding 'The Horn' the *main* aim of all the effort that I had put in.

I'm not laying any blame, it was my fault as much as anyone else's. I am just incompatible with a crowd, and always have been. I should have known, in fact did know, but had hoped that the adventure of sailing around the world would have submerged such petty feelings on my part and on other peoples – but it didn't.

As I worked on the oil rig equipment in the docks at Bluff, I had a lot of time to myself and did plenty of thinking. A recurring thought came to me. 'Well' it went, 'if you want to round Cape Horn and you can't stand crowds, DO IT ALONE! Why not? I was a natural loner, I'd had no fear of the sea on the 15,000 miles from Portsmouth to Auckland, not even when we ran close to Antarctica on the second leg, SO WHY NOT?

I returned to the U.K. in May 1978, determined to keep with the sea which I had virtually deserted since leaving the Navy in 1966. I resumed my job with Sedco, an American drilling company, and worked as Assistant Driller on the Cormorant drilling and pumping platform 150 miles Northeast of Sumburgh airport in the Shetland Isles. It wasn't much fun, nor was it meant to be, but it paid well and the two weeks on, two weeks off routine allowed for thinking and planning. When 'On', I had more than enough to occupy my mind.

In November 1978, I bought a <u>bare</u> Glass Reinforced Plastic hull of a Corribee – a 21ft fin keeler by Newbridge Boats of Bridport, the fine lines of which attracted me. I partly fitted her out during the winter of 1978/79 in Brighton Marina, during which time I also worked as a Rigger there when not on the rig. I'm an energetic chap!

I had bought the hull already designed to take a Chinese Lug-Sail, or Junk Rig in order to try out a different sail system to the Bermudan rig which had given us such hard times changing out the Jibs on the plunging foredeck of Debenhams. I didn't fancy doing that operation singlehanded! So, in the Spring of 79 I had this smart, little blue boat with an alloy mast and attractive Tan Junk Rig sail, working my way in and out of the Marina under sail, and oars when necessary as there was no engine at first.

I used "Aries" for the next three years as a prototype to "discover" the Junk Rig and I never did a lot of sailing in her, the furthest West we went was Weymouth and the furthest East, Dungeness, but I learnt a lot from these short voyages.

Meanwhile at work, I had gained promotion to Driller, now in charge of the Rig Floor drilling crew still on the Cormorant platform, but it was a terrible life for a would-be loner. It is hard to imagine two wider opposites of the life I wanted to lead, of sailing alone in peace and quiet with pleasant music (as in my off time) and the mad life on the rig. 900 miles to travel twice a month from Brighton by crowded trains, planes and helicopters to a world of noise and hurry-hurry, in charge of a crew of half-mad Scotsmen living in constant bustle. All this surrounded by literally hundreds of men in air-conditioned quarters full of smoke and stale air. My only pleasure out there was the fact of actually being on the sea and noting all its moods.

In December 1979 came the offer of a job from a British drilling company, as Driller on a land rig which had recently started working in the Wytch Farm area, near Wareham in Dorset. I jumped at this job mainly to escape the long journeys North every month, and found myself working the same 'two weeks on, two weeks off' routine, but this time on land with less pressures and only 110 miles from Brighton.

I bought a retired ambulance, which had been named Bramble by the children of the previous owner, and lived in this comfortable home while at the rig. During the two weeks on we worked shifts of 12 hours on and 12 hours off and on finishing the crew dispersed. My time then was my own and I used to drive Bramble to a quiet quarry or park somewhere on the Purbeck Hills with wonderful views of the English Channel – all this in utter silence and being able to eat exactly what I liked. This was wonderful after the claustrophobic living conditions offshore and I loved it. I became a happy man and did my very best work.

During 1980 I worked happily on the rig in the Isle of Purbeck area, drove to Brighton and sailed my bonny wee boat and settled down without any grandiose plans at that time. In September of that year though, I started a Journal, or diary, in which were recorded my thoughts and ideas for the future. They centred round a steel boat capable of going round Cape Horn, but it seemed a remote likelihood.

In the Spring of '81 though, things began to happen. I was doing pretty well at work, when all my bosses, for various reasons, took off for other posts. I found myself promoted to Toolpusher, or Rig Manager at the very respectable salary of £25,000. I lived a fairly quiet life and managed to save quite a lot of money. And so the year passed with plenty of work, the occasional bit of sailing on Aries and also on the 'Biche', a converted French Sailing Tunny Fisher, on which I sailed as Mate to Capt. Chas. Booth, quite a character but a difficult man to get along with.

JOURNAL 5.3.82 "I have almost decided to settle on a Three Year Plan to retire on my 45th birthday which will be on the 27th of March 1985 and by then to have organised myself to be able to sail around the World alone." It seemed very optimistic at the time, yet I made the "retirement" six months early!

"Aries" was sold at the Brighton Boat Show in May 1982 so that I could concentrate on <u>my</u> "Big 'Un". I was still sailing on the Biche now and then, had plenty to do at work and so was always busy, just how I like it to be.

I feel neglected in not doing two or three things at once!

Chapter Two

1982 – Roamer Takes Shape

In mid-1982 I started looking around for "The Hull", having already decided that steel was to be the material, for reasons of strength, safety, flexibility of design, and "reparability". I wrote off for various study plans and visited boatyards on my travels. I like the Weston Farmer – designed Tahitian Ketch, which looked a fine seaworthy craft, but on actually seeing one in Bristol, I decided that at 32 feet with an aft cockpit, it was too small. I always think that you lose a third of a boat with an aft cockpit and be suitable for a Chinese Rig.

Viewing various hulls cleared my mind greatly as to what I wanted. I am a great believer in the saying, "If it looks right then it probably is" and went about it with that motto in mind, inspecting hulls with a sailor's eye rather than an engineer's.

So what was I looking for? Firstly a good seaboat, a traditional displacement hull with a full length keel for stability and to encourage her to steer a straight course down the great Southern Ocean Seas. I wanted a centre cockpit as a safe control point to allow me to handle the sails from there without putting myself to unnecessary risk. The centre cockpit would also allow me to have an aft cabin, with the facility to walk from one end of the ship to the other. The aft cabin would have a strong "doghouse" over it to help break up any waves which might poop us. The hull, as previously mentioned, had to be compatible with a two masted Schooner Junk Rig.

I planned to live aboard permanently so wanted the boat as large as possible, but the size was limited not only by my budget but by how large I thought could be handled by myself, in harbours and marinas as well as at sea. All these criteria led me to the ideal craft between 35 and 40 feet, which slimmed down the short list somewhat.

On the 22nd June, '82 I arrived at the works of "Oceancraft", in Wadebridge, Cornwall. It was a small workshop, reached down a lane called Bradford Quay, where many years ago schooners used to berth on the River Camel, awaiting their cargoes of slate from Bodmin, 9 miles inland. With Les Savage, the owner of Oceancraft, I viewed some 33ft hulls in the workshop and outside on the bank of the river. We discussed costs of the 36 ft version of "Ebbtide", and my special design requirements at this first meeting, then I drove off to Norwich where I was to go offshore on temporary loan to a jack-up drilling rig, my rig having been laid up. I wrote to Alan Pape, the hull's designer, and to Alan Boswell, who designs Junk Rig sails, asking for their opinions on the suitability of the hull for the Junk Rig and vice versa.

Journal: 7.7.82. "The summer of the planning". "At this time 'The Project', as I was calling my plans, was just that, a project to get an ocean-going vessel capable of letting me carry out some if not all of my dreams and ambitions. These naturally revolve around a singlehanded circumnavigation, rounding Cape Horn, visiting the cold and lonely parts of the world, the unvisited and peaceful places, to see grand vistas and high mountains from the sea. Being naturally unselfconfident, I can hardly believe that it could come true, so am broadcasting no great plans about it."

I started detailed planning, not only for the ship and her equipment, but also on a personal level. I looked at myself and wasn't too displeased with what I saw. At 42 years old years old, I was fairly fit, very active, hardly ever subject to illness, I had a few problems, one was alcohol, in that I tended to go on a "Bender" after each two-week work trip.

So I vowed to cut down on the booze, and did, though it took some time. Medically I had no great problems, my teeth were mostly still there, in need of a refit, but all mine. My eyes were a potential problem, having splashed the left one with Caustic Soda on a rig some years ago. It tended to close up in the late evening , especially indoors in smoky atmospheres.

The most serious problem was my left ear, the drum of which was perforated due to an infection of many years ago when wearing earphones as a sonar operator in the Navy. This perforation allowed water to ingress into the inner ear and sinus tubes, and would prevent me swimming underwater to work on the hull. I planned to solve these problems.

Journal: 16.7.82 "Big item for the diary – today I wrote off to Oceancraft and ordered the vessel. An Ebbtide 36 to have a centre cockpit." That was after having received letters from Messrs. Pape and Boswell approving the hull and the junk rigs compatibility.

So we press on. I visited Alan Boswell at Bosham and discussed the rig, storm sails and light weather sails. Alan undertook to draw up a design which would give the required mast positions in the hull so that Alan Pape could modify his construction drawings to accept them.

I paid a further visit to Les Savage and went into more detail with him. On the 22nd of July I noted, "some of the prices are shocking, and it seems certain that my £20,000 budget will be exceeded." I was to be a lot more shocked than that!

In early August I paid Les an initial deposit to get on to his building schedule. Whilst in Wadebridge I scouted about for possibilities of fitting out down there, and launching and mooring facilities. Padstow looked a friendly place, out of the tourist season, and Falmouth was only 40 miles away.

In Wadebridge I found cosy digs with Eileen Clark in her very old stone cottage "Spring Gardens". at the town end of Bradford Quay. Eileen looked after me splendidly, her cooking was wonderful, mainly fish and vegetables, I lived well there.

I visited Alan Pape on the 16th of August and had a long and wide discussion with this traditional ship designer at his home at East Looe, overlooking Looe Bay, with the Eddystone lighthouse visible out to sea. Alan gave a good reception to my ideas, even unconventional ones, like the designed-in jury mast rig-up, inside steering position, and standing legs. He agreed to redesign the "36" to meet my requirements for a very reasonable sum, and I departed rejoicing to the "Punchbowl", a famous Cornish pub at Lanreath, for a pint and a pastie.

Journal: 18.9.82. "Visited Southampton Boat Show this week and had a sail with Robin Blain of Sunbird Yachts to view his "swing-wing" rig. I was partly impressed with this aerofoil Junk Rig, it pointed high on the wind, and was very quiet, but I didn't like all the moving parts and the framework of the aerofoil sections looked like a big problem should it get damaged. It was also 50 percent more expensive than the basic Junk Rig, which, simple as it was, flat, and made up of rope, wood, and canvas, appealed to me more as being capable of repair and maintenance at sea.

I received two quotes for the two masts. £2,800 from Harry Spencer in Cowes, £1,800 from Richard Mason in Bristol!

I had a first appointment with Mr. Elcock, an ear specialist, to try and solve the problem.

Journal: 27.9.82. "This being my 42½ birthday, I'm one sixth of the way into the 3 year plan." I reviewed the "state of the project" and asked, 1. Can I have this ship, 2. Can I afford it, and 3, Am I capable of carrying out the long term plans??? To which the answers were Yes, Yes and Yes!

In October I wrote many letters to manufacturers of the wide range of equipment needed and accumulated a fat file of information and specifications. My land Rig has been shut down during the Summer but was now due to start up and drill a hole for British Gas near Wareham, which kept me busy on that front again.

Journal: 16.11.82. "I have the construction drawings from Alan Pape and they are impressive. Took them to Les Savage who sees no problems. I need more fuel capacity than the 60 gallons in the drawings. I put a plan to Les to use the 90 gallon water tanks as drawn, for fuel, and build in extra water tanks forward of the "Engine Room bulkhead". We agreed on some prices and on the engine I'm planning to install, a Perkins D3-152. Costs are somewhat frightening but I'm getting used to the shocks!

22.11.82. Paid Les S. half the cost of the hull which set me on to a lot of detailed thinking about costs versus bank balance. I started visiting ship scrapyards for deck fittings and anything useful to the project. These were at North End Portsmouth, the Belsize yard near Southampton, and the well-named Aladdin's Cave at Bursledon on the Hamble. I bought a lot of goodies there, including a 45-year-old anchor winch, for £75.

13.12.82. Visited David Hunt of 'Needlespar' at Warsash to discuss the proposed jury mast rig. He soon cleaned up my crude drawings and designed the four-part sheer legs. Even better, he came up with the idea of using the lower parts of the jury rig as my standing legs.

14.12.82. At Wadebridge again for further meetings with Les Savage. He is now building "36" No.1 . His first 36-footer, with mine planned as No.2. There were two 33's outside, one with portholes in the hull and no toe-rail and one with no ports, but with a toe-rail. I shall have the latter system. No portholes in the ship's side but with glass prism deck lights set into the deck. "Les hopes to start in mid-January and finish by the end of April", the journal reads!

I was doing a lot of reading at this time, books like Bernard Moitessier's "The Long Way" and "Cape Horn - The Logical Route", David Lewis's "Ice Bird", Hal Roth's "Two Against Cape Horn" and "After 50,000 Miles" and the Pardey's "Self - Sufficient Sailor." They are full of interesting practical ideas. I also became a collector, of just about anything, plastic bottles, boxes, plastic sheeting, wood off-cuts, all sorts of things got carried up to the spare room in my flat in Brighton, and eventually spilled out onto the landing, into the lounge.

Just before Christmas 1982 my drilling rig was shut down again after drilling the well at Waddock's Cross, near Wareham, Dorset, and I went to supervise its laying-up. This took in the Purbeck Timberyard by Wareham Railway Station and I rigged up a 40ft office Portakabin, which is also my living accommodation on the rig so that I could get power and water. This was now used as home, to "hide" from the Christmas and New Year revels, which I have never enjoyed much. In this quiet refuge, I worked on the design and planning of the ship, on deck and below, and made detailed drawings of all aspects long before any building took place.

Chapter Three

1983 – Year of the Building

Journal, 4.1.83. "At last! Christmas and the New Year are over. There was even a Bank Holiday on the Monday! But now it's all systems go into the "Year of the Ship", and me, not being one to hang about when it's time to go, shot off to London, visited Thomas Foulkes, Davey & Co., and Telesonic in that order, and spent £700 on a wide selection of equipment for this ship of mine which is still in theory stage. Have spent £9,280 on the project thus far and the £30,000 budget looks like being about right. "Hmmm. I spend quite a lot of time calculating income and savings against the cost of the project.

I went to Earl's Court Boat Show in January 1983, and did some useful work there. A chat with Chris Fletcher of Whitlock Marine Steering laid the basis of my steering system, and in the same department, John Holden of Levanter Vane Gears and I had an initial talk about the self-steering gear. I found a supplier for my proposed perspex bubble dome over the inside steering position, and spoke with Henry Browne Ltd. for the compass equipment.

I also bought "Adventures Under Sail", a selection of writings by Bill Tilman, edited by Libby Purves, which has been a source of constant enjoyable reading.

Back in Brighton enjoying the second week of a useful two-week holiday, I worked on the drawings again and "cracked" the steering system, my preferred one, of wires running along the upper deck. I drew it all up neatly, sent a copy to Whitlock Marine, and another to John Holden, complete with a photocopy of the hull construction drawing. John H. was to design the self-steering gear from day one to suit the hull.

It may appear to any potential planner of his own "Project" that I was premature in all this planning, but I can assure him that I was not. In some cases it took many months to get matters organised.

I did more travelling, bought the viewdome for £82, visited Bristol for early talks with Richard Mason about the masts. There was no hurry for these, but I needed some specifications for the deck and hull fittings for the builder. Continued my tour by seeing Les Savage again, visited Falmouth to check the place out, and liked it. I had the fine sight of 26 ships of a fishing fleet at anchor in the bay. On the way back to Wareham, I called in on Alan Pape again, and found Jimmy Green Marine's rope shop hidden away on the hill above the village..

My rig was still laid up in the Timber Yard at Wareham, and I was able to use the office as stowage for all the gear I was collecting, as well as accommodation when not at Brighton.

Journal, 15.1.83. "Back at Wadebridge for more talking with Les S. Les reckons to start by the end of the month and take until the end of May, which sounds O.K. "Hmmm. Shall probably have to exceed the increased budget of £30,000, £35,000 more likely now. Still, am fully committed and will stick with the plan of getting everything I need and get the cash somehow."

I had the name in mind for her at this time of Black Beauty, for black hulled she was to be, black and beautiful, to ride the seas with spirit. This didn't last long though and was soon overtaken by "Roamer", to go with the World Wildlife Fund's print of a whale's tail, with the added verse, "He roams the seas in freedom, with no enemies save man". Just how I wanted to be.

At the end of January, Les Savage asked me if I would let him build a 33 footer next on the production line, and although it hurt to delay things further, for mainly financial reasons I said "Yes", but it was a decision which caused me a lot of trouble and expense.

I was in Wareham at the time and arranged a R.Y.A. day's Skippers' Theory course to bring me back to thinking about Navigation and Seamanship, and to prepare for my Yachtmaster's Certificate. I passed the Day's Skipper's course on 28th March, the day after my 43rd birthday and one third through the 3-year plan. Into the Spring of '83, I was plenty busy with the organisation of getting my rig to work for Carless Exploration near Basingstoke. I still managed, however to get to a 2-day Diesel Course at Perkins' factory at Peterborough. A fascinating and terrifying place. No wonder they have strikes at car factories and the like. How terrible to have to work in one of those places each and every day.

I paid a visit to the Beaulieu Boat Jumble Sale in mid-April and bought two Canpa hatches, 14 guardrail stanchions and many more minor bargains. It's always worthwhile going, and great fun too.

I paid Perkins for the D3.152 engine at the end of April which just about cleared out the bank account. In between haring all over Hampshire and Dorset organising the rig move to Herriard, near Basingstoke, which is held up by excessive rainfall on the site, I'm chasing up equipment for the boat. I know I hadn't even started building yet, but some items can take an age to acquire.

My rig got drilling at last, which kept me fully occupied and I was hardly able to get away from work, my planned relief having fallen sick, I did what I could for the project, ordering equipment, keeping in touch with the builder, and so it went on through the hot Summer of '83, most of the time at the rig, using the phone a lot, keeping the project going. "Roamer's" building started in late June, but I wasn't able to get to Wadebridge at all.

By August I had drilled two wells for Careless and had moved the rig to a site near Rownham's Services on the M27 near Southampton, for Amoco, and was very much tied up with supervising and all that. We drilled a quick well for Amoco, and by mid-September the rig was laid up in Wareham again. I had been hoping for a long holiday after my hectic summer but it was not to be. I was packed off to Great Yarmouth to act as Rig Superintendent for the Jack-up rig, Shelf Driller, working for Amoco. This was presumably because I had got on well with the Amoco bosses during the Rownham's Well. I wasn't at all pleased at this turn of events as it meant being at the opposite end of the country to where the boat was being built, but I wasn't offered the choice. I made the best of it, at least I was ashore, had my own office with a free telephone and a photo-copier. I stayed in a posh country hotel, all paid for of course, and apart from the fact that I had to be in the office by 0700 each day to take the Morning Reports from the rig, I had a fairly easy life. I went jogging in the early morning, gave up drinking, and joined a health club, but what about my "Roamer"!!

The hull was my main concern, but no way could I get away from Great Yarmouth. Mark Gamble visited me there, and we discussed the possibility of his fitting out at his workshop at Ilminster in Somerset. I had all my interior design drawings done by now so we were able to get into detailed costs, which were another shock.

My 43rd birthday passed by with me assessing that the project was on the right lines. Budget was going out of the window but there was no real choice but to keep on. The Budget is now up to £50,000, a previously unbelievable figure.

Journal. 12.10.83. "In Wadebridge!! Hurrah, I have escaped from Great Yarmouth and work for a while."

Journal. 13.10.83. "Red Letter Day, Maggie Thatcher's birthday, but that's not the reason, the reason is that I saw "Roamer" for the first time, and she is beautiful. Everyone agrees that she is the best looking hull to come out of Les Savage's workshop. I was stunned when I first saw her, her lines are gorgeous, everything lines up, and boy, does she look strong!!!

I spent only a few days in Wadebridge for further planning discussions with Les S., and got back to Brighton to see my ear specialist. My "escape from work" didn't last long as I had a phone call from Aberdeen "asking" me to go to Hong Kong for a few weeks to help out on a rig drilling for B.P. offshore of China. Ready for anything, I agreed, and was in Hong Kong by October 25th.

The rig was about 100 miles offshore of the Pearl River, south of H.K., and there was some delay in our getting out to it due to bad weather. We oilmen waited in a hotel in Zhu Hai, near Macao, and although obviously a frontispiece for tourists, I was most impressed by the friendliness and humility of the Chinese people, in contrast to the behaviour of my "fellow" oil rig workers. I eventually got to the "Nan Hai II", did what was required, and flew back home by the 10th of November.

Back at Wadebridge it was "on with the project", with my bonny ship nearing completion, and me pushing Les to complete before the end of the year. The situation on the 17th November was that "The doghouses, decks and cockpit are finished, most of the padeyes were on, toe-rails were O.K. with stainless steel fairleads and rigging eyes. The stemhead anchor fitting was on with a cunningly contrived forward towing eye incorporating jury rig rigging eyes. In fact she's looking good, though there's still plenty to do."

Journal. 26.11.83 "Paid Les the second half of the hull payment of £7,452, as he reckons he is getting short of cash. He is!! Have now spent £26,084 on hull and equipment, plus £893 on travel, digs, etc. a total of £26,977!!!

I did a lot of work aboard at this time, drilling hundreds of holes for deck fittings, portholes and hatches etc, and generally helped as I could to speed the project along.

I was away for a few days in late November to visit the Land Rig, fix a date for my ear operation, and attend to my Brighton flat and the mail and bills which accumulated in it. Back in Wadebridge by the 1st of December.

Journal. 1.12.83. "To Les's early and here's the situation. Still not ready to blast and paint her. I again helped where I could, mainly in grinding down welds all over the exterior of the hull, and cleaning out the rubbish which accumulates in the bilges. Les's lads were putting the final welding touches to the hull which is looking really good.

Journal. Sunday 4.12.83. "First day alone on Roamer. Had a happy and contented day inside the hull in peace and quiet on my own and perfectly content, singing away, looking forward to when I shall be on my own for long periods."

On Monday 5th Dec. I had to leave Wadebridge, but before leaving I had a good natter to Les and agreed on a completion date of the 16th Dec. by which time she would be built, blasted, and primer painted. I left at 1630 and had a dark miserable 5 hour drive to Brighton with the car playing me up, not delivering full power.

In Brighton I got after the usual business of banks, bills and visiting, also had my eyes tested as I had been having difficulty with reading. I ordered two pairs of glasses with hard carrying cases, for £105.

I moved into Brighton Ear Hospital on the evening of the 7th Dec, taking plenty of books and drawings to make my enforced stay a useful one. I had a private room c/o B.U.P.A. which was helpful for working on the plans. The operation a "Myringoplasty" took place on the 8th, and I wasn't much use that day, but was soon back at work again on the 9th. I nearly starved to death in there and only survived by chatting up the night nurses for tea and Marmite sandwiches! I checked my head was O.K. by completing Daily Telegraph crosswords, and pressed on with the boat paperwork.

I agitated for release, although I did feel a bit weak and wobbly. Quote "Left side of the face is swollen and left ear is a bit bloody" but a nice young nurse dressed and cleaned it up. No news on what happens next. Am worried that I might not only get stuck in here till Monday, but then, on getting out, have to attend as an out-patient, which would be difficult…

Am trying to work on the project but feel lethargic and the eyes are not good. Must take it easy.

I was released by 1200 on the Saturday, was cold and weak and vomited up any food I tried to eat, so maybe I wasn't 100% fit yet! Spent most of the weekend visiting and drinking Guinness and rum, to keep the cold out!

I got away from Brighton and visited Mark Gamble who was to fit her out in his new premises at Rose Mill Works, just to the West of Ilminster. The premises weren't impressive, a large barn, part of an old silk mill, full of dust and cobwebs, no doors on, no power on, and the approach road a morass. These defects would be rectified soon, said Mark. While at Ilminster I took a bold step, bought a caravan, and installed it in a field not far from Mark's works. This was to be my "digs" while I helped with the fitting out. It all looked like a good scene, fairly quiet, within walking distance of the Five Dials pub at Horton, 1½ miles from where Roamer would be, and 1 mile from the "Lamb", at Horton Cross, a friendly pub noted for its meals, and, in particular, its vegetarian meals which were cheap, wholesome and enormous.

Back to Brighton, and the usual story of running around visiting everyone in pouring rain and mad traffic. "How this place wears me down, running around in the rain, giving my money away for Christmas. I keep telling myself it'll be for the last time."

Thursday 15th Dec. Escaped from Brighton after fixing up the transport of Roamer by Exonia Transport of Exeter, for the 21st. Visited the Ear Hospital for removal of stitches and the ceremonial "pulling out of the wick" from my ear. It felt about 100 yards long and was pulling my complete head contents out! Eventually hit the road and at Wadebridge by 1840. "Went straight to Les's and there she was, my big beauty, out in the open at last". Had a look all round her and into Eileen Clark's for a nice meal and an early night. Again, "it has been a busy week, but a useful one."

"Life is but a struggle", says my journal on Thursday the 22nd December, and this past week certainly has been. I worked like a slave to try to get my bonny ship blasted and painted before the Christmas shut-down but didn't succeed. I had some bad times arguing with Les S. about the inefficiency of his men and equipment, and even him.

Journal. Monday, 19th December. "An interesting day this, down to Les's at 0815 and in the office for a chat..., I suggested to Les that now the hull was outside the door he had no further interest in it, to which he agreed!! Further pressed, it seems he has no intention of having it back in to paint it, and indeed, to do as little as possible to it!! Not surprisingly, I was not too keen on this plan... His reasoning is that, he says, since he has made no profit on my hull, he must press on with his next one, which the presence of my hull in his workshop would delay."

More bad times followed, with the discovery of rust breaking through work which had already been done. That was grit-blasting followed by molten Zinc sprayed on through an oxyacetylene flame, which was supposed to be an A1 treatment. The trouble was, we were trying to do it in between showers in the cool damp air of late December. Les's spraying equipment actually sprayed water at times due to condensation in the air lines. It was all not very clever. Now I was paying for my allowing Les to build another hull before mine. Three months ago the weather was fine, but then the finances weren't!!

To get a break from humping sacks of grit and doing some of the blasting myself, ("Do all owners do this?" I asked myself at times.) I popped up to Ilminster to see Mark Gamble. Still no doors, no power, no road. So it's just as well Roamer isn't ready.

Back at Wadebridge the blasting and painting was not going well, but at least Les relented and agreed to take her back inside after blasting and priming, to apply two more coats of paint. (Not that he ever did!!).

By Thursday the 22nd December I had abandoned the hope of getting her finished before Christmas, and cancelled all the moving plans. The job didn't look good, everyone, except me, was in high spirits at the thought of packing up for the long holiday, so I gave in. I packed my gear, and drove off to my caravan at Ilminster to be alone with my thoughts, which weren't happy ones. The time schedule was slipping, costs were getting out of hand, and finances looking bad.

I soon got over the blues though, and by 2015 on Christmas Eve I was "feeling fine and relaxed, no duties, no responsibilities, no visiting, no traffic jams. I like being alone." During the period I had access to Mark G's old workshop at the Old Donyatt Pottery, and did some useful work drilling and countersinking the Perspex ports and windows, and making teak pads for various deck fittings. How I loved being out in the countryside, in perfect peace, on my own, working with my hands. Not that I am any craftsman, but I made a respectable job of the work I did.

To Brighton on the 28th December and safe from Christmas for another year. Interesting item in the Junk Rig Association Newsletter, quite apart from my latest report on Roamer, was that the J.R.A. had been invited by the Australian Institute of Navigation to enter a boat in the "Sirius Event". This was to be a cruise-cum-race from Sydney to Cape Town and back to Sydney as part of the Australian Bi-Centenary celebrations in 1987-88. Interesting!

On New Year's Eve I hit the road again down to Ilminster, visiting Norman Hamper at Fareham en route, he has my sail battens and booms about done, and they look good.

I had a quiet night in the caravan while the outside world celebrated a date change. I never did go for this New Year's Eve madness.

Chapter Four

1984 – Hull into Ship

Another year and pressing on with self-appointed tasks, having got the Jury Rig spars from Needlespar, I laid them out on the floor of Mart G's new workshop, and drew up a rigging plan, the weather was terrible at the time, cold and windy, and I spent most of a few days in the caravan working on drawings and plans.

Between the 2nd and 16th of January 1984, I circulated between Ilminster, Wareham, and Brighton, sorting out the myriad of matters involved in keeping the project going, keeping my drilling rig up to date and looking after mail and personal business in Brighton. It was a busy time, as usual. Mr. Elcock, my eardoctor, pronounced the operation a success and am very pleased about that. I also had my teeth attended to, which only required two fillings and a clean-up.

I was mulling on the long-term plans, involving money to a great degree, how much is needed, how soon I could retire from my job, which continued to be complicated and uncertain, with plans for "my" rig fluctuating between selling it , to sending it to Indonesia, or elsewhere. Thought had to be given as to what I was going to do with this boat of mine when it was ready for the sea, plans at the moment look like getting the blasting and painting finished by February, taking her to Mark Gamble's for fitting out which should take about four months, at the end of May, and thence to Brighton or Falmouth and have her sailing by late Summer (Ever the Optimist!!)

Thoughts ran along the lines of work-up trails in late Summer and during the Winter while I kept my job going, until March, 1985, when I would "retire". More trials in the early part of 1985, ready for a possible circum-navigation in Autumn '85 until spring '86. This would just about rule out participation in the B.O.C. "Around Alone" starting at Rhode Island in August '86, but would give me the experience and confidence to plan for the Sirius Event in Australia in 1987, possibly taking some "paying guests". I wrote to the organiser in Sydney with some ideas of my own regarding linking up in a commemorative voyage from the U.K. to Australia in an historically correct sequence.

On the 16th January I set off once more on my travels with the car as usual loaded. I called in on Norman Hamper, collected the battens and booms, and took them to Lucas Sails as Portsmouth, to try them in the sails. Just as well I did, for there were several minor but essential modifications needed, Kevin Lee undertook to have this work done, Peter Lucas being away on holiday at the time. Apart from the above, the sails look just fine, including the lightweight "ghosters". We measured up for, and designed, two sail covers while I was there.

I spent the night at my Rig office in Wareham and did some more worrying about finances and about how the blasting and spraying was going.

On my return to Wadebridge, my worries about how the operation was going, were to be fully justified.

Journal: Wednesday 18th January, 1984."Bad day today, on visiting Les and Roamer the situation is that all I have in good condition is the forward ten feet of the foredeck which has been reblasted clean, zinc sprayed, and immediately covered with epoxy primer. Some of the cockpit and some of the doghouse is O.K. but not much. Naturally I'm not too pleased about this, also, it was pretty nice day but not a thing is happening to her. So I go straight into Les about the situation".

"We can't go on like this, Les." "I'll get it done," says Les, "It depends on the weather!" I groan. "In January, in Cornwall, with gales and rain roaring up the river from the Atlantic!"

I put it to Les that I planned to take the hull away and get it blasted and primed properly under cover. At this he produced his account for the work done on this item so far for which I have ten feet of foredeck in good condition. The discussion became rather heated with charges and counter charges, going on for some hours until I suggested we rest from it over separate lunches and take a fresh look in the afternoon. This we did and when we resumed, were more amenable and put each other's positions.

Les's was that he wasn't making any money out of the hull anyway and couldn't afford to pay for the abortive blast/paint job. Mine was the basic one that I hadn't got a good job done so why should I pay for it? After more discussion we came to the compromise that we would split the cost 50-50, Les would get the hull moved from outside where it was blocking further production, and I would take it elsewhere to get the job done to some sort of acceptable time schedule.

This was particularly unsatisfactory to me as it cost several hundred pounds for nothing. But there comes a point where decisions have to be made and it was either that or the hull sitting out in the rain till... when...??

So, it was back to Eileen Clark's for a cup of tea and a sympathetic ear. Then an attack on the Yellow Pages where I set my fingers walking all over the West Country looking for shot blasters and painters.

Next day, the 19th, I visited five "possibilities" on an itinerary of St. Austell, Plymouth, Ivybridge, Newton Abbott and back to St. Austell where I got the only "probable" high on the hills above St. Austell, in the village of Penwithick., I found Cornwall Metal Treatments and its manager, Brian Boynes, who was keen to do the job. He had a shed large enough to take Roamer, with a recycled shot-blasting system. He would undertake to not only blast her clean and prime her but would do the full paint job, that is, after the primer, five coats of epoxy paint, and quoted me a reasonable price for doing it. He seemed a good old-fashioned honest Cornishman, so we agreed terms and tentative dates and I went back to Wadebridge fairly relieved. Les has agreed to install the engine and prop shaft for a price, and have her ready to move by the 31st of January.

Phone calls to Penwithick produced a time-table which would give me Roamer blasted and fully painted by mid-February, which sounded like good news, something I could do with after the harassing times of late.

So I organised all the crane and transport arrangement again, plus calls to Blake's Paints for the full paint order. Technical discussions with Blake's changed the plan again in that they didn't recommend that their paint system should be applied to sprayed-on zinc, but should be put straight on to the blasted steel!! Shock upon shock!! What did Les think about this? "That's only Blake's opinion", says he!

One of the things which will be learnt throughout an operation such as this, is that there are many experts with as many "absolutely right" opinions as there are birds in the sky, and it's very difficult for the lay - man to pick his way through the minefield of these opinions. Books are the same, how you do it depends on who you believe, or what you read. It's a hell of a game.

But we must press on – and did. I spent a few days at Wadebridge working on the hull, getting more rubbish, grit, welding rods etc, out of the hull. At least she looks good inside even if the exterior is red and rusty. I suffered another blow in that one of Les's lads had filled up my designed-in deep forward bilge pump sump with cement, and left me with one only 6" deep!

Sunday the 22nd, Drove from Wadebridge to Exeter and popped a note into Exonia Transport office giving full details of the dimensions of the load they would be moving, soon, I hoped. To Ilminster and off-loaded some gear from my long-suffering car. Had lunch with Mark Gamble in the 5 Dials, then to Wareham and the sanctuary of my office in the Purbeck Timber Yard. I was glad to relax in the armchair and watch T.V., as my back was playing up again, a hangover from the days of humping sacks of grit.

I spent a while at Wareham working on the rig equipment with the storeman and mechanic, to justify my salary. I was lucky to have all the time off which I did, but I had earned it from my exertions of the previous Summer and Autumn and so had no guilt feelings. I worked on the rig during the day, and the project during the evenings.

Journal: Thursday, 26th January. "1100 - Disaster?? Bob Jones called to say that half his roof had blown off and could we put the move off for a week? Stunned!! I managed to talk him into continuing with the move and if necessary, finish his other blasting jobs, and repair the tie roof with Roamer inside, it won't do her any harm. I'm desperate not to have to cancel all the moving arrangements again". Brian Boynes was also having problems getting a crane, but was fixed up with a tractor to pull her into the blasting shed. I kept him on course for the arranged dates. Later in the week I had more problems with Exonia saying they couldn't keep to the dates. I was pretty much past being stunned, told them straight to "keep to the arrangements" and rang off.

I had a busy weekend, (aren't they all?), on Saturday drove to Beer to see Jimmy Green Marine about my rope order, to Weymouth to look at some anchor chain, but it was no good, back to Wareham, and then on to Brighton.

On Sunday at Brighton I had a further clean out of the flat, arranged with a friend who has a decorator to smarten up the place for selling, and of course, visited half the town. I had a pleasant drink in the "Wellington", Elm Grove, with an old friend Charlie Piedot, who introduced me to one

Syd Crocker, a tug skipper from Simonstown and Cape Town, a member of the Royal Cape Yacht Club, who said he remembered me from 1977 Whitbread Race visit there, but I couldn't recall meeting him. He was a right old sea-dog and we got on well. He was to become a good friend.

Journal: Tuesday 31st January 1984. Wadebride 0700.

"So here we are at the first move day, it's been a struggle even arranging it, so I'm hoping all will go well..."

"Went to Les's at 0815 and was shocked at his final invoices". (So I am still shockable!!). Paid him off though and got on with business of the day. Crane arrived at 0900 and truck at 1000, problem with truck due to Exonia's taking no notice of my information that the hull would be on a cradle, so when we put it on the truck it was 15' 4" high. Exonia had told the police that it would be 11' high and they had planned a route which included a 14' 4" bridge! After many minor adventures of getting her out of the yard, down the narrow line with me on top lifting telephone lines etc... Out onto the main road and to Penwithick by a long and circuitous route, we were at Brian Boynes' place by 1300, off-loaded and safely into the shed by 1500. "Phew - good to see her in... the tractor towed her in via a wire through a small hole in the back wall, communications were a problem!!"

I was back in my office in Wareham by 2030, Wednesday the 1st of February feeling somewhat weary to say the least. Life ain't easy for a would-be sailor.

Of course my boss in Aberdeen had been yelling for me as soon as I left the office, he never wants me when I'm there. Carless Exploration and Sun Oil wanted to visit the rig and I had to arrange everything.

Journal: Thursday, 2nd February. "Another stunning blow! Richard the mast builder called to say he had revised his calculations and the apertures we had cut on the decks to take the masts were now not long enough!! ...Now he tells me, just when I've moved her from the builder to the painter, but Richard was right to increase his specifications if that was to give me that strongest possible design for the mast fittings. It's hard on the nervous system though!!"

During the next 14 days I stayed at Wareham for a rest, getting and making the odd phone call to keep the projects on the right lines. Thursday the 16th found me back in Wadebridge for the last time, ready to move Roamer from Penwithick to Ilminster, but staying in my cosy digs with Eileen Clark for a last delicious fish and veg meal.

At Penwithick I had the first sight of my bonny shop in her livery of black hull, grey topsides, and cream anti - fouling primer on the underneath section. She looked pretty good. Not wonderful in the way of straight waterlines or filling-in of the welds along the chines, but good enough, I thought.

Friday the 17th of February. At Penwithick by 0140, loaded up excess paint plus my bollards which Brian B had re-galvanised. The crane arrived and with only a little bother we had her outside by 0930. Waited on the truck until 1000 and had her loaded and ready to roll by 1100! Great!! The police escort arrived and away we went by 1115. This all seemed too good to be true – and was. "Old Bill" took us to a lay-by on Bodmin Hoor, said "Wait here", and drove off. We waited an hour for the next escort who took us 15 miles, dropped us, and drove off. This was at 1400 and I'm thinking of the crane I had arranged for Ilminster for 1300! But the next escort took us to the dual carriageway East of Okehampton and we took off up the A50/M5 at 70 mph and arrived at Marks Gs place by 1715. We had a little trouble getting her in the shed due to the sharp ramp in the workshop entrance but did it, even though part of the floor collapsed! She was in and jacked up by 2200. I went to my caravan, collapsed, and slept like the dead until 0700 – another major stage accomplished.

Next stage – Fitting Out. Saturday, 18th February, 1984.

"The workshop has doors on now, but it was several weeks before we got full power supplies, and the approach road never did get surfaced." the fitting out stage is where I really lost control of the spending. Mark Gamble did a good job of workmanship, she is strongly and beautifully fitted out, and he worked to my designs very well, BUT he took too long and cost too much, and didn't finish it.

I cannot advise strongly enough, to anyone contemplating having similar work carried out, to, (A) get a firm price fixed, (B) a firm completion date, and (C) get it all written up legally with the I's dotted and the T's crossed. I really don't think that Mark G. planned to drag out the job consciously, it was more of a case where a young chap setting out in business promised more then he could deliver, with the situation arising where he had to charge me for all the hours spent on the boat to pay his lads' wages, and I had to pay him or take the boat elsewhere to be done, with all the extra costs and trouble involved. I wanted my boat in the water as soon as possible and would pay to get that. Even at this stage I could not envisage running out of money.

So, the fitting out took from the end of February to the end of October, 8 months instead of the 4 we had agreed on, and cost twice the sum we had agreed, and even after all that the aft cabin wasn't finished.

During this summer, I had a lot going on with my rig working for the B.B. in Lincolnshire and near Manchester, with new crews and a new man working opposite me, which didn't help keep a check on how the fitting out was going.

The details of fitting out a 36ft boat would be enough to fill a separate book and which I have no intention of setting down here, but basically, we, and I did a lot of work on her myself, had to turn a cavernous steel frame into a home. First tasks were to make sure all the paintwork was good in the bilges, forepeak, and other places which would not be sprayed with insulating foam. After fitting out the main bulkhead and securing 1" battens to the frames that would be our furniture, that would be our first big job. Or rather the task of Chris Underdown of Aqua -Insulation. After that, Mark started forward to get the workshop made, which would give him a 10ft workbench to help with fitting out the remainder of the hull.

So the summer rolled on, I spent the duty tour on the rig of 37 days in May/June, not quite the 14 on, 14 off that I'm supposed to work. That didn't help me get the boat finished. But was good for the finances.

On the 4th of June I put in my notice to quit, giving me 3 months more on the rig, and then I'd be free to concentrate on getting Roamer afloat. I put my flat up for sale for £25,000 and am confident that the finances are O.K., in spite of "stunning blows" in the form of Mark G.'s ,monthly invoices. During this time there were plenty of things to do in the way of ensuring that all required equipment is ordered, manufactured, or found in second-hand chandleries. It was a constant worry to wonder if I had forgotten anything in the whirlpool of activity.

At this time I bought the only really expensive mistake of the project, a 10ft Glass Reinforced Plastic dinghy. I had this plan to have a rigid dinghy as a tender, and convert it to act as a life raft , with a mast and sail, on the self-sufficient principle. It seemed right, and was, in principle. I needed the dinghy so that we could try it for fitment on the fore deck, and install teak blocks to act as chocks for it. So I brought it from Brightlingsea, and after drawing in its shape on the foredeck, had Norman Hamper, who made my sail battens, fit it out very nicely, with a centre board, rudder and tiller in teak, very neat indeed but very costly as well. It wasn't a mistake at this time, but would become one.

The fitting out progressed slowly, I visited Ilminster and helped out whenever I could and started laying down completion dates, arranging transport, and the launching, which was to be at Brighton.

In mid July the masts arrived from Richard Mason, and, with a little time off from the rig at last, and the weather settled, I treated them with 25 coats of Decks Olya, a penetrating wood oil from Scandinavia, then a further 6 coats of the D2 sealant. They looked really good, beautiful, and strong.

The organisation seemed to be going really well, having various degrees of success with various outfits. The exhaust system was being made in Plymouth, propeller stem gear and anchor bow rollers in Teignmouth, stainless steel fittings for the rudders in Chard, and the self-steering gear "nearly ready" in Colchester, amongst others.

By mid August I had the good news that the flat sale was almost completed. Good, finances were low!

Journal: Tuesday 4th September. In the caravan at Ilminster. Well, the deed is done, this is Day One for Bob Burns in retirement, having quit my job and now a free man."

During the early part of September Mark took a two-week holiday, the rest of us pressed on with the project. I took two days off to visit the Southampton Boat Show and to pick up my sails from Peter Lucas, I also brought a radio receiver from Smith Midlands Communications at Totton, Southampton.

At the boat show I met Captain Brian Evans R.V., who is the secretary of the R.N.S.A./ Whitbread Round The World Race Committee. He was very interested in my project and agreed it would be in our mutual interest to be in contact about the race. I plan to be well ahead, in time and distance, of the race fleet but it will be nice to know where they are.

Back at Ilminster I resumed the never-ending work. The forward part of the boat, that is, the workshop, heads, midship cabin etc, was going O.K. but the after cabin was being neglected, so I tried to get some action in there. I wanted at least the ply cladding in, which required a lot of hacking off of excess insulating material. I was working a fairly average day from 0700 to 2200 on the boat.

"Still a million things to do, only thing is to press on." top priority now was to get all the large sections of cladding into the boat, so that I could get the Engine Room hatch on. After this was on, there was only access for items under 24" wide. We made a date for "Move out" of the shed for Tuesday 25th September, which also happens to be my niece Sandie's birthday, An omen? I believe in them.

Tuesday the 25th duly arrived and though it took us from 1000 till 1430 to get her out of the shed, as last she was sat on her cradle, out in the fresh air, away from planing machines, dust, and Radio One!! There was still plenty to do, and I pressed on, pretty much on my own in the interior now.

Journal: Monday 1st October. "Disaster!! I had started rubbing down the underwater section ready for anti-fouling when I noticed some bubbly-looking paint on the anti-foul primer. On attacking it with a scraper I found – RUST!! I spread the attack with the scraper to non-bubbly paint with the same result, rusty metal with no bond to the paint and it hardly looks as though it has been blasted. Rust!! after 8 months of sitting in a dry shed. What a blow. I tried to keep calm over it, but had a struggle not to become depressed over the way things were going.

I screamed for help, and Blake's paints had their S.W. agent visit me. Rupert Dove-Meadows, a real nice chap. He took paint thickness all around the hull and had a scrape here and there. The story seems to be that Brian Boynes and his merry men at Penwithick did a lousy job for me. The paint on deck is O.K., on topsides nearly O.K., and below the waterline, where it really matters, useless. On the starboard quarter, where I found the first rust, it appears not to have been blasted at all and only has two coats of paint on. Charming!!

That's the story, what's the solution? In theory to blast off all the underwater section and start again. Who pays? How much? That's the problem. No wonder I'm depressed.

After a sleep on the problem, things seemed clearer, there was no way I was going to bodge the job, it had to be a blast off and paint again. So, I asked around for local blasting outfits but got little joy or interest. I drove S.W. towards Brian Boynes.

Eventually I reached Penwithick and confronted Brian B. with the facts. I was always of the opinion that he was O.K. and it was his young work force which had let him down. He seemed genuinely distressed and surprised that they hadn't done it properly. 'They took some time", he said, "and used all the paint". Yes, and perhaps they threw it out of the back door as well. Anyway, the outcome was that he agreed to get his mobile blasting outfit organised to come to Ilminster and do the job again.

This would take place in 10 days time, so on my return to Ilminster I made up a paint requirement list and phoned it through to Rupert Dove-Meadows. I pressed on with the work aboard, there was still plenty to do – of course.

Saturday the 6th October was an occasion for a "Red Letter Day" entry in the journal. "First night aboard" it says. "I had a really good sleep for my first one aboard, turned in at 2215 and slept till 0630, then lay there enjoying it till 0720!"This was a big practical step forward as well for morale as it meant I could operate from the boat instead of the caravan for meals etc, and, maybe more importantly, keeping me from the temptations of "The Lamb" and "The Five Devils". It was much quieter too, with no lorries roaring past on the busy A303 from 0400 onwards. Well, maybe they still did, but I didn't hear them anymore.

I carried on organising for the blast and paint job, fixing up the hire of some tarpaulins while I was applying the seven coats required. This time it would be done properly – I would do it.

The rudder and trim-tab were taking shape O.K., and various fittings for it appearing from "Joe the Welder" in Chard.

I played sailor and rigger's games, rigged the jury mast and hoisted the dingy aboard, turned over and sitting on its chocks, I didn't like it. Due to the sheer of Roamer's foredeck, and that of the dinghy when upturned, there was a very unsafe and unseamanlike gap between dinghy and deck, not one that I could live with. I rigged it all down for the moment and prepared the lower section of the jury rig legs for their secondary role, that of "standing legs". They are bolted onto mahogany blocks at the ship's side, and , with mahogany feet, will enable the ship to be driven onto a beach and dried out to allow inspection of, and repairs to the underwater section of the hull, in parts of the world where there might not be the facilities which are accepted as the norm in European waters.

Friday, 12 October, 1984, the day began with the shocking news that the I.R.A. had bombed the Conservative Party Conference at Brighton. The lovely old Grand Hotel had been wrecked, with 4 killed and 20 injured, but Maggie is O.K., and the rest of the Cabinet.

I had a difficult day. "Rupert Dove-Meadows arrived, but with only the primer. The main paint order arrives next Tuesday. A bit tight for this time!" The rudder is glued up, but needs more fittings from Joe. Tried to hook up the cassette player speakers but the connectors don't match. Tried pressure test cooker tank, but found a pin hole in the brazing. What do I think of these suppliers?

Undeterred, I started organizing the move to Brighton and the Launch, for the 31st/1st Nov.

Will I ever be ready for it?

On Tuesday the 16th the blasting job took place, and a dirty messy job it was, with grit and dust all over the ship, even though I'd covered her with tarpaulins. We blasted everything off below the waterline up to one foot above it, then got a coat of wet primer on while the steel was still warm. (If only I had known about this system while at Les Savage's!!)The job was done by 1800. "I am now faced with the task of a solid week's work applying four coats of Epoxy Pitch, 1 coat of Anti-Fouling Primer, 2 coats of Anti-fouling and the water line cutting in job. The Epoxy Pitch has to be applied by brush, one coat every 24 hours, and to do one side today took me three hours. I did it all though. I did it, so it's done right now.

Hopefully, things are looking up. Mark and the boys hung the rudder for fitment test, it swung freely, and looks good. The companionway ladder was rigged and also looks good, I sold the caravan and got a cheque from my Company Pension Scheme pay off. I could do with some good news.

Journal: Saturday, 20th October. "Well, if anyone was paying me for doing all this I'd certainly be earning my money!!" There follows a whole page of the day's work, still painting the hull, emptying the caravan and moving all the gear aboard, buying and stowing provisions, etc. etc its never ending, but no-one else is going to do it, that's for sure.

By Monday the 22nd, I'd applied five coats of Epoxy Pitch and was able to put a coat of anti-foul primer on the starboard side, easy work after the thick pitch, and it went on so quickly that I did the port side too. Next day I put on a coat of the Green Anti-foul and was very pleased with its looks. The rudder and trim-tab were about finished and we had the hangings at last. I'm counting down to 'Move Day". 7 days to go.

During that 7 days, somehow, I got everything done. Waterline cut in, rudder and trim-tab together and painted, all gear aboard and stowed ready for…

Journal: Tuesday, 30th October, 1984. 'Last day at Ilminster, all packed up and ready to go.

At last, on Wednesday the 31st, Roamer was loaded onto Phoenix Marine's low-loader, and, in few words, and not many hours, was whisked to Brighton Marina by 1930. I slept aboard still on trailer, parked right in front of the travel-lift, so that they couldn't miss us.

Chapter Five

Afloat – Early Sea Trials

And, so at 0830 on the 1st November 1984, with no fuss and ceremonies, my bonny ship at last reached her element. By 0930 she was berthed quietly at pier 32 while I helped the boatyard lads off-load the masts, which had been on the low-loader, and stow them on the mast racks. I have to get them rigged and ready for stepping by early Monday morning.

Mum was my first visitor, bringing welcome sandwiches and tea, and she was duly impressed. The rest of the day was spent visiting around Brighton, and organising my Marina berth.

Over the weekend I had more visitors but they had to be content with a quick look at Roamer, and chatting to me while I carried on working on the masts. All the masthead lights had to be wired up, that is, a Xenon bright-light flasher on the foremast, and a combined tricolour/all-round white light on the main. The radio aerial ran up the inside of the foremast and terminated at an insulator under the mast cap fitting. All the cables were taped together and had a piece of foam rubber taped to them every foot. No tapping cables in my masts, thank you!

The Firdell Blipper 300 Radar Reflector was screwed to the foreside of the foremast as high as possible.

All the running rigging was then made up, there being no standing rigging, of course. It is fairly simple, on each mast, a four-part main halyard, on the fore, two ghoster halyards, and on the main (there ghoster halyards). The radar reflector prevents my having three ghoster halyards on the fore. The halyards are all secured to strong eyes on the mast cap fittings. The only other rigging is the "Lazy Jack" sail-gathering system, which can be seen in diagrams of the sail-rig.

I devised a simple system to step the masts, the normal one of having strops under the spreaders not being possible, of course. Four coachscrew eyes were screwed into the octagonal section of the masts, but above deck level, my nylon strops passed round under them, and the crane's lifting strops shackled to mine. We passed a half-hitch round the masts about two thirds the way up, and they hung beautifully for stepping. Remember, I used to be a rigger in the boatyard. I still think I should have got a discount price for the job, for the masts went in very quickly. By 1000, the boatyard work-boat had towed me off to berth 51/49, and I was stowed away for the last stage of the completion which took until Tuesdy 15th January 1965, when we at last went to sea, with a liberal coating of snow and ice. Cliff Groves and I took her out of the harbour entrance for her first feel of the sea.

The previous ten weeks had been the familiar long story of attending to every little detail, struggling to get people to do things for me, even though I was paying most of them. I had to hope that they would turn up when they said they would, and grind the teeth when they didn't, but, the bottom line is the fact that, during that long, cold winter, Roamer was turned into a sea-going ship.

The First of February was a notable day when Cliff and I took Roamer to the Outer Harbour and Roger Muir swung and adjusted the two compasses for deviation. That went well, he got the deviation down to two degrees except on a N.E. heading where it is three degrees, but we shan't worry too much about that.

On Sunday the 3rd, Cliff and I went out again, there wasn't much wind, which gave us the opportunity to give the ghosters an airing, and to test the anchoring system. All went well with that, we finished the day by groping our way back into the Marina by its foghorn, in the dark.

Monday the 4th was a much nicer day, and a good day's sailing was had by Cliff and I in the delightful company of Barbara Holder, the Editor of Junk Rig Association's Newsletter. She brought along 2-year-old Emily who, well wrapped up against the "cool" breeze, seemed to enjoy the sunny day as much as we did. I had met Barbara at the J.R.A.'s A.G.M. at the East Coast Boat Show on the 12th. She wanted to write an article on Roamer for the Newsletter.

Next day I ran off to sea in Roamer, on my own, for the first time. Having had a N.E. wind blowing all night, I wasted it by having to go into town for a few hours. We sailed out of the Marina by 1200 and ran off to the West, and though we ran out of that N.E wind before the Looe Channel off Selsey Bill, we made it to the anchorage off Seaview, Isle of Wight, by the evening.

I had to settle for Cowes the following day, the weather was lousy, with fog and rain. Thursday dawned wet and windy, but I was determined to get away from this noisy place, for if the hovercraft weren't bad enough, the pile-driving operations were. So we ran off down the Solent towards, Hurst Castle, shot through the Narrows on the tide with a N.E. force 6 behind us, and on past the Needles. Once out in the open sea, the waves were big enough to be "interesting" and to give a "George", the self-steering, a real test. With only the foresail up, and that with the first big reef taken in, we were making 6 or 7 knots. Then the self-steering trim-tab started vibrating badly. I had always worried about this trim-tab, ever since I first saw it made, a blade, 10 ft long, with fittings only at top and bottom must vibrate in the water, I had thought. At that time there had been no chance to get extra fittings made, and now my fears were borne out. Speeding along, the trim-tab transmitted its vibrations right up through the gearing to the wind vane.

This problem, combined with forecasts of Easterlies of force 8 & 9, made me deem it wise to run into Weymouth that evening, rather than attempt to pass Portland Bill.

Sea trials after that amounted to fighting my way back to Brighton to get the trim-tab modified. I had to make my way to the East into a bitter East wind which blew between force 5 and 6 for 16 days. I had a few excitements like the exhaust pipe setting fire to the ply cladding in the engine room, in the middle of Poole Bay in a bit of a blow. Reaching Lymington, I had a cold night there, so cold that on leaving in the morning, a layer of ice on the sea surface took the paint off the waterline.

I painfully worked my way and made it back to Brighton by 2130 on the 20th February, after trials which, while not teaching me much sailing, certainly showed some problems I was glad to find out about in the Channel, rather than further afield.

Back in Brighton, I resigned myself to being "harbour-bound" while carrying out the modifications. As soon as I was back in my Inner Harbour berth, alongside Roy and Carol's "Spray", I applied my rigging know-how, and design planning of the rudder, and in an hour, rigged a pole across the pushpit, hooked up a block and tackle, and lifted that rudder right out of its gudgeons. In fact, it popped up once free, surprisingly buoyant. Once it was on the jetty, I measured it up for the additional pintle and gudgeon required to stop the trim-tab vibration, and ordered the piece right away, which was just as well, as it took four weeks to get.

I was grateful for a visit from Mike Richey, owner of the famous "Jester", who was kind enough to give me some valuable advice. This was, to have cringle eyes inserted at the "Clew" of each sail panel, in case the present webbing tabs should part, also to have the Norway Spruce battens sheathed in G.R.P, both of which suggestions I had carried out

Peter Lucas's van picked up my sails from Brighton, and while he had them at Portsmouth, I asked him about putting in the cringle eyes, to strengthen the area around each eye, as that was the clew for the sail at each reefed position.

The battens I took up to Garth's G.R.P. shop at the boatyard for sheathing, but due to costs, and to the time it took me to sand the paint off them, I had to settle for just the top three battens receiving this treatment.

My brother Terry and I were mounting a sponsorship drive at this time. We made up 24 packs of literature, containing details of my background, description of Roamer, and the plan, and sent them off to a wide spectrum of business concerns, Banks, Department Stores, Breweries, the Marina, etc., but received only negative replies. I did get the odd bit of minor backing, for which I was grateful, and which is acknowledged in the introduction.

I wasn't entirely surprised, but certainly disappointed with the reaction of Brighton. Here was a working class chap, born and bred in the town, about to set off on a singlehanded world voyage from the town's marina, not something that happens every week, and no-one was interested. We had plans to involve local schools, to make a living Geographical Adventure Project out of the voyage for the children, and to benefit the local Lifeboat Institution, but no-one appeared interested in funding the voyage to the minor amount of £5,000, which I asked for as a back-up fund, should anything go wrong. Everything else was paid for, by me, to the amount of around £60,000.

Maybe if I was 5' 6", Blonde, 42-26-36...??

I made a trip to London for yet more equipment, and to return my Concept compass to Munro-Sestrel at Barking for repairs to damage suffered when it had jumped out of its bracket. While in town I visited the Embassies of South Africa and Australia regarding visas. Surprisingly in view of reputations, South Africa was no problem, no visa, "Just turn up and we'll give you a 6 month visitors visa." At Australia House I had to fill out a large form mainly assuring the Australian Government that I would not be seeking employment, or become a drain on their finances!

Back aboard, all the modifications were finalised, and the rudder re-installed. I bought 120 fathoms (720ft) of 2" hemp rope cheap from the chandlery, (it was blocking their doorway!), and stowed it in the aft cabin. This is to be my "Southern Ocean Brake".

It was an all-action time, but then when wasn't? I felt that I had been working on "The Project" for as long as I could remember. But at last I felt my bonny ship was about ready for the ocean. This is a good time for us to take a tour of her.

Join me in gazing at this ship of mine. She rather stands out in the crowd, wouldn't you say? The black hull with high freeboard, low grey deckhouses, two beautiful, gleaming wooden masts shining in the surrounding forest of alloy of the other yachts, the tan sails, neatly bundled on their booms all say "I'm a one-off, and proud of it".

Step aboard this fine craft, my ship, my home, my everything. Most people's first impression is that she is more of a small ship than a yacht This impression is encouraged by the steelwork and the colour scheme. The matt black hull with no fancy "Cove line" between the black and the green anti-fouling paint, and deckhouses of light grey. The "small ship" aim was entirely deliberate in my design. I wanted a vessel which could cope with all sea conditions, small ships go to sea in all conditions, so... a small ship design. Hence the low-profile deckhouses, with a centre cockpit for safety and as a control position for working sails. A deep cockpit surrounded by grab rails and padeyes for securing my safety harness. Note the strength of the grab rails, including the high ones on either side of the forward deck house. Note the 30-inch-high guardrail stanchions with their matching pulpit forward and pushpit aft, a massive guardrail of one and three eighths inch galvanised pipe which extends right across the transom, protecting the rudder head and giving me strong protection when working on the steering equipment. The guardrails along the ships side are of half-inch rope, but not wire, the rope being equally as strong as wire, but kinder on the hands and easy to cut away should the need arise.

Note the small portholes set into the houses, twelve altogether, so much stronger and safer than the windows seen on most yachts. The portholes are made of half-inch thick Perspex, very strong to begin with, but then their eight inch diameter is bolted onto the steel from the <u>outside</u>, so the sea, to get in, must push the Perspex through the six inch diameter hole in the steel. There are two ten-inch by six-inch windows to allow light into the after cabin, but these are on the aft face of the cockpit and thus not in such an exposed position as the portholes. The teak surrounds on the ports and windows are to protect the edges of the Perspex, and to make the installation prettier, but they play no part in the strength or the watertight integrity of the portholes.

On deck are two 20-inch square hinge hatches, one on the foredeck, and one on the after deckhouse. There are for access below, but are also important for ventilation. The forward hatch is hinged on its aft edge, the aft hatch on its forward, so that whichever way the wind is blowing, from forward or aft, the breeze will be directed below and keep the ship well ventilated.

The only other entry to the ship is the main hatch-way, which is much smaller than is normal. This is deliberate, the smaller the hatch, the less water can get in. The hatchway can be closed off with a one-inch thick washboard which is in two halves, so that the lower half can be left shipped in rough weather but still allow access. The washboards have sliding bolts which prevent their falling out in the event of a capsize. The sliding hatch-top also has a locking system, inside and out, and slides under a steel "garage".

On deck are six pairs of mooring bollards, two towing bollards aft, and two more forward for being towed and for mooring. The towing bollards aft are substantial, with steel strengthening welded beneath them. They and their matching fairleads are designed not only for towing and rescue work, but also for trailing my "Southern Ocean Brake", 720 feet of two-inch diameter rope which I plan to drag astern in the Southern Ocean storms, to both slow the ship down, and to aid in keeping the stem directly in the line with the monster seas "down there".

On the foredeck, in chocks, are four alloy spars, which comprise my "jury" mast. Should the great waves ever overwhelm even this sturdy ship, I am confident that, so long as I can keep the water out of her, she and I probably would not. As a contingency plan for such an event, David Hunt of Needlespar, at Warsash, and I, designed this jury mast which, when rigged up, becomes a pair of sheerlegs 27 feet in height, with a fore- and a back-stay, and a halyard, to set either the junk rig sails, if I had been able to save them, or special jury rig sails which have aboard, to get me to a port, or an island, where I could replace my lost masts with trees, or telegraph poles. I carry two spare masthead fittings. The sheerlegs can be used to install the new masts. As an extra facility, the lower halves of the sheerlegs can be adapted, with special fittings, to bolt onto the ship's side and form legs with which the ship will stand up when driven gently on to a suitable beach, to allow inspection and repairs to the underwater hull.

Also on the foredeck is the anchor winch, which looks antique, and almost is. Simpson-Lawrence, the makers, were unable to give me specific technical details on it, as their memories and records only go back 45 years! I am confident though, just looking at its construction, its open gears and general impression of simple strength, that. given the occasional ration of oil and grease, it will not let me down. The 3/8 inch chain leads from the winch to the 60lb C.Q.R. anchor, 15lb heavier than most yachts of 36 feet carry. It is stowed on the stemhead fitting which projects to be self-stowing on its four-inch bronze roller, without the tip of its plough hitting the hull. Note the high sides of the stemhead fitting, protected by stainless steel chafing plates, and the bolt across the top to prevent the chain, going back to the anchor winch, passes over the chain gypsy, round its aft face, and then forward again to a roller set in a stainless steel cowl over the navel pipe which leads into the chain locker, thus giving maximum grip for the chain on the gypsy.

Look at these beautiful masts now, specially made for me by Richard Mason, in Bristol Docks. They are of Douglas Fir, in segments, made to a patented design, wherein each segment is keyed into its partners, giving extra glued surface and, using the modem recorcinol glues, immensely strong. They are mostly eleven inches outside diameter, and round, but are built up to a fourteen inch octagonal shape at the deck partners for extra strength, and taper off to eight inches in diameter at the truck, or top. They are hollow, having a four inch hole right through them for running electrical cables for lights, and the radio aerial. The cables have a piece of foam rubber taped to them each foot, to prevent tapping and chafe. The masts are both thirty five feet in height above the deck, and are unstayed. The gloss on them comes from the application, by me, of thirty-one coats of Decks Olya, a Norwegian wood oil. I promise myself that one day I will calculate how far I travelled up and down the masts whilst applying that oil!

The sails were made by Peter Lucas of W.G. Lucas & Son Ltd., of Portsmouth. They are of Tan colour, in eight ounce Dacron, except for the "top triangle", which is ten ounce material, Peter's "bullet-proof" sailcloth. This top triangle design is my own idea, being a simple way of designing out the conventional junk rig yard and top angled batten, which, when reefed right down, are not controlled by the sheet, and tend to "fall off" to leeward, causing a broaching effect. The weight of the yard also gives it a tendency to roll about in rough seas.

Alan Boswell did a good job on the basic design of the sails, and they are just fine. He was happy to advise me on my plan for the top triangle, but it is my idea, and I take full responsibility for it. The full length battens and booms are of Norway Spruce, made by that good chap Norman Hamper at the Upper Quay, Fareham.

You will have noticed the Perspex "Astro-dome" on the starboard side of the forward deckhouse. This is the "roof" of my inside steering position, a designed-in facility to enable me to steer the ship, and/or keep a lookout from inside the midship cabin, a real boon in cold weather.

Before we go below, let me show you the steering equipment. The 24-inch wheel in the cockpit has a twelve-toothed sprocket on its shaft, from which a length of chain leads to the starboard, connecting to two 5mm stainless steel wires which continue to the starboard and pass through a conduit in the starboard cockpit coaming. Out on the side deck the wires pass round a pair of lead blocks, and lead aft, past two guide blocks, to the aft deck and round another pair of lead blocks. From there one wire goes to the port side, round a single lead block, and thence to a crossbow quadrant, the other wire goes direct to the quadrant. The quadrant has an n arc which keeps the wires taut when the rudder is turned. The system is in line with well-known K.I.S.S. principle, Keep It Strong and Simple. The thinking being that, with the wires on deck, I can see that they are in good condition, and can grease and oil them and their lead blocks to keep them that way.

Mounted on the pushpit is the "Levanter" self-steering gear, designed by John Holden of Levanter Vane Gears from the construction drawings before the hull was built. It consists of a wind vane mounted ten feet above the sea, and connected through John's sturdy gearing to a cross-link arm which drives a trim-tab trailing on the main rudder. The method of operation is to set the ship on the desired course, get her balanced with the sheets and the main rudder, put the brake on the wheel's shaft, and engage "George", the wind vane. He can be adjusted to any angle to the wind by an endless rope turning a worm drive. The endless rope is controlled from the cockpit The system has three major virtues, (1) The equipment is fitted high up on my strong pushpit away from most waves, (2) It has nothing trailing unprotected in the sea, and (3) I can use the main rudder without having to disconnect the Levanter system. The self-steering worked well on early sea trials, particularly in following winds, which is comforting.

Let us go inside my bonny ship now, be careful as you enter the main hatchway, use the four F's method, feet first facing forward, and keep a firm grip on the sliding hatch handle, it's a long way down. Seven feet to the cabin sole, or floor. You'll notice that the companionway ladder is rather narrow and has 45 degree wooden blocks on each side of each step, which is a little inconvenient in harbour, but very useful at sea when she is rolling or heeled.

Isn't it cosy here? Very snug and compact, with no wide spaces to be thrown across in rough weather, grab handles in useful places. The woodwork is strong, beautifully fitted, and finished with a matt varnish.

To port is the galley area, with a Taylor's two-burner paraffin stove and a warming oven under the burners, surrounded by stowage lockers for ready-use food items, crockery and cutlery. A bilge pump is mounted at the aft end of the galley area, over a deep stainless steel sink which has a water pump. Forward of the cooker is a small work-top, and forward of that, a very important space, my "cosy chair". Designed for me to take short naps in when sailing alone, it has blue vinyl cushions and a seat belt for strapping myself in when the seas are rough. There is a reading light over the seat, and, if you have an "inside leg" dimension of 29 inches or more, you may rest your feet on the side of the chart table!

There is a bulkhead forward of the cosy chair, which extends right across the ship, it has a door, but we won't go through it just yet. Towards the starboard side of the bulkhead is the chart table, the centre-piece of the saloon, at which I can sit, on my sea berth, and do all my writing, some of my thinking, and, of course, the navigation work. There is a drawer under the table top, for ready-use chart stowage, compass deviation tables are on the bulkhead, as are navigation instruments.

Also on the bulkhead, forward of the chart table, is the beautiful photo-print, from which Roamer gets her name. It is a colour photograph of a whale's tail fluke, magnificently caught by photographer Tom Bean. Ted Sherman has added the following words,

"He Roams the Seas in Freedom, with No Enemies Save Man".

How sadly true.

Above Roamer is the main switchboard, controlling all Navigation Lights, Compass Repeater power, Radio, and Chart Table Lamp. A "Fastnet" paraffin lamp hangs between the switchboard and the radio receiver, which has excellent coverage from 150 KHz to 30 MHz. It is a Yaesu FRG 7700, and is aboard mainly for receiving time signals and weather forecasts, but picks up general entertainment programmes as well of course.

On the starboard side of the cabin is my sea berth, a 6 feet, 6 inch long bunk, very cosily built into the corner so that the lower half of my body is in an enclosed space under lockers, and my shoulders and chest are alongside the chart table, which prevents my being rolled out at sea. The bunk has a reading light. From the sea berth I can see the main compass repeater in the "Wendy House", the Echo-sounder repeater and the luminous alarm clock, which are on a part-bulkhead over the bunk and facing me. The cassette player is close at hand as well. Above the bunk, on the ship's side, are shelves packed with navigation books, pilots, and general reading. My favourite books are kept here. The bunk has stowage lockers under it, as does the cosy chair.

The aft part of the midship cabin is my inside steering position, basically a raised platform to give sufficient height for all-round vision through my astro-dome. Its aft face is the bulkhead between the midship and aft cabins, and mounted on this bulkhead is the inside steering wheel, facing aft, as its main purpose is to allow me to assist the self steering system to keep on a direct down-wave course in the mighty Southern Ocean Seas. Standing at this wheel I have a part-bulkhead at my back, which has a hinged seat on it. This bulkhead started off life as a blank wall of one inch ply, which I found uninteresting, and a little claustrophobic, so I had the carpenter cut two "windows" in it, high up, and then two more lower down. On cutting these windows, the inside steering position was dubbed, "The Wendy House", and that is its name now.

On the starboard side of the Wendy House are large lockers for more books, ship's papers, files, and technical equipment manuals. There is also an emergency Camping Gaz cooker stowed in here, with two 10Ib Gaz bottles, carefully checked for leaks. On the aft bulkhead, to starboard, are stowed the V.H.F hand-held radio, the Lokata Radio Direction Finder, and a charger unit for both of them. Lower down are inside stowages for the two compasses, the Sestrel-Moore Master Compass, and the Concept Sailing Compass, both by Munro-Sestrel, who used to be Henry-Browne. Above the wheel on the aft bulkhead is a repeater compass which works off the Sestrel-Moore. Alongside it is the Seafarer 700 Echo-Sounder, which, mounted on a wooden pad, can be moved to a matching pad in the cockpit, forward of the wheel. There is quick and easy access from the Wendy House to the companionway and on deck.

The floor of the Wendy House forms the top of a locker, the upper part of which is a long-term chart stowage, and the lower part, the fresh vegetables store. These being stowed in plastic baskets screwed to the floor. The onions, potatoes, and carrots, etc., like it in here as it is cool and dark. Also in this locker is the very basic plumbing manifold, allowing either pump, galley or heads, to pump out of either tank, port or starboard. Each tank holds 65 gallons, and I carry about 15 gallons more in small containers around the ship.

In sunny weather, the midship cabin is light and airy, having the main hatch, the astro-dome, six portholes, and two decklights to let in plenty of light. These decklights are glass prisms set into the steel deck, which magnify and project into the cabin, any light shining on them. There are three more in the workshop, and one in the heads.

Let's go into the workshop now, through the doorway forward. The main feature is the ten foot workbench, filling the port side and allowing me plenty of elbow room to make the repairs and fabrications which are bound to become necessary during the voyage. There is a stout vice half way along the bench which is removable. Outboard of the bench, on the ship's side, hang lengths of spare wood and metal, saws, and a grease-gun. Above those are small lockers holding a variety of ship's stores. At the aft end of the workbench is the 1½ gallon paraffin pressure tank safety measure. Two fire extinguishers and a fire blanket hang nearby. Under the workbench are two strong drawers holding tools, and six open-fronted lockers, my "Hardware Store", a large collection of tools, wood, metal, rubber etc., a veritable ironmonger's shop.

Right forward in this compartment is a steel bulkhead across the ship with a watertight door in it to port. This is a collision bulkhead, designed to maintain the watertight integrity of the ship in the event of a head-on collision splitting open the bows. Unlikely, but possible. The compartment forward of the bulkhead, the forepeak, is used as a stowage for lightweight spares and stores.

Immediately aft of the bulkhead, is the foremast, well, the base of it anyway, secured into a strong fitting with wedges and coachbolts. The base fitting is designed to allow drainage and ventilation.

Abaft the mast is the chain locker, a specially tall and narrow one, to avoid the chance of the incoming chain piling up in a pyramid, falling over, and jamming itself. The locker has an inspection hatch, and drainage into the bilge system. There is 270 feet of 3/8" chain. The inboard end of the chain is secured to a strong nylon rope which is in turn secured to a "clench" or padeye on the keel. The rope is long enough to allow the "bitter end" of the chain to reach the deck, to allow extension of the chain, with more chain, or with nylon rope "rodes", or maybe to buoy the chain and let it go temporarily.

On the starboard ship's side hang lifejackets, harnesses, a crowbar, and spare ropes. A 'Victory" paraffin heater is stowed here, close to two "Tilley" paraffin lamps. Also to starboard is the sail bin, a small one, holding my Jury rig sails, two "Ghosters", lightweight nylon sails for light wind sailing, and two 150 foot, 5/8" nylon ropes, the anchor rodes. Around the chain locker are netting stowages containing paint and grease etc. There are hatches in the floors, giving access to stowage in the bilges. The hatches have catches to prevent their opening should the ship ever turn upside-down. There are similar hatches and stowage throughout the ship.

In the starboard after corner of the workshop compartment is the washroom, the "heads" to a sailor. In this "little room" is a sink with a water pump, a formica work-top, a mirror with a fluorescent light, and lots of stowage for washing materials, toothpaste, razor blades etc. I stow my electrical spares and ready-use paraffin and methylated spirits containers in here as well. The "main attraction" is the toilet itself, a good old reliable "Racasan" galvanised bucket, with wooden seat and lid, bought cheaply at the Beaulieu Boat Jumble Sale, it is absolutely reliable and foolproof. No smelly plumbing problems here, the famous "Bucket and Chucket" system. I initially installed a plastic "Porta-Potti" toilet, but threw it out as too complicated! There is a grab handle in front of the toilet for holding on tight in rough seas, which doubles as a step for exiting up through the foredeck hatch which is immediately above the toilet. The builder was most surprised that I could accept having a hatch over the toilet, but why not? Who's looking? Under the floor of the heads is the echo-sounder transducer.

Let's move aft now, back through the midship saloon. Keep to the right, between the companionway ladder and the galley, and through the doorway to the aft cabin. Mind your head now, this is the only part of the ship without full headroom, as we pass under the port cockpit seat. If you go right aft and sit on the midship seat we can see all that is in this "State-Room" as I used to call it, as it always seemed to be in a right old state, but it's better now.

The centre-piece in here, which draws all eyes, is the "Iron Top-Sail", "The Big Blue Beastie", alias the Perkins 03-152 Diesel engine, all 1100 lbs of it, which cost, with its accessories, over £4000. Pure sailors try, and sometimes do, manage without an engine, and they have my admiration and some envy, but I am a realist, I know where I'm going, and what I'll be doing, so decided long ago that I needed a big strong engine to help me, as I sail single-handed, into, and out of, marinas, crowded anchorages, and ports and harbours which have the wind blowing out of their entrances, which is surprisingly often the case. I know that my Junk Rig won't go to windward at all well, and it's a desperate business for a weary single-hander trying to make port, to beat into a fierce wind to gain his refuge.

So the engine sits proudly and unashamedly in the centre of the aft cabin, under the cockpit well, but, with plenty of headroom work to allow work on it, I have no plans to box it in. I like to be able to see if all, and to be able to see oil and water levels without dismantling the woodwork. Visiting another yachtsman's beautifully fitted out boat once, I asked him where his engine was. He removed several bulkhead panels, revealing the motor crammed into a tiny space. "Where's the dipstick?" I asked, he waved vaguely over the engine, "Over the other side somewhere," he said. I couldn't live like that.

There is an instrument console abaft and above the engine with the starter/heater key, a tachometer dial with engine hours read-out, water temperature, oil pressure, and ammeter gauges. The engine is fitted with an audible alarm system for warning of low oil pressure or high water temperature. The alarm sets off a klaxon in the Wendy House, a two-tone, "police car"- type horn. There is no engine instrumentation in the cockpit, only the single-lever throttle and gear control. This is deliberate policy to "encourage me" to look at the engine, in the engine room, and "Think Before Starting". Is the Lube oil ok? The Cooling water? Are the seacocks open? Is the fuel turned on? The engine can be stopped from the midship cabin.

Still on the engine, observe that it can also be started by hand, from either end, and that it has a Jabsco mechanical pump, worked from a power take-off belt, which will pump out the deep engine room bilge, and contain any major leaks, while I get after solving the problem. There are fuel tanks in the keel, and more across the forward part of the aft cabin. Capacity is 150 gallons. Fuel is pumped from the tanks, by hand pump, by me, to a header tank. This system should keep condensation and "gunge" down in the keel tanks. Even so, the header tank supplies the engine via a water trap and a fuel filter so I reckon the engine has a fair chance of getting a supply of clean fuel.

The main mast base sits on the fuel tanks, which were strengthened to take the strain. It is secured similarly to the fore mast. Two 110 Amp Hour 12-Volt batteries live in a box alongside the mast to port. In the starboard forward corner is a locker holding work clothes, rucksacks, etc., and aft of it, a double locker of pigeon holes designed to hold square ice cream boxes. There are about 40 of these boxes, holding more ship's stores from stainless steel bolts to sprouting seeds, and Tilley lamp spares to needles and thread, a veritable floating shop. The boxes were collected by my mother over a long period when I was getting the ship built. Thanks Mum, and the ladies of the "Whitehawk Co-op".

Aft of this locker is a 6-foot, 6-inch bunk, with lockers outboard of it for books and general stowage, there is a matching bunk and lockers to port. Right aft amidships, is an area which started out as a 5-foot, 6-inch bunk, but ended up as stowage for my 720 foot, 2-inch diameter, "Southern Ocean Brake" rope. More spare rope, and the 25lb Kedge spade anchor, 30 feet of chain, and 150 feet of rope are also stowed here.

Forward of the port bunk is the wardrobe, with plenty of airy hanging space, and stowage for boots and shoes under it. One more locker forward of the wardrobe holds more clothes. The exhaust pipe exits through this locker and has a sea cock valve.

The aft cabin is light and airy with its creamy foam-backed vinyl headboarding, six portholes, two windows and the 20-inch square hatch. There are two dorade air vents to supply air to the engine when the ship is battened down, and a Solarvent air extractor, powered by a solar cell in the cockpit. A Fastnet paraffin lamp and an electric fluorescent lamp supply light at night.

There is stowage available under the two bunks, and more in some of the bilges. The floor sections all lift to give access to seacocks and the propeller shaft stern gland. Some of the polyurethane insulating foam can be seen on the hull aft, where I never managed to get it boxed in. A 1½ inch layer of foam was sprayed over the entire interior surface of the ship's sides and deckheads before fitting out and proved itself well worth the expense during the long cold winter of 1984/85, which I spent living aboard finishing the ship off, in Brighton Marina.

So there we are, we have had our tour, a fairly exhaustive one, and if I missed anything, we can pick it up as we go along. You will now be able to follow me as I go around my ship on the voyage.

I am entirely happy with her, and would change very little if I were to start the project over again, which I definitely would not want to do anyway!

A big day arrived on the 1ˢᵗ April when my "Winter rent" ran out for the Inner Harbour and I moved out to a berth on Pontoon 9, in the Outer Harbour, close alongside H.M.S. Cavalier. I was the yacht nearest to the sea, her bow now pointing South and lifting gently to the swell which rolled in through the entrance.

My nephew David and Mike Richey helped me out through the lock and we had a brisk sail to celebrate the day.

Various friends were taken out for "Jolly's", including the happy family from "Kirinka", who came out one day, for a fun day's sailing which included putting Father, Inyake Beguiristain and his daughter in their rubber dingy while I sailed round them for a photography session.

And so at last – at last – we came to the long-awaited day when Roamer and I were to sail off to the West Country for approximately 2 months "Final Sea Trials". I left at 0700 on Monday the 15ᵗʰ April, and the Kirinka crew were on the breakwater to wave me off.

Thanks Gang.

Chapter Six

Sea Trials

Monday 15th April 1985

There wasn't much wind, so I motored for a while until a light Northerly came on just off Shoreham. By Littlehampton the breeze had gone to the South but was still light, so, in decreasing visibility we sailed slowly towards the Looe Channel, South of Selsey Bill. I had obtained a precise position from the Winter Knoll Buoy off Littlehampton and it was just as well, for I never saw any more land or buoys until I came to clearer weather to the West of Selsey and sighted the Nab Tower.

I wouldn't recommend that practice to anyone, the Owers Shoals off Selsey are very shallow in places and the tidal currents run strongly. So, luckily (or skilfully?), I found myself in the Solent and, with the evening drawing on, was glad to motor into the Chichester Harbour entrance to a peaceful anchorage off East Head.

Peaceful is the only word for this spot, flat calm and absolutely quiet except for the bird calls from the sanctuary on the sand dunes ashore. I enjoyed a fish and veg stew, with wholemeal bread washed down by a bottle of Guinness. The tides are good for an early start to the West in the morning.

Tuesday 16th April. 1900hrs. Studland Bay, Poole.

Today I had the best day's sailing yet in my bonny boat, we were "on the wind" the whole way but she did very well in the short, choppy seas.

In these conditions she stood about 55°- 60° off the wind, and did best when it was at the top end of Force 5. With anything less, she lacked the drive to push through the waves, and fell off to 65° - 70°. I got the self-steering to be more positive by adjusting the counterweight on its sliding arm, and the system worked much better.

I tried out the Davis Mk. 25 Master Sextant in taking a first Meridian Altitude Sun Sight and found it pretty simple. After working out the sums, I appeared to be 5 minutes out, equalling 5 miles of latitude, BUT it WAS a bit bumpy, and it WAS my first sighting since 1977!!

And so – we tacked our way round to the South of the Isle of Wight and N.W. to near Bournemouth, where I found myself pinned on the coast by the wind and tide, so I cheated little a bit and motored over to Studland Bay just outside Poole Harbour. Anchored in 5 metres at 2100. All in all, a good day, made some Westing, the weather is fair and I'm hoping that an anti-cyclone drifting round France will move North and give us a South or an East wind. As always I'm ever hopeful!

Wednesday 17th April 2000hrs

Anchored in Weymouth Bay. Aren't I just the high speed record-breaking Junk Rig sailor? I'm sure that the folks ashore think it's a beautiful day, but I can't say that I appreciate it much. Very light winds and these from the South West, so we struggled and pinched our way into them, using the Ghoster sails for several hours. I certainly learned more about how to fly those.

After rounding St. Albans Head mainly with the aid of the tide and ghosting in the breezes, I found myself in a position where I would have arrived at Portland Bill just as the tide turned foul.

I considered anchoring just North of the Bill and going round on the next tide, but inspection of the chart showed no anchoring is allowed in that area, so I gave in and trickled across to drop my anchor off Weymouth. We'll try again tomorrow, the forecast is much more hopeful, talking of Southeasterly 3-4 which is a following wind!

The Navy put on a special display for me this evening by parading a fleet of eleven N.A.T.O. ships entering Portland Harbour. Ah! What memories I have of Portland, that's where the ships and crews 'work-up', that is, getting trained for any, and all, eventualities. I've had some times there, good and bad! I listened in on their Operations Channel which brought back more memories.

It's very peaceful here in my cabin but noisy on deck with the sounds of traffic, people shouting, all the usual shore noises drifting out to me. I'm glad I resisted the temptation to go alongside because there's no need to go ashore – I know Weymouth well enough!

Tomorrow I should realise a small ambition, to sail further West than Weymouth in my own boat, on my own.

Thursday 18th April 2000hrs Torquay Marina.

This is really coast-hopping! Rounded Portland Bill at 1000hrs this morning with no trouble, I had the tides right and it was pretty calm, but the Bill can be a nasty place in the wrong conditions. We picked up an Easterly wind to the to the West of Portland and ran across Lyme Bay before it. This was so unusual that I kept hitting my head on the Main Boom as it lay across the main hatchway. I'm so used to being close-hauled with the boom fore and aft. We ran out of wind in the evening, wallowed around in the mist for a while, homed in on the Barry Head Aero beacon. I felt rather pleased at this as I was in charge of a team of riggers who had constructed the beacon some years ago in my rigging days. I snuggled into Torquay Marina for the night. Most of the day had been terrific, running in beautiful weather, the ship steering herself ten degrees either side of the set course, everything hunky-dory. I shall hold an inquest into how we came to be off Perry Head when I thought we were off Start Point, but it was almost certainly caused by the tidal set, its Spring Tides and the currents are fierce.

Saturday 20th April Plymouth.

Yesterday lasted quite a long time! Up at 0530 and rarin' to go – motored out into Torbay ever optimistic – into a calm. Off Berry Head I shut down the iron topsail and, there being a whisper of a Northerly, hoisted the Fore Ghoster and experimented flying it in next to no breeze. Played some games like rigging the boathook across the pulpit, bearing out the ghosted tack and flying it like a spinnaker - it works!!

The whisper died away though, visibility fell to half a mile, and so I motored to the River Dart and anchored off Wash Point. It's nice and quiet if a bit rolly. I experimented in some sun-bathing but it's not an exercise I've had a lot of practice in!!

The 1750 forecast was for Northerlies and improving visibility, so I weighed anchor and found a South-Westerly. This gradually veered though, allowing me to reach Start Point on a semi-circular starboard tack. She sailed well close-hauled in the calm sea in the lee of the Start Peninsula, and followed the wind round. The sunset was very lovely, all 'Orangey' and peaceful.

We sat off Start Point in the later evening waiting for the tide to turn, counting Start's 3 flashes from 2300 until 0200. THEN it was all change as a Nor'westerly came out from the land, the tide turned and we shot off to the West at great speed, scattering coasters left and right. It was an exhilarating ride along the coast through the starry night, the wind veering to the North and strengthening. At 0400 I found myself being bounced around rather roughly in Plymouth Sound with a Force 7 howling right out of the harbour. It was a good time to practice reefing and some fun THAT was, as the tide against wind kicked up a horrible sea. A mini disaster struck during this time as, during all of this action, my very best sea-going hat, a Harris Tweed trilby, veteran of many stormy nights on land and at sea, and which was being worn over my Damart balaclava (it was very cold) was whipped away to its doom by the dark, rushing wind – bad news indeed.

By this time I was getting pretty weary of trying to make to windward in this confused sea, so it was time to engage the engineering department and motor-sailed through the chop to anchor in Cawsand Bay just after 0600. After a short nap, coffee and a bite to eat, I motored into Sutton Harbour Marina for a weekend's rest and rehabilitation.

Roamer and I, having reached Plymouth in fairly good time, with all the headlands behind, and only an easy run to reach Falmouth, were able to relax a little. A very enjoyable part of the weekend was to take a day sail round Eddystone Lighthouse on the Sunday.

It was whilst at Sutton Harbour that I managed to part-exchange my 10ft GRP dinghy for a canvas and rope folding dinghy and a Walker Log. A poor bargain for me but the dinghy had to go.

Monday 22nd April. By the time I left Sutton Harbour in mid-afternoon, there was a Northeast gale blowing, so I dropped anchor for the night in Mountbatten Bay, spending a quiet evening writing and listening to Baroque music followed by a good night's sleep.

Tuesday 23rd April. We celebrated St. George's Day with a brisk and quite eventful run down to Falmouth in the still-strong Nor'easter. I practiced sailing off the anchor by hoisting half the mainsail and sheeting it in, but not too tightly. She then makes a little headway until the anchor chain pulls the bow into the wind, thus luffing her up. She then falls off on the other tack, and repeats the process. This works well and saves me a lot of heavy hauling on the winch.

Once out of the harbour, I tried to get her settled on a course for Falmouth, with both sails up, each with two reefs in. With the wind nearly dead astern though, the mainsail blanketed the fore, so the main was reefed right down to its top triangle. It still spoiled the fore's wind so I stowed it. The Levanter gear steered her quite happily like this, but only up to 5 knots. If I hoist more sail for more speed, she drives excitingly off to windward and "George" (the Levanter Vane), can't bring her back. I'm working on this problem – probably the answer is a bigger vane to have more effect on the trim-tab.

The day was invigorating with plenty of wind, clear skies, and good visibility, giving me a grand vista as we sailed past the headlands of Cornwall. We reached St. Anthony's Head and Falmouth by 1630 and motored up to the friendly Marina to spend the night.

Wednesday 24th April. Anchored off St. Mawes. After a busy day during which I went into town for cash and provisions (mainly Pasties for which I am a glutton!), bought an Irish courtesy flag in case I get there, and also tried to get a replacement for my broken engine tachometer cable. I also endeavoured to get the faulty V.H.F. radio fixed. Eventually I departed the Marina and came across a peaceful spot to the South of St. Mawes. And very pleasant it is too, at anchor all on my ownsome a few hundred yards offshore. It's very quiet, just the slap of the wavelets on the hull and a whisper of the wind in the rigging. I really do like anchoring!

Earlier, there cries of 'Hello' from some walkers in the fields and I was glad to return their greetings. A herd of cows munched contentedly close by. Now, at dusk, I sit in my cabin writing by the light of a Tilley lamp, while my other Tilley hangs from the main boom as an anchor light, which I will replace with a masthead electric light before turning in. I try to save the batteries as much as possible.

Having worked out the tidal streams for around here and the Lizard, I plan a reconnaissance of the coast South of Falmouth, and to anchor in the Helford River tomorrow night.

Thursday 25th April 2000hrs. Well, this evening I'm not anchored in the peaceful Helford River as planned, but at an isolated spot on the coast of Mount's Bay, just West of Porthleven. I can imagine it to be a wild place in a Sou'westerly, but this evening the stiff North has died off to a breeze and it's beautifully quiet and calm. My day began at 0500 and I awoke feeling fine and ready for a quick and easy breakfast of coffee, biscuits and marmalade. Up anchored at 0630 and sailed away across Falmouth Bay on a gentle Northerly. Popped into the Helford River to look at possible anchorages, hove to for a coffee break, and then sailed out again. The wind picked up a little and we made off to the East to round the Manacles Buoy, the rocks looking menacing inshore of us. Down to the Lizard we ran with George doing a pretty good job of steering, though I had to take over for a dead down-wind stretch when the sails were goose winged. She goes along nicely like that but is very critically balanced and usually gybes one sail or the other when she rolls. The Lizard Lighthouse looked very smart in the sunshine, but the wind was light off the Point After making to the West of the Lizard, we picked up a brisk Northerly and made a long tack to Tater Dhu Light on the Land's End Peninsula. Went about there and made another long leg to Porthleven where we dropped anchor about a mile West of the village, close in to the cliffs. For the very first time I sailed to my anchorage, using just the mainsail, and found that she handled very well, moving at 2 to 3 knots in the stiff breeze and calm seas. She tacked well under one sail, and, when ready to anchor, I let the sheets fly, the sail quietly weather-cocked while I laid the anchor out.

Now it's nearly 2200, there is a Tilley lamp on deck, but I don't plan to leave the electric light on all night tonight, I doubt if any one will come along here in the dark, and Roamer is well tucked away in a bay. I shall pump up the Tilley before turning in, which should keep it going for several hours, and if I wake up during the night, which is likely, pump it up again. But now it's bedtime, and this laddie has had a long and windy day!

Friday 26th April 2100hrs

I had a lovely quiet night off Porthleven, calm and not a sound. Up and about at 0500 for a quick coffee and biscuits and in good time to catch 2 the 0555 forecast. Then it was haul in 50 metres of chain and my trusty C.Q.R, drift off the cliffs and hoist sail. It's difficult to describe the satisfying feeling of being up bright and early, heaving in the anchor in the still of the morning and getting under way with no noisy engine to shatter the peace. Just the gentle sounds of small waves and light breezes, the cliffs receding and the coast of the Lizard Peninsula in the morning mist under the rising sun. Just as sailors have been doing for hundreds of years. All this tranquillity lasted only until we reached the Lizard again, where the East-going tide met a stiffening North East wind and threw a very nasty short sea through which we bundled our way We weren't making much progress, and, being keen to get to Falmouth before the end of business hours so that I could chase up my tacho cable and radio problems, I cheated again and used my big Perkins to push me through the waves. Well, that's what it's there for, to a degree! At the Manacles Buoy the tide eased and I was able to sail the rest of the way to Falmouth. The Bay was busy with many boats and ships about, divers down near the Manacles, helicopters buzzing about so I'm back to civilisation again. Safely berthed in Falmouth Marina at 1300.

Saturday 27th April 1730hrs.

Here I sit, still in the Marina, ruminating on the day's operations. I had quite a busy day, did some chart work for the trip to Ireland. Thanks to Mike Richey in loaning me an "Irish Pilot" and some charts, I have enough information to make a trip to Cork and Crosshaven. My plan is to head for Cork via the Kinsale Gas Field Platforms, make a token visit to Crosshaven, sail down the coast to Cape Clear, then a long leg back to the Scillies. The whole idea is for me to get some sea-time in, practice my navigation, and try out all the ship's equipment and systems.

Later, I went into town for fresh provisions, got my tacho cable and repaired radio, and also bought a paraffin anchor light guaranteed (!) not to blow out. Back aboard, I tidied up the ship (that always seems to need doing), fitted the tacho cable and ran the engine to check it. On looking around the engine I discovered two port mounting bolts were loose, and I was very glad to find them.

Les Savage, the boat's builder paid a visit and made some complimentary remarks about her. A man of few words is Les, and he commented that she "looks very competent". I'll certainly drink to that! Les is coming out for a sail tomorrow.

Sunday 28th April 1900hrs.

At anchor off Durgan in the Helford River. Took Les for the sail, but the winds were light and I wasn't able to show her off much. He had a good look round though and seemed to enjoy his day. I dropped him back at the Marina at 1500 and sailed from Falmouth to the Helford on a nice Nor'westerly which had sprung up. Dropped anchor in 6 metres off Durgan and paid out a healthy 40 metres of chain to cope with the wind which had gone to the West and was blowing briskly down the river.

During the day we had sailed close to a monster oil rig, the "Ali Baba", anchored in Falmouth Bay, and also viewed the old school ship "Uganda", looking desperately neglected and absolutely running with rust. How I hate to see a ship approaching the end of her days and I believe she will shortly be heading for the scrapyard.

Monday 29th April. Up early and in with the anchor by 0830. We sailed up the river a little way to have a look at "Obo", obviously, to me anyway, a steel yacht. She was of a very interesting design, with a tripod-construction mast which looked very strong. Waved to her Skipper, his wife and young daughter. How friendly live-aboard sailors are, always ready for a chat and a tour of each others boats – it must be due to the absence of most of the noise and pressures of modern life. We sailed across the Bay to Falmouth and made a short stop at the Yacht Haven while I popped ashore to clear Customs for my forthcoming trip to Ireland. Whilst ashore I picked up some more provisions, including a healthy supply of Pasties, of course! Back aboard and away by 1200, cleared the harbour and ran down to the South, past the Manacles Buoy and anchored in 8.5 metres off the village of Coverack, 10 miles South of Falmouth. Laid out 45 metres of chain, it being quite windy. The recommended ratio of chain is from 3 to 5 times, but I always pay out at least 5, unless my swinging arc is restricted, this on the principle that chain is doing no good if its in the locker!

During the evening I listened to the forecasts, which weren't too good for making to Ireland, W to NW., 5 -7. We shall see what arrives, I can always take another step and make for Penzance.

Tuesday 30th April 2000hrs.

And that's exactly how it turned out! The wind was N.W. 5 - 7, and we had a hard beat to get to Penzance after rounding the Lizard again. However, we are another 30 miles to the West.

I passed H.M.S. Shetland, a Fishery Protection Vessel, near the Lizard, and, visibility being none too good, I called them up on V.H.F. and asked how my Radar reflector showed up on their screen. I have a Firdell Blipper 300 mounted near the top of the foremast. He replied that I showed up well and that they had picked me up at 12 miles range, which is a comforting piece of information. I am relaxing after a long day of fresh winds, and, after having had a good supper, I'm off to bed early.

Wednesday 1st May 2100hrs Porth Cressa, Scilly Isles.

Up at my usual 0500 I was raring to go, but the 0555 forecast, being for N.W. winds, 5 - 7 again ruled out any plans for going to Ireland. But, I say to myself, N.W. is a fair wind for the Scillies, so, weighed and set off at 0630 in a light Northerly breeze. Past Mousehole, Tater Dhu, Gwennap Head, the Runnel Stone Buoy (what names to conjure with!) and set course for the Scillies on a bright and beautiful morning. Passed Wolf Rock lighthouse at 1000, bounding over the Atlantic swell at 6 knots in the fresh Northerly and it was cold too. "Land Ho" was the cry at 1030 . "Land Ho on the starboard bow" By 1300 we were closing the Islands , looking like South Seas atolls with their golden, sandy beaches. I looked into St. Mary's Harbour at Hugh Town but didn't like what I saw, a swell from the West was a-rollin' in, and so I took the Customs Officer's advice, went round to the South a little, and anchored in this cosy little bay, Porth Cressa. It's a little bit restricted, with rocky reefs close at hand but no problem on a day like this. Anchored in 6.5 metres, secured the ship, rigged the folding dinghy and was able to row ahead of Roamer and look down at the seabed to check the anchor was dug in, so clear was the water.

In the evening I rowed ashore, phoned the folks in Brighton, and paid a visit to the Atlantic Hotel for a few pints of Guinness and a couple of Pasties (I DO like Pasties!). It had been many moons since I had been on the Scillies, when I used to carry out maintenance work on the radio aerials at St. Mary's Airport back in my rigging days.

Thursday 2nd May started misty and drizzly, so I stayed in this cosy bay during the forenoon, relaxing and watching the weather for a break to get to Ireland. With the weather clearing in the afternoon, I decided to go and look at another anchorage to the NE of St. Mary's Island, Watermill Cove, in Crow Sound. So, in with the anchor and motored out of the calm Porth Cressa, I was to see it in a different mood on my next visit. On arrival at Watermill Cove didn't like it one bit, not much of a cove at all, and there was a NE blowing into it. HMS Beagle was anchored further offshore, what an appropriate name for a Survey Ship.

A NE wind did I say? Just right for Ireland, so, turning my back on this uncomfortable anchorage, I sailed off round the North of the Islands. It being late evening now, I soon picked up Round Island's distinctive red light, and later, on making some Westing, Bishop Rock light. The sea was now uncomfortably short and steep, but this improved as we moved away from the Islands.

We made a course of 320° (M) during the night and dawn found us out of sight of land, with a falling wind. We made only 3 miles from 1000 to 1400! Then a Northerly breeze gave us a, little headway to the West. And so the evening and night passed us in utter silence and peace, making very little way but not much bothered about it – who's in a hurry?

Unfortunately, Friday the 3rd was similar, becalmed most of the day, wallowing in the swell, with the sails hoisted to damp down the rolling, but slatting and creaking. It wasn't until 1400 on Saturday the 4th that I got a wind! A breeze came in from the South, gradually became a West Force 4, which was great and had me making a good speed directly on course for the Kinsale Gas Field platforms, which I intended to use as an offshore mark. During Saturday evening the weather turned wet, cold, and dark. I was glad to keep lookout from my viewdome rather than the cockpit. Not many people about though. As my log says, "It being Saturday night, they're probably all in the Crosshaven pubs".

By 0100 I was feeling pretty pleased with myself, having picked up the two platforms dead ahead, but my reward for this fine (or lucky?) piece of navigation, was a blast of wind to come roaring out of the North, and drive me to the West. A real snorter, with heavy rain and 50 yard visibility, I felt it safer to run off to the West, rather than East, where the platforms were now. I didn't want to be blundering around them in the gale and murk.

I reefed the rig right down to the top triangles of both sails, hove her to on the starboard tack and retired below, for naps in the cosy chair, and lookouts through the viewdome. I saw nothing during the stormy night, while we drifted to the West. On the Sunday morning it still blew a full Force 9 with a big sea to match, so I reefed the foresail right down and lashed it to the boom, letting her ride out the storm. She did this very comfortably, almost beam-on to the seas, fore-reaching at about 2 knots. This is the practice I wanted on my sea trials, so I didn't mind this blow at all.

Come lunchtime I thought there was a lull in the storm, so hoisted the fore top triangle and gybed her round to the port tack to try to make up the lost ground and make to the East or Northeast. She gybed very steadily and positively in the big seas and still strong wind, and settled on a course of E.N.E. All day we crept to the East, but the wind didn't start easing until the early hours of Monday the 6th, when I was able to get a little more sail up and head N.E. and then a Westerly leg to the North of the platforms trying to close the coast. The weather gradually improved the way it does after a blow, with clearing skies and lessening winds and by the afternoon we were romping to the W.N.W. with full sail up in a Northerly Force 6. Made it to the Old Head of Kinsale lighthouse and, using Mike Richey's 20-year-old Irish Pilot book, holed up in a tiny cove just outside Kinsale Harbour. Sandy Island Cove was the name of this very welcome calm and quiet anchorage for the night.

Tuesday at 0900 saw us, cleaned up, well fed and rested out of our cosy harbour, having a pleasant sail along the coast, N.E. towards Cork Harbour. A brave sight my bonny ship must have been, making 6 knots in a calm sea with an offshore wind. Full sail up, Red Ensign flying aft, the Irish Tricolour to starboard, Customs "Q" to port. We entered the impressive Cork Harbour, turned to port into Crosshaven and tied up at the Boatyard Marina, my first visit to Southern Ireland.

My brave flags were wasted, no Customs men or the Cardai came dashing down to inspect the stranger who might have had a ship full of drugs or machine-guns. I found out later that the Customs were "In dispute", and not handling any yacht inspections, and the local Cardai policeman, (all one of him) was playing football with some boys in the car park. Ah, to be sure, that's Ireland for you!

Two words will describe my short stay in Ireland, "Very pleasant", but I was here to get some sea time in, not Guinness time, so after a look round, some pints of the "Real McCoy" Guinness in Con's Haven Bar in the evening, I sailed out again by 1200 on Wednesday the 9th, bound, having changed my plans, for Falmouth.

On hoisting sail and stowing the engine, once to seaward of the buoyed channel, I was shocked to find the wind from the South! Not head winds all the way back too? I pretended not to notice, made furtive notes in the log about "Coastal Anomalies", and made the best course I could. The wind veered to S.W.3 - 4, and I made 160° towards the Gas platforms. Sighted them at 1700 and altered to 150° for the Seven Stones lightship. During the night the wind veered more toward N.W. and abruptly increased to Force 7, giving me a busy time reefing in the dark.

A bright brisk dawn on the Thursday heralded what was to be a long and eventful day. During the forenoon we rolled down the waves and swells with just half the foresail up, making 5-6-knots, but steering herself well. She yawed some 10-15 degrees either side of the course, but always came back to 150°. The coast of Cornwall was in sight at 1300, and the Scillies at 1400. I decided to run into Port Cressa for a night's rest rather than spend another night up in the busy waters around Land's End and The Lizard. Having decided this, and altered the course toward the Islands, the wind increased to a full gale and turned bitter cold. Wet and weary by the time I got to Port Cressa at 1800, I was dismayed to find it full of yachts and motor cruisers. Not keen to try to anchor in between this crowd of boats in the blast of winds which were sweeping across my former calm haven, I motored round to try for more room in Watermill Cove again. On arrival there, I found the wind absolutely shrieking across the anchorage, ruling out that plan. I had a choice – Port Cressa again, or back to sea. I chose wrongly and went back to Port Cressa. On entering the Bay, although I was really cold, wet and tired by now, with dusk approaching, it didn't look so bad. I found myself a space right in the middle of the bay, prepared my anchor, with a buoy and buoy-line in view of how crowded it was, motored to my chosen spot, stopped the engine and nipped forward to let go. As I did, a blast of wind swept across the bay, the anchor, chain, and anchor buoy shot over the side and I paid out 20 metres of chain as quickly as I could. I stopped for a look, we seemed to be dragging, I looked for the anchor buoy, couldn't see it – Oh No! I dashed aft, looked over the stern, and, Oh Yes! there it was, jammed in the blades of the propeller. I tried to free it with a boat hook but it was too tight, we drifted towards the reef on the East side of the bay, I had seen that reef at Low Water, not a pleasant sight. Having nothing to lose now, I turned the propeller to try to shake the buoy off, but the engine strained, it was jammed! Now we really have had it, "That's it, Robbie boy," I said to myself, "The project is over". But was it? We were getting close to the reef, with no engine, no steerage way – but – it's High Water, maybe we could slide over it? I heaved in the anchor chain to pull the anchor up under the hull as close as possible, and, as we hit the reef, I felt the hull bounce over the rock, once, twice, three times, horrible sounds, the anchor chain snagged and freed, and – we were over it!

Now we headed for the cliffs! I rushed forward and cut the sail ties on the foresail, back to the cockpit and hoisted a scrap of fore, enough to give us steerage way. I was able to alter the course 60° degrees to starboard and head out of the bay – we were safe – for the moment. I nipped down below to check for leaks but all was well. Hurrah for steel hulls. But – we were heading out to sea with no anchor, no engine, cold, wet, tired, and night coming on with a full gale blowing. Not a good situation.

Just then I saw a yacht approaching, a man on the foredeck waved a rope at me! Good chap! In a fine feat of seamanship, the yacht passed to leeward and passed a tow rope to me. With further fine skill, the crew not only towed me back into the anchorage, but put her anchor down with me still in tow. Mind you, there were four people aboard, and the wind had abated a little. It was still a great piece of work by Ashley Woods and his crew aboard "Magnum". Thanks again, Ashley!

Lucky as I was to have been rescued, I was even luckier in that there was Diving School ship also anchored close by, the "Dunedin". The tow line was passed to her stern and I laid to that for the night, the wind having eased considerably by then, as usually seems to happen after a drama. After making sure I was secure, I retired below, for my first food and drink for ten hours, shaking with the cold, tiredness, and nervous reaction to almost having wrecked my dream.

Next morning at 0600, I paid out the anchor chain forward, heaved it in aft, and recovered the anchor. Dunedin's divers cut the buoy and rope from the prop, reporting no damage. I turned the shaft by hand, started the engine – and – all's well. What a relief!! Having no money aboard, I sent my best bottle of rum to Dunedin, a bottle of wine to Magnum, and scuttled out of Port Cressa with my tail between my legs, humble and ashamed of my poor performance.

The remnants of the gale blew across to the Lizard and I was anchored in the peace of the Helford River by 2230 on Friday night – another long day.

After spending a weekend recovering in Falmouth Marina, Monday the 13th found me again at anchor off Durgan. Whilst in Falmouth, I booked a berth on the scrubbing posts, in order to inspect the hull, after bouncing on the Scilly rocks. It being a period of Heap tides though, I couldn't get on the pad until Friday. So I am anchored in the Helford, relaxing quietly and cheaply, waiting until then. The mind always being active though, I looked at the beaches ashore... they looked smooth and fairly level. I recalled that the lower halves of my Jury Rig sheerlegs are designed to be bolted to the ship's side and act as standing legs – my own scrubbing posts in fact! An inspection of the beaches made me think that one of them, at Grebe, would be suitable. Decision time – am I brave enough to try out my Legs system? It would be a bold step, especially having just survived the Port Cressa crisis, but then, if I don't try out the system, I'll never know if it'll work if and when I might really need it. So – next day I rigged up the legs with their mahogany side blocks and feet extensions, and, having been ashore and laid out landing marks on the beach as a guide, prepared to do the deed. 20 minutes before High Water, I upped anchor and made a dummy run to see how she would handle in the slight side breeze blowing. All went well, and shortly before H.W. I beached her, laying out the Kedge anchor over the port quarter to hold her at right angles to the beach, and using the engine to keep the bow steady until the tide had reached its peak. H.W. passed, the tide began to recede, she leaned slightly to starboard onto that leg, which creaked ominously. I held my breath for 15 minutes or so (!), but the creaking gradually stopped, the tide continued to recede – and – we remained upright! Relief!

I went all round the hull, cleaned off the weed, and when the hull was dry, patched up the scars from the Cressa Rocks, which are minor scratches, thanks again to a steel hull. I also raised the anti-foul line 3" all round, as she sits lower in the water than I had planned, and gave her a new coat of anti-foul paint.

During the night, I nursed her through the 0300 H.W. keeping her straight up and down the beach with the kedge line and a bow line which I'd taken ashore to a handy tree.

On a fine Wednesday afternoon, I gave her a second coat of anti-foul, and, after a trip to a nearby village for bread, cheese, and pasties, (big, beautiful hot ones), I was ready for lift-off on the afternoon tide. An unwelcome onshore breeze had sprung up, but with fairly vigorous use of the main engine and rudder, and pulling on the kedge line, off she came. Back at anchor in the Bay, and rigging down the legs that evening, I felt pretty pleased with myself.

The major plan now, was to get to the River Hamble by the 25th May, for the Junk Rig Association Rally to be held there over the weekend 25th/26th. So I started off to the East, which was a sign to the gods to send East winds, no winds, and a package of haze and mist. I made it to Plymouth by the 17th. On the Saturday, we spent a day visiting the River Yealm. I made off to the East again on the Sunday and had a difficult time with light and contrary winds. Called in at Dartmouth for two nights, hoping that the prevailing poor weather would clear, but it didn't so I had to press on across Lyme Bay towards Portland Bill, spending a hair-raising night out in dense fog off the Bill, with ships passing close by – too close by!

I hope my radar reflector kept them away, however, we survived that, made Swanage Bay on the Wednesday, Beaulieu River on Thursday, Friday in Cowes, and, as planned Saturday and Sunday in Port Hamble Marina. The J.R.A. Rally was a bit of a non-rally, as I was the only boat to attend, but we made the best of it, and I took everyone out for the day on the Sunday. It being a typical British Bank Holiday, it blew, rained, stormed and calmed, the normal weather. We sailed and motored around the Solent, visited Buckler's Hard on the Beaulieu River, and back to the Hamble in the evening. It was an "interesting" day, but I hope the folks enjoyed it.

After that, I was keen to get back to Brighton, and make my final preparations for my "Big Voyage", having now decided to "go". First though, I spent a few days in Poole, and having written articles about the sea trials, the Scillies grounding, and the Standing Legs event, sold them to Practical Boat Owner magazine.

And so – after a quite an adventurous set of sea trials during which I learnt a lot, I was back in Brighton by the 7th June.

Following my return to Brighton Marina, I made the final decision to "Go" for my circumnavigation. The decision was made easier by several occurrences and changes of plans by other people. (1) was the collapse of the Australian Bi-Centenary "Sirius" event for 1987/88, due to withdrawal of sponsors, (2) was a letter from the organisers of the B.O.C. Singlehanded Race for 1986 informing me that I did not qualify as they had set a minimum L.O.A. of 59 ft., and (3) news from Terry that sponsorship potential was Nil, for my project. At times like that I get very stubborn, so my answer to all these setbacks was – to hell with the lot of them! I'll go – on my own.

So – June was spent making final arrangements. A naming ceremony was planned for Sunday the 30th June, and maybe a little party at the Marina, after which I would sail off.

Some minor sponsorship help was obtained in the way of supplies, for which I was very grateful, as expressed in "Acknowledgements", and another great help was the donation of a Wind Generator by L.V. Motors, of which more later.

I held a sale on board of excess equipment and books, which raised some much-needed cash, finalised my food stocks, charts, navigation books etc., and by the weekend of the 29/30th of June 1985 was "set to go".

My nephew Mike got married on the Saturday, which was a good reason for relaxing and having a day off from the project, and by Sunday the 30th, we seemed to be ready.

Chapter Seven

Off to the Start – Brighton to Falmouth

Sunday, the 30th June 1985. Brighton Marina.

Not an auspicious start to my big day, a low damp mist sat over the Marina, and an equally damp Southerly wind blew more mist in from the sea. There was nothing to be done about that though, I continue my preparations for the "Naming Party", and for going to sea having been in the Marina for over three weeks.

At 1000 my sister Doreen arrived with David and Gareth, plus some items from Terry's house. She left 10 year old David with me, and went off with 5-year-old Gareth to continue preparing the food for this afternoon's "Do", a task she has voluntarily undertaken, and for which I am very grateful. David, my "First Mate", is a useful little lad, and together we slipped from Pontoon 9, Berth 45, and moved up alongside the Main West Jetty.

Here, after securing her, we found my collection of flags, which wasn't a lot, and dressed the ship with them. This amounted to flying a large Union Flag from each foremast ghoster halyard, the courtesy flags of South Africa, Australia, and New Zealand on the main ghoster halyard to starboard, and the Burgee of the Junk Rig Association and of Brighton Marina Yacht Club to port. Not exactly dressed overall but the flags gave a slight air of gaiety to the scene. She looked good to my eye, lying alongside, heading South, strong and seamanlike, ready to go.

Shortly after 1300 Doreen returned with Gareth, and with Mum, and together we rigged a table and laid out the food they had prepared, sandwiches, sausages and sausage rolls, Hors D'oeuvres etc., and something special I wasn't allowed to see, covered over! We laid out 40-

odd pints of Bitter, courtesy of Phoenix Brewery, plus wine and soft drinks. It looked a goodly spread.

The "Fan Club" began to arrive, friends from over the years, all the family of course, more friends, and friends of friends. Soon the ship swarmed with children, and their parents, I conducted as many tours of the ship as I could squeeze in, kissed the girls, hand-shook the fellas, and a pleasant scene it all was.

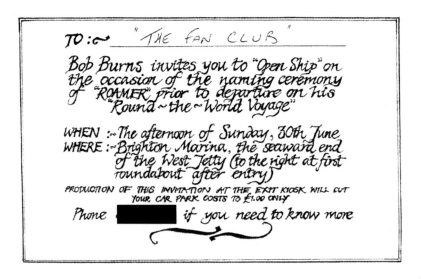

Now to the Naming Ceremony. I made a short speech of sorts, mainly thanking everyone for coming, and for their presents. Terry popped the "Champers", my lovely niece Sandie said in a clear voice, "I name this ship "Roamer", may the Gods of the Wind, and of the Sea, Bless Her and all who sail in Her", and poured a liberal dose over the bows of my fine ship, who will carry me many miles. I took a token drink from the bottle, which made my head buzz, the only alcohol I took that day. Terry had a taster, and passed the bottle to Tom, Landlord of the "Wellington", who had donated it, Tom had a glug, and passed it round as far as it would go, there wasn't any more.

After that, more rounds of kissing and handshaking, interviews with the Press, and the cutting of Doreen's surprise, a cake, beautifully iced with the words, "Bon Voyage, Bob and Roamer". Thanks a lot Gal, that was lovely of you.

But it's "Time to go Time". Starting the engine dispersed part of the crowd by the exhaust discharge. I said final farewells to Mum and the Family, telling them not to worry, but I know that they will. Willing hands let go my lines and we, my bonny ship and I, now partners, motored away from the jetty to loud cheers. I took her over to the Outer Breakwater and hoisted the sails, then made a close pass by the end of the jetty to more cheers. One more circuit through the horde of incoming Sunday Sailors and Motor Booties, and we made a final pass, further off, with a flourish at six knots. I waved, everyone waved and cheered, hooters and horns blew. Carrying on towards the Marina exit channel, I gave a final two-handed wave and turned my back on Brighton, family and friends, to concentrate on weaving my way out through the traffic. We're off. The adventure had begun.

With the excitement of the departure party left behind, we motored out of the Marina, as more day sailors motored in. Out here, and unknown to all these boats, I felt a little foolish with all these flags flying, and stowed them as soon as I could. There was no wind, so we motored off to the West, stowing all ropes and fenders as we went. Still no breeze showed, so I had to motor all the way to Worthing, and anchored at 1900, to rest and await a wind. It was very pleasant to sit on my own at a peaceful anchorage, after the past hectic week.

I slept a little but was awakened at 0230 by the tap of rigging on the masts, and the slap of wavelets on the hull, announcing the arrival of a small wind from N.W. After coffee and a biscuit, I weighed anchor, hoisted sails, and proceeded to the S.W. towards the Owers light buoy. During the day the wind backed to the West but with help of a fair tide during the afternoon, we tacked our way through a lumpy sea to anchor between the piers of Sandown and Shanklin at 1630, to sit out the evening's foul tide.

A customs launch paid me a visit right on the 1750 Shipping Forecast which earned him a disparaging remark, and he went off. I slept from 1830 to 2030 and awoke to the sound of propellers thrashing the sea. With my steel hull, underwater sounds are clearly audible. I popped my bleary eyes up the hatch to see a 70 ft launch, the "Searcher", almost alongside, more Customs men. Answered their questions and they went away. I returned below to put the kettle on and think whether to stay here the night or sail on the 2300 tide. More thrashings of propellers, the Customs men are back and want to search me! O.K., they do so, I am entirely legal and have no worries, all my papers are in order. I think I sounded too good to be true to them. Only one aboard, nothing to declare, no Duty Free stores!! I chatted with the man in charge while two others had a poke about and they left.

At 2133 a shipping forecast on V.H.F. Channel 28 from Niton Radio just around the corner spoke of N. or N.E. winds so I decided to "Go".

Weighed anchor at 2300 and was rewarded for my industry by a beautiful North Wind Force 3 to 4 and a fair tide which transported us through a delightful moonlight night, at no cost, to 4 miles South of the Anvil Point Light, near Swanage, by 0430. I am ever struck by the wonder and thrill of weighing anchor, hoisting the sails and proceeding silently on my way on the free wind, with only a little calculating regarding the tides to ensure a speedy passage.

Dawn came a little after 0400 and "Phoebe", the sun, "rose in my eyes" at 0510. Such simple pleasures are not available to everyone.

We sailed steadily West to find Portland emerging from the mist at about 0800. Approach to Portland was confirmed by the "pings" of warships' Sonar echoing through the hull. Music to the ears of an ex-Asdic Operator.

Becalmed to the East of Portland, I engaged the services of the Perkins Diesel at 1020 and pushed Roamer to the Bill to ensure I got a full 6 hours of fair tide. As I had hoped, there was a N.E. wind to the West of "The Isle of Portland" so was able to turn off the "thumper" at 1120 and sail on peacefully. The notorious Race was well-behaved today and gave me a good push to the West, but having seen it in all moods I know that it's not to be fooled with in stormy weather.

The wind settled dead astern on our course of 245! so I goosewinged the sails and made 4 knots on the Force 2 - 3 breeze. It was a splendid day, clear sky, calm sea, has Summer come at last? "And so we sailed on", the wind veered to the S.E. and I returned the foresail to its fore and aft position.

A 1600 R.D.F. check put Start Point dead ahead, which was nice to know, and to celebrate this good news I held a "Happy Hour" party on the bows, treating myself to two (small) glasses of Port, a can of Foster's, and a bag of Planter's Peanuts. This is the life for me.

During the evening the wind fell off, the tide turned foul, and I found myself 4 miles off Dartmouth drifting N.E. when I wanted to go S.W. On the principle of using the tools of my trade to best advantage, the motor was started at 2130 and again used to get us to the optimum position for riding the fair tides. Motored until 2330 by which time we were South of

Start Point Lighthouse and on the fair tide. I was lucky again, a North wind picked up and carried my bonny ship and I along the Devon Coast to Plymouth on another lovely moonlight night. The moonlight was very welcome, as there are few lights on the coast West of the Start. I took the odd snooze in my cosy chair, but never more than 15 minutes naps as I was having difficultly in getting her to steer herself in the fickle offshore breeze.

Lowering the sails near Plymouth Harbour Breakwater, we motored into the grand harbour and dropped anchor in Mountbatten Bay at 0400 just as the sky was lightening. Having tidied the ship, I retired below for a cuppa well pleased with progress, having made 124 miles in 29 hours and more importantly, I am within an easy day's sail of my objective, Falmouth, with no major headlands to round.

I slept, but not for long, and at 0930 weighed and motored into Sutton Harbour Marina, tying up at 1015. Some visiting French yachtsmen helped me to squeeze into a small berth, "Merci Messieurs".

My main reason for coming to Plymouth was to try to sort out a problem with my original two batteries, which were condemned by electricians in Dartmouth as "gone", only four months after being initially charged up. I paid a visit to the man who supplied them, who we shall call B.K. He was very busy and disorganised as usual and cost me a lot of time and hassle trying for a solution of my problem between him and Lucas Services. The outcome of 2½ days of being stuck in Plymouth while East winds were blowing towards Falmouth was that Lucas will "reconstitute" the duff cells in the batteries and send them to Falmouth. What a struggle it is dealing with "Shore People" who are always busy, and always in the same place, never in a hurry to help once they have your money. They know that we wanderers only want to get away on our ships and have done with them as soon as possible.

I hurried out of Sutton Harbour on the afternoon of Friday the 5th of July, though the staff there are always friendly and helpful, and anchored in the peace of Cawsanu Bay. How lovely anchoring out is, after the hassle of several days in a noisy town. It seems so pure and clean after the bustle of being alongside. I spent a quiet night having gone early to bed.

Awoke at 0400 and up at 0430 on a lovely morning, I planned to stay and watch the start of the Round Britain Race, but decided to get away, and sailed off my anchorage in utter silence.

Sailing off turned out not to have been a good idea as the wind, which was N.W. 5 at first, fell off to a 3, leaving a nasty choppy sea from the West, into which my bonny ship wasn't at all keen to travel. The tide was foul and by 0900 I found myself only mile from the Eddystone Light, not exactly on the direct line to Falmouth. So it was on with the motor for 2 hours to a point South of Fowey, after which we managed, with a light N.W.'ly and the now fair tide, to get to. the Helford River by 2015 and anchored in almost peace and quiet. It being a Summer Saturday evening, there were two barbeques on Crebe beach, and plenty of noise with them. Not that it worried me any, I had a bite to eat, a read, a little music and was away to my bed by 2200.

Sunday the 7th July was spent at anchor off Durgan. The weather was fine and I had plenty to do. I got up to date with my Jobs List, wrote many letters, sorted out much paperwork. Running off to sea isn't easy!

On the Monday, I motored to Falmouth Marina and booked in for a final two weeks of socialising and preparation. It's quite amazing how much sheer work is involved in getting a small craft ready for a long voyage. I had now been working full time on her since September last year, preparing for and carrying out sea trials, writing this book and magazine articles, trying to cover for every possible eventuality, and now it's the end of July, ten months since launching and I'm only just ready.

My situation is not as good as I would have like it to have been. I never did get my batteries back from Plymouth. Lucas and "B.K." came up with a story that they hadn't been charged properly, and couldn't be "reconstituted" (after I'd left Plymouth), and I have to admit that I just couldn't face dealing with "land sharks" like that any more and gave up on that operation. This means that I go to sea with only one 12V 115 amp hour battery, which has effectively cost me £250. I wrote outraged letters to those two people in Plymouth and to Lucas's Head Office, so something may come of it yet. "Land sharks" an apt description.

I had asked Golden Arrow Marine in Plymouth for some engine spares, was assured there would be no problem in getting them to me in Falmouth, but they never arrived. How do these people stay in business??

My financial position is precarious, to say the least. I will sail with £250 in travellers cheques, to cover living expenses at my stops. That's all. If I suffer any major damage or need repairs, I'm in trouble. I leave £250 in my bank account to pay interest on the £500 I drew from my Barclaycard, and to pay Mum's telephone bill. The taxman wants £298 for back taxes he says I owe, he has no chance. As I wrote and told him, he should have taken it when I was earning!

On my priority list there is only one item. To carry out my ambition. The other matters are minor and will be attended to on my return.

Civilised, happy and human amidst all of the hassle going on around me. We put Roamer on the Marina's scrubbing pad for a last clean off and touch up of anti-fouling paint. Then we motored up the River Fal to a quiet anchorage. I did a little exploring, commiserated over the fate of the "Uganda", who was moored up there, ate well, and walked ashore. A lovely few days indeed.

Sunday the 21st of July saw us back in the Marina.

But that's the way it is, the deed must be done, I shall hurry back.

I had farewell drinks in the Marina Club with Alan and Rosie, "Smokey the Boatman" bought me a last rum and treated me to a big Cornish kiss on the cheek, but I was still away early to my bed.

Chapter Eight

The Voyage – Falmouth to the Equator

> So – o, fare thee well, my own true love,
> And when I return united we shall be,
> It's not the leaving Old England,
> That is grieving me,
> But my Darling, when I think of thee.
> ('The Leaving of Liverpool')

Falmouth Marina, Monday the 22nd of July, 1030.

So, my reader, that's the background story of how Roamer was created, and how I had to work hard and struggle to get her. But, the bottom line of that story is the fact that here we are, in Falmouth Marina, and almost ready to go.

There are still a few things to do, but today is the day I said I'd leave, and leave I shall. I'm not actually planning to start the Voyage today, but I need to get away by myself and make the final preparations.

I was up early, and had topped up the water tank by 0700.

Then, on checking the fuel tanks, was dismayed to find only five gallons aboard. When I checked the keel tank at Brighton, it had indicated full, but on removing the dipstick this morning, there were a lot of gurgling noises, so I have to assume there was some sort of air lock in the system. I'll have to buy more.

1130. I've tidied the ship, and moved her, in the strong wind, out of the restricted berth we were in, to the fuel jetty, and bought thirty gallons. I popped ashore, bought bread, butter and cheese, and rang B.B.C. T.V. at Plymouth.

Their camera crew should be here soon.

While we're waiting, let me tell you that, although up to now I've been telling the story after it has happened, in the past tense, I now plan to tell it, as far as possible, as it happens, in the present tense. So, here we go.

It certainly is a foul morning, a strong West wind brings curtains of heavy drizzle over the grey hills and houses of Penryn. The T.V. crew arrive, and we do a fairly short interview in between showers. They don't like the weather.

They leap ashore with their equipment, and I'm ready to go. A few friends from the Marina Club are there to wave farewells.

'See you next year!' and we're off. Out of the Marina Channel, down the river, down the wind, we motor towards the sea.

My plan is to motor and sail to the Helford river, to anchor there in peace and quiet, and finally make ready for 'the off'. I also want to wait for a few days in the hope that the Jury Rig sail will arrive from Jeckell's.

It ought to be here now, and I very much want it aboard.

Coming across the Bay from Falmouth we have a wet trip with a strong wind whipping up short steep waves. Spray flying across the decks, heavy rain showers keeping me cool. All my usual weather in fact.

1800. At anchor in the peaceful Helford, just off Durgan, we are protected from the worst of the weather. The 1750 Shipping Forecast was for S.W. force 6 to 8 winds, So we are in a good place here. I have a goodly feed of mackerel and vegetable stew, with wholemeal bread, washed down with a strong cup of tea. Very nice too.

The Fishing Vessel 'Penolva' FH 479, passes close by and calls out good wishes. Lovely, friendly people they are down this way. I have a quiet and an early night.

Tuesday is spent at anchor in surprisingly nice weather. I have a good sort out down below and stow more equipment away. Then I haul myself up to the Mainmast head in the Bosun's chair for a last check and modifications to the topping lift system.

I change the 'bulldogs', the wire grips, on the steering wires, tighten them while I'm at it, and grease the system.

On the paraffin cooker, I change the burner which has been in use since I started living aboard, and will service the old one later. Whilst doing this I hear a lot of noise up top, and here's 'Smokey the Boatman' come to visit, with a boatload of 'Grockles' (holidaymakers). As I appear on deck, with oily, sooty hands, they all cheer and applaud, which surprises and embarrasses me. Smokey throws over a can of beer 'Cheers old Pal'. 'You were on T.V. last evening', one of the grockles tells me. Ah, that accounts for the applause and for the constant flow of other boats which have been passing by. Smokey motors off to Falmouth with his holidaymakers, 'See you next May!!'

Wednesday, 24th July 1900

At anchor off St. Mawes, Falmouth Harbour. I've had to move back into the shelter of Falmouth, due to Easterly getting up which blew straight in Helford. An Easterly!! – Just what I'd like, but can't use, as I have to hang about for that sail, to clear customs, and get last minute fresh fruit and vegetables. How I hate letting fair wind go to waste. We could have been a hundred miles to West by now.

Thursday, 25th July 1985

Ow! this is a painful day, shopping in Falmouth, due to the Yacht Haven being full, I have to anchor off, rig the folding dinghy, and use it for my many trips ashore. I spend all day running around a hot and crowded town centre, and achieve all my aims to get, or even trace, that sail. I'm very peeved, considering all the trouble I took to ensure its safe arrival here.

I go on a last-day buying spree, plenty of fruit and vegetables, four large loaves of wholemeal bread, pasties and cheeses. Four gallons of paraffin and one of meths, and a spare plastic sextant. What a day though! it seems that everything I want is at the Town Centre, and I have to make many trips through the crowded narrow High Street. I even go right out to Penryn for a sheet of plywood for spare wind vanes, and check at the Marina for the sail, but no.

In the evening, on a last run ashore, I post a couple of letters, ring Mum, Terry, Doreen, for a last chat and to tell them that it's 'Time to go time'. Four pints of Draught Guinness and some Fish and Chips, my favourite meal, use up my last pennies.

Friday, 26th July. 0700.

After an unpleasant night that was warm and humid, with too much noise and light coming from the decks astern, and the town ahead, I'm up early, and decide to leave without the sail. I can't face another day like yesterday. I've cleared Customs, so am O.K. to go. I pop ashore to ditch the gash, and with a few spare pennies lying around, buy a newspaper, for its weather map. I'm so glad to be back aboard, for the town is disgusting, with the streets filthy with food refuse which has been ripped out of plastic bags by really big and bold seagulls.

I prefer seaside resorts in the Winter!

Let's get to sea, aboard with the dinghy, on with the engine, in with the anchor. We motor out past the docks, the Governor Buoy, Pendennis Head, hoist sail, and off to the South!

Bob sails on deep sea trek

LONE SAILOR Bob Burns (right) is due to start his solo round-the-world adventure this weekend.

Brighton-born bachelor Bob, 45, will set sail from Falmouth for the start of his 27,000-mile ten-month journey. He hopes to reach his first stop, Cape Town, in eight weeks and after that he will head for Sydney and the Falklands Islands before returning home next spring.

Bob left Brighton Marina to a tearful farewell from family and friends last month and since then has been stocking his 36ft. 12-ton cruiser Roamer with supplies for the voyage at Falmouth Marina.

His brother, Terry, who lives in Brighton, said the family were expecting a telephone call this weekend from Bob to say he is on his way.

"If weather conditions are fine he will be off on Saturday or Sunday," said Mr Burns.

"He is very excited and he cannot wait to set sail."

His family will keep in touch with Bob's progress through a radio link organised by Lloyds of London. During the trip Bob will contact passing ships by radio and they will pass on the sailor's position to Lloyds.

Bob has been planning the journey since 1977 when he joined John Ridgeway's crew for the Whitbread Round the World race, only to leave the ship half-way after a difference on opinion.

The former Royal Navy man sold his house and spent his life savings to fund the trip.

Evening Argus 25th July 1985

Off to the South maybe, but not very far, for the weather has turned nasty again, and Sou'westerly, Force 6, with rain and poor visibility is hardly favourable for rounding the Lizard and making it to the South West.

Its time for 'Discretion to be better than Valour', and we anchor in a little bay I know off the village of Coverack, about ten miles South of Falmouth.

It's pretty windy, and I have a busy time stowing the sails, and motoring under the lee of the land. Using the echo-sounder, I gets as close as possible to the village and the tiny harbour, but we still roll quite a bit in the swell which comes in from the South. Having anchored, I watch the antics of school windsurfers trying their art in the strong wind – they spend more time in the sea than on their boards. A dinghy is in constant use towing them back upwind from where they have been blown.

It looks like a cold and wet hobby – like yachting??

As always, there is plenty to do, and dismantle the anchor winch, which was very stiff on the anchoring. Generous applications of oil and grease solve the problem.

All shore gear is stowed away, fenders, ropes, boat-hooks, etc. I rig down the canvas lifebuoy holders, and lash the lifebuoys to the guardrails.

There will be no-one to throw them to me, should I go overboard!

The aft cabin is now my greenhouse, with most of the fruit and vegetables laid out in plastic trays, the onions hanging in string bags. Potatoes, carrots, and more onions are in the locker under the Wendy House. The cabin smells very pleasant, like an orange grove.

After another tasty supper, I'm in luck. It must have been Coverack's Fete Day, colourful floats and a red-coated band from Constantine Village I read through the binoculars are gathering in front of the Bay Hotel.

Further round the Bay, the Paris Hotel public house, and old Lifeboat House, are bedecked in flags.

1930. They're off, the band marches towards the Paris, the floats and crowds following on behind a pretty girl on a horse, all wind through the village street to the square in front of the Paris, where floats are judged, and prizes awarded. It is a cosy, friendly scene, very different from my situation. I leave them to it, and go early to my bed, in case we should sail during the night...

... Which we do, the 0033 forecast gives only Force 6's, but a deepening 'Low' is approaching Lundy from the Nor'west. Not so good, but not so comfortable in Coverack Bay either, so let's get away and see what it's like out there, we can always come back. At 0200, in with the anchor, and out with the Bay without using the engine. All is well...

...at first, we pick up a breeze from the Sou'west, and head South, the Lizard's light flashing clearly to the West.

At 0530 the tide turns to the West, and so do we, but the wind falls light, and, two miles South of the Lizard, we are becalmed!! Rolling and slatting in the Channel chop, what a place this Channel is for weather. This is no good, so I start the engine, hoping to motor to a wind in Mount's Bay, but there is none there either, and I motor all the way to Penzance, where, frustrated and weary, I lock into the Inner harbour, and tie up alongside the old coaster, 'Crazy Diamond'.

I'm pretty unhappy at having come in to a harbour so soon after 'setting off', but we have to be sensible as well as adventurous, and out in the Bay it's blowing hard, with heavy rain showers and poor visibility, it's just not the weather for a singlehander trying to make to the South West, and that's a busy piece of sea out there, with ships coming and going in all directions.

So, reluctantly but sensibly, I spend a quiet night in harbour, locked inside the lock gates. There is no 'run ashore' for I have no money, so it's early to bed again.

Sunday, 28th July 1985

Well, this morning looks a lot better, clearing skies, and the wind down somewhat. The 0555 forecast speaks only of Nor'westerlies, which will do us just fine. So I'm champing at the bit, waiting for the gate to open.

I'm well fed, and rested and raring to go. This must be it – there's nowhere else to run and hide except the Scillies, and after my past experience there, would be hard-pressed indeed to seek shelter among those islands.

At 1100, the lock gate hinges down, the sea swirls in and beckons us out. I follow the Naval Training Yacht 'Kukri' out, she looks like a Camper & Nicholson 55 and has a dozen people aboard, all dressed up to the ears in oilskins and safety harnesses. Quite rightly so, it's still breezy outside, and they are probably trainees.

As I pass through the lock, Jeff the Lockmaster calls, 'Where are you bound?'

'Cape Town.'

'Where??'

'Cape Town, South Africa,' I shout up.

'Bloody Hell, best of luck to you!' he cries.

'Thanks, I'll need it.'

Following 'Kukri' out, we turn into the Southerly swell which still runs, Kukri is hoisting sail, going slowly. I plan to motor across the Bay to the lee of Newlyn to get the 1355 forecast. I wave as I overtake them, but no one waves back, perhaps they have orders, 'No waving on Sundays'.

Off Newlyn it is calmer but still windy, the forecast is as expected, N.W. 5-6, becoming 4. that's it, no mention of anything nasty to come. Right then, let's go. Up with both sails, one reef in with respect to the strong breeze still blowing, off engine, close it's seacocks, and away we go to the South – Again. Will we escape this time?

Conditions are difficult at first, with the wind falling light and my long – suffering ship pitching up and down in the Channel chop, short steep waves that stop her dead in the water. By 2000, however, the N.W. wind has picked up, and, the tide with us, we make off to the South West, gradually dropping the Lizard Light astern below the Horizon, and replace it with the Longships, and the Wolf lights, to Starboard. Aptly for this British Summer, my last sight of Old England is washed out by the sheets of drizzle as we plough on through the dark, wet, night.

Bishop Rock Light shows up the during the night as the weather clears somewhat, but when dawn arrives at 0515, there is nothing to be seen but the cold, grey, Atlantic waves. A more alarming sight is the L.V.M. wind generator tottering atop its pole and looking as though it is about to plunge in to the sea, much as I am glad to have this piece of equipment aboard, it does worry me some. It is rigged above the Walker Log position, and, as its blades spin at a terrific speed in a strong breeze, as now, I have fears of it causing me a serious injury when I go aft to read the log. It is howling like a banshee now, but I approach it very carefully from behind, feather it by turning the vane, and, as it slows, throw a lashing on the blades. Then, in a very precarious position on the pushpit, I tighten its three grub screws as much as possible, take off the lashing and retreat, fast.

Ship's Log; Monday Evening. 'My bonny ship plugs bravely into the short, steep waves, only making about 3 knots now. At 1800 it is still blowing Force 6, and more at times, I have all sail up save for the first big reef in each. My feelings are mixed at this time, it is painful to be fighting to windward, but the way this year's summer has been, who can say when an anti-cyclone, with North or East winds, might come along. We must make the best of it, and battle to get as far West as possible.'

We will plug on and hope for better weather. Time to cook some supper now, perhaps a fresh vegetable stew ??

On a visit to the bow to check all is well, morale is given a boost by a school of porpoise playing in the bow wave. I feel they find me poor sport at 3 knots, but they are a fine sight, a dozen or so, wheeling, diving, and arching out of the waves, such beautiful creatures.

At 1200 on Tuesday the 30th, I estimate we are at 48 - 12'N, 7 - 35'W or 120 miles West of Ushant, and on our way, no turning back now. The weather continues to improve, clouds lifting, sky clearing, can things be looking up?

At first light on Wednesday morning I notice that No.2 batten on the foresail has jumped out of its forward pocket, so I lower the sail and lash it back in. At the same time, I repair No. 3 batten's running luff panel block, which has broken out of its webbing tab. There is always plenty to do aboard, and I rig a 'MK I Falmouth Line', 120 feet of floating orange rope which tows astern as a safety line. Its inboard end is tied to the self-steering tiller, so if I should fall overboard, and grab the rope, the tiller goes hard over, steers the ship into the wind and stops her while I (hopefully), pull myself back aboard. I hope not to have to use this system.

At 1200 on Wednesday, the last day of July, our position is 47 - 26'N, 9 - 24'W, or 180 miles W.S.W. of Ushant, and 263 miles from Falmouth.

Ship's Log; 'Question, have we made it to the Tropics? We have sun, blue sea and sky, wind N.N.W. 4, it's calm and lovely, all is well.' Probably not the Tropics, but it's a great improvement!! During the afternoon the wind picks up to force 6 and we are making 6 knots on 240 degrees, isn't it grand?

I have a small battle when the 'Falmouth Line' becomes tangled with the spinning log line and gets itself into a mighty bunch of knitting, I have to haul the whole thing inboard to sort it out. While I am doing this, sitting aft, a cheeky wave jumps inboard and gives me a dousing.

1950: 'Have just had a good feed of new potatoes and cabbage, with Ham Risotto, which I improved with Oxo and peas. Followed by bread and jam, tea, and a piece of Shirley Boon's delicious fruit cake.

Saturday, 3rd August. 'I notice this morning how clean the ship is. Rigging, ropes, and burgees are bright and white, and the decks free of dust and dirt. Lovely.'

Breakfast is taken on deck, 3 courses too; half a grapefruit, a bowl of muesli/wheat flakes/nuts & raisins with water and condensed milk, followed by coffee, biscuits and marmalade.

And so we roll South, down the big Atlantic swells, and I mean roll, we have a following wind and she does throw herself around a bit, but it's a good progress.

Sunset is beautiful, but too late, so I put the ship's clocks back an hour to G.M.T, and an end to British Summer Time. This action brings sunrise on Sunday at 0545, a civilised time to start the day. 'On this ship, I say when the sun will rise!!'

We stride on South, and our noon position is 41 - 28'N, 11 - 25'W. or 120 West of Portugal, so we really are getting somewhere now.

Ship's Log 1900; 'The time passes quickly, from sunrise, until now, when it won't be long till sunset, has been a day of wonder and pleasure. Wonder, that this really is me, sailing down the wide Atlantic in my own little ship, in glorious conditions on my great adventure. And pleasure in the feeling that at last all my struggles have got me here.'

I keep busy all day, reading, writing, or maybe just standing in the cockpit enjoying it all. The morning sextant sight is due at about 1030, after which I spend half an hour working it into the chart. Then I'll relax in the cockpit thinking about anything which might cross my mind, while I nibble some nut and raisins. Lunch usually arrives just after 1200, a salad these warm days, served a la cockpit with a can of Foster's Lager and a lime juice in my pewter mug.

The noon sunsight is due at 1250 in the Longitude, so I take that and plot it, and scratch my head over which position is true, sunsights or dead reckoning? I don't know which to trust, it's like having three watches aboard, is one right and two wrong? or two right and one wrong? or...?

The afternoon at present is given over to sleeping and sunbathing, for a couple of hours. I'm trying to get some immunity to the sun for when it gets hot soon. At about 1600 I roam around the ship checking the sails, rigging, steering gear etc., check around below too, a peep in the bilges, all gear secure? Just normal daily checks.

I try to use the cooker only once a day, so when I do light it for the evening meal at about 1700, it is fully utilized. First I put the kettle on with half a pint of water for a cup of tea, then on with whatever fresh veg I'm having, cooked in the sea water to save water, and salt.

Noon, Thursday the 1st of August. We are now 215 miles N.N.W. of Cape Finisterre, far enough to the West, and can alter course from 240 to 210 for Madeira.

I stow the anchor chain in its locker and fit the cover over the chain locker pipe. The anchor remains on the bow roller, securely lashed down. I grease and oil the anchor winch and wrap it up in plastic bags and canvas, then rig a MK II Falmouth Line on an outrigger to keep it away from the log line. The mast wedges at the deck fittings are checked and tapped down securely.

Now that we are toddling South, fairly easily, in fair weather, I'm improving my navigation techniques. It will probably surprise you to know that when we started the voyage, I didn't know how to navigate by the Sun, Moon and Stars. I made sure that all the correct books and tables were aboard and relied on the expectation that if all the voyagers could work it out, then so could I hopefully, that seems to be the case.

Now, we have a first, though minor, milestone coming up. At 2300, Friday the 2nd August, we have travelled 500 miles in 6 days. Interestingly, they have all been done on the same starboard tack which was set up at Newlyn last Sunday.

I'm now settling into a routine of sleeping, eating, working etc., still stowing items, finding new homes for them.

When the veg is cooked I stand its pot on the unused burner and put on the other half of the meal. There is a pretty basic choice, Ravioli, Spaghetti Bolognese, Fish, Corned Beef etc.. but I 'improve' it with the use of the herbs, soy sauce, curry powder etc, to increase the variation. When the meal is ready, and put in a bowl, on with one and a half pints of water in the kettle. This is for the vacuum flask and my midnight and breakfast drinks. It boils while I eat, then I pour the water, very carefully, into the flask and stow it in the Wendy House foot locker. On with the kettle once more with one cupful for my after supper tea or coffee, which is usually taken in the cockpit with the biscuits, cheese, and jam. The cooker is then off for 23 hours, very economical, 10 cc of meths to light it, and very little paraffin to operate it.

Shortly after coffee I'll wash up in a bucket of sea water and tidy up. Before dark, a good check all round the ship again, before bedtime. If all is quiet I sleep for an hour or two before midnight when I like to be up for the log reading and a good look round.

Tuesday, 6th August. Well. Isn't this nice? Here we are a-running down the Trade Winds towards Madeira which is about 350 miles away Running downwind isn't all easy though, there is a price for everything in the life and the cost of 'Running Down The Trades' is 'Rhythmic Rolling'. This is a phenomenon which shows itself as a tendency for the ship to hurl itself from side to side... for no apparent reason. Actually it is caused by there being no sail set fore and aft, the sails in a following wind obviously being set across the ship to catch the wind. It is surprisingly violent. She will sail calm and level for maybe 30 seconds, then dive one of her quarters into a sea and roll to the opposite side very quickly, and back, and back again, every 1½ seconds – I timed it. Multiply this by all day and it becomes exhausting and painful.

To make maximum speed I have the full foresail up, with the main reefed down to three panels, and this really lets us roll. We will have to put up with it during the day, but there's a little trick I do just before dark, so that I can get some sleep. I hoist the mainsail fully, and sheet right out, to the port side for this wind. The foresail is now blanketed and flops about across the foredeck. I sheet it in hard – and – the rolling stops!! this is because we now have a fore and aft sail which damps out most of the rolling. We have lost about 120 sq. ft. of driving sail and our speed drops a little, but I must have some sleep. And so must suffer the slower speed.

This evening I have changed charts from 'English Channel to Gibraltar and the Azores Archipelago', to 'Lisboa (Lisbon), to Freetown;. Very exciting, and makes me feel we are really on our way.

Wednesday, 7th August. Always seeking more speed, today I rig the sails for 'Goosewinging, that is, with one sail swung out on each side. The full main rang out to Port with no problems, but I can't get the full fore out to Starboard, due to its wind being spoiled by the main, and have to be satisfied with it reefed down two panels. They both have a foreguy tied to the boom, preventing them from swinging back inboard in the rolling.

At 1500 I'm down below writing up the log when I sense something is wrong. I look up the hatch and see that she has gybed herself. That is, she has yawed off course and the wind has got round the wrong side of the sails. Worse, the main-sheets, having gone slack during the gybe, have tangled with their friend the L.V.M. blades. There is a lot of strain on the L.V.M. wind generator assembly, and more on the mainsail foreguy, which is bending the guardrail stanchion it is tied to. I put the helm over to Starboard but she won't come round, I have to untangle the sheets from the L.V.M. first, and haul in the sheets tight to take some of the wind out of the sail, all the time expecting the foreguy or the stanchion to break, but neither does and I gybe her back on course. This of course, gybes the foresail, but with two reefs in it, there's not such a problem. It takes me half an hour of struggle to get the mess sorted out and I give up goosewinging for a while.

At 0810 today we have our first 1,000 miles on the clock, this being day 11 I'm quite pleased with progress.

We're getting near to the Madeira now and I'm picking up signals from the Radio Beacons. These help guide me to the islands, as I must admit, my navigation is not yet 'spot on'. The chart, a work of art, full of information gathered by seamen over the centuries, is covered with lines, comments, D.R. positions, sunsights... It's a mess. Thoroughly ashamed of myself, I rub everything out and home in by R.D.F.

Dawn on the 9th August reveals Ilha Porto Santo to the South, and the mass of Madeira Grande to the South West. The wind is light and variable and it takes us all day to get though the passage between the two islands. I take sunsights at noon which put us where we are, so I am doing the sums right.

As we near Sao Lourenco Lighthouse at the Eastern end of Madeira Grande, I hold a discussion with myself. It involves communicating with 'the folks back home'. One part of me says that since I am so close to civilization I ought to make an effort to get a message home. Another part says, 'No, you must press on, to get a letter home you'll have to (a) Break your non-stop voyage, (b) 'Enter' the Portuguese Territory, and (c) Anchor, rig the dinghy, go ashore, change and spend money. No – it's all too much trouble!'

However, the wind falls lighter, the sea grows choppier, and darkness approaches. I start the engine to get me out of the area before dark, as I have no charts, only an 'Atlantic Crossing Guide', with a few chartlets, with the...

... 'thumper' going through, temptations to stop and communicate grow again. The guide tells me there is a secluded anchorage just around the corner from the Lighthouse. Perhaps there might be a cruising yachtsman there who would post a letter for me. So – as dusk falls we round the 300ft lighthouse, and, in gathering gloom, with the guide, echo-sounder, and a powerful flashlight, we find our haven. It is empty, and I drop the anchor in 15 metres of water in Baia Da Abra. We are stopped for the first time in 12 days.

My, it's very dark, but calm and peaceful. I tidy up, have a cuppa, and scuttle off to bed, It's been a long day.

Friday, 10th August. 0600. A lovely, cool morning, here we are in a tiny bay, (how did we get in here in the dark?), well sheltered, but close to the rocks. It's beautiful to see hills and grass.

I have plenty to do though and must press on. Taking advantage of our being calm and level, I top up the paraffin ready-use container, the coffee and Ovaltine tins etc., I have a good wash and shave... I have a plan to go to Funchal, 10 miles to the West, looking out for someone to post them for me. I make up 'Barter Gear' as payment, since I have no money. One Barter Bag holds a tin of ham and two cans of beer, the other is half a bottle of Scotch. I dig out my 'Yachtsman's 8-Language Dictionary', but it's not much help. The best I can manage is Por Favor, O Correio (Post Office),Os Selos (Stamps)', which I hope will do the trick.

In with the anchor and away out of that cosy bay by 0900. At first I motor, thinking that Funchal is where I saw some lights last evening, but that turns out to be the Airport. So up with the sails and along the coast as much the same speed ten times the pleasure.

A Swissair jet takes off with a roar, it'll be in Europe in 2 hours, and could be in England in 3, a distance which took us 12 days. So what, they don't have the pleasure that I have.

The island is very picturesque, colourful houses are scattered along the coast and scramble up the foot-hills, thinning as they go. Above them are the 6,000 ft high mountains, topped with cloud, a lovely sight. We round Punta Santa Katarina (St. Catherine's Point? sounds familiar.), and Funchal is revealed. Quite a big town, spread around the bay and climbing up the hills I head for the harbour, dropping the sails as we are headed by the wind.

The plan is to enter the harbour and look for a British yacht, or a foreign one, or... anything afloat which will take my barter bag and post the letters to save me 'entering'. I am flying all the right flags, 'Q' to port, Courtesy Flag to Starboard, Red Ensign aft, but I don't want to go through all the formalities.

We might be lucky, there's a sizeable yacht just coming out. I range alongside him, the crew look wary. The 'Tricoleur' flies brightly, I hail them, 'Bonjour, parlez-vous Anglais?" "Oui" is the reply. I am in luck. The crew of the 'Oscar', from Nice, two men and an attractive lady, agree to post my mail and accept the Scotch for doing so, they are more than welcome. They are amazed that I don't plan to go ashore. 'What about fresh fruit and vegetables?' they ask, 'Madeira is famous for them'. 'It would be nice, but I don't have the time – I must make to the South, I have 6,500 miles to go yet! "Au revoir, Bon Voyage', we call to each other. I turn my back on the delights of the town and motor out to the N.E. wind which still blows, away from the lee of the high land.

I feel very pleased with myself for taking the trouble to get those letters away. They will cheer a lot of people , I hope. I reward myself with two cans of beer with my cheese and biscuits lunch.

Monday, 12August, 1500. position, 20 miles S.W. of Palma, Canary Islands. We were further rewarded by the best two days run of the voyage so far, 135 and 148. the N.E. Trades blew more from the East and I was able to keep both sails full on my course of 210 degrees. It was terrific sailing, tramping along at 6 or 7 knots. We ran like that until 0500 this morning, when, with Punta Cumpida Lighthouse looming to the S.E., and fixed lights high up on Ilha Palma, the wind became somewhat more than boisterous as it funnelled round the N.W. shoulder of the 7,000 ft island mountains.

I left the reefing too late, and, having to round up into the wind to do so, got the main sheets wrapped up in the L.V.M. blade again. I had a hard battle in the wind and lively seas, reefing, untangling the lines, and getting underway again. We passed within 5 miles of the island, which was too close, causing us to suffer light winds most of the day before we worked our way out of its lee.

It was an impressive sight though. I wonder what land we will see next, because I'd rather not sight the Cape Verde Islands and get becalmed again.

So we sail on. Course is now 230 degrees towards those Cape Verdes, nearly 800 miles away.

The red stain on the towel reminds me that I suffered my first injury this morning. While undoing a tight knot in some shock cord on the foresail boom, the marlin spike I was using shot free and stabbed me right under the nose, between the nostrils. That made my eyes water! It was rather painful and messy, but no serious damage done I think. 'Must be more careful', I write in the log.

Whilst sailing across this empty piece of sea, I'm reading up on what my future courses should be. It might be thought that I'm on my own out here when it comes to making decisions of that sort. Not so, I have plenty of company and advice in the form of books of other voyagers to help me on my way. My favourite two are Robin Knox-Johnston's 'A World Of My Own', with Suhaili, and Alec Rose's 'My Lively Lady'. Their boats were similar in size to mine and make similar speed. Then there is Bernard Noitessier's 'The Long Way', when he sailed 'Joshua' this way. His book is a mine of information, but somewhat sketchy about this part of the world. Bill King in his Junk Rigged 'Galway Blazer' doesn't give much useful information either. I have Bill Tilman in 'Mischief, John Ridgway in `Debenhams', plus my own diary of that voyage. So I am not short of information and tales of the sea as I sail along the way. My 'Bible' of course, is 'Ocean Passages For The World', and its pocket with charts of sailing and steamship courses, weather maps, and surface currents. A wonderful book. It advises me to pass 'To the West, but in sight of, the Cape Verdes, where 'the winds will be stronger and steadier'. I am taking its advice.

Saturday, 17th August. 1800. V.H.F. Radio contact is made with the German Container Ship 'Avon', bound to the Nor'East. Her Captain promises to 'Report Me To Lloyds'. A system where merchant ships will then pass on the report to a previously designated agent of the yacht, Terry in my case. All for free! A marvellous service in these expensive times.

Sunday, 18th August. At 1500 we have been at sea for 21 days, time passes so quickly. We have logged 2,220 miles at a daily average of 104, which isn't bad, but not as good as I would have liked. I need a higher average really, to make up for the slower speeds we will make in the Doldrums.

After 21 days, the health is fine, the nose pain has almost gone, and morale is good, ₁ always subject to progress of course. All moods are dependant on the progress made! Eating habits are O.K., somewhat basic but I ring the changes on my food stocks, using Soy Sauce, Curry Powder, Vinegar, Herbs and Spices to vary the flavours and make the meals 'interesting' The potatoes and onions are my only fresh foods now - a welcome addition to the cans and packets.

Tuesday, 20th August. Overnight we pass about 15 miles West of Santo Antao, the Northwesternmost of the Cape Verde Islands, without seeing it. I spend an anxious night looking out in fairly gloomy visibility, but see nothing I had turned away to the South West at dusk for safety. Punta Malgrade light has a visibility of only 9 miles, which is too close for comfort anyway. This morning we bound South on a Force 6 Nor'Easter, full of hope and happiness that this bonny wind will carry us well to the South.

Tuesday, 20th. 1600. Ship's Log. 'Course 190, Speed 4 Kn., Position 16 - 15'N., 25 - 35'W. Oh Dear! The wind is falling light, I hope this isn't the end of the Trades'.

But it is... By 1800 we are stopped, becalmed, just like that, the Trade Winds gone. So – the Doldrums start here, at 2,480 miles logged.

Since we are becalmed and the engine is overdue for its weekly run, let's give it an airing. Damn! The battery won't turn the starter motor, never mind the engine. Looks like I have more battery problems. I start the engine by hand and motor for an hour, stop it, and the battery still won't start it. Damn again. It's luck I never did trust electrics or electronics. I can carry on starting the engine without the battery, using the L.V.M. to put a little charge into it for lights and radio etc. Another problem for Cape Town. I have plenty of Paraffin for Tilley lamps if I really need to show a light. We can carry on. We have to.

We enter the Doldrums, an area of light variable winds, thunderstorms, squalls, and slow progress. I had worried about this area, not so much on account of Roamer, or of progress, but rather more about how I would handle it mentally.

I need progress to keep me happy, and I feared that going slowly in light wind conditions, which Roamer doesn't like, plus hot and humid weather, which I don't like, might cause my temperament to boil over. But it hasn't happened. I had mentally prepared myself for the slow going, resigned myself to 50 m.p.d. for a couple of weeks, and am now making the most of the calm weather. There are fantastic sunrises and sunsets to enjoy, and, as an added bonus, I sleep on the upper deck, under a canopy of magnificent stars, much clearer than they are ever seen in the U.K., with its polluted atmosphere. Millions upon millions of stars, from horizon to horizon, casting their own soft light so that there is a night – long twilight.

We make slowly South. I take to having a daily swim, after a good look round for sharks. I dive off the bow and swim alongside until the stern catches me up, and

Sailor Bob sends a message

LONE round-the-world sailor Bob Burns has sent a message to his family in Brighton to say he is safe and well.

Bachelor Bob, 45, set sail in July on his 27,000-mile adventure aboard his 36ft. cruiser Roamer.

He passed close to Madeira earlier this month and decided to scribble a hasty note to his brother, Terry, in Brighton, to let the family know of his progress. A local fisherman posted the letter which arrived at the weekend.

"He assured us that everything is OK and the boat is going beautifully," said Terry. "He is determined not to step ashore until he reaches his first scheduled stop, Cape Town, in October where he hopes to telephone us."

Brighton-born Bob has been planning the solo trip since 1977 when he joined John Ridgeway's crew for the Whitbread round-the-world race, only to leave half-way after a difference of opinion.

Bob, who served in the Royal Navy for 19 years, sold his house and is spending his life savings on the trip.

After reaching Cape Town he will head for Sydney and the Falklands before returning home, hopefully next spring.

Evening Argus
19th August 1985

haul myself up the steps on the starboard quarter. While in the sea, which is beautifully clear and warm, I attack, with a plastic scraper, Goose Barnacles which are beginning to grow on the rudder and under the stern.

Thursday, 22nd August. Ship's Log. "0700 – Awakened from my slumbers on the foredeck at 0600 by a shower of rain. Hurling the bedding below, my first reaction is to hide down below, muttering mild curses. Second thoughts though, are that this is my long-awaited shower arrived. So I strip off the shorts, grab the soap, and have a glorious dawn bath in the cockpit in the heavy cool rain. Quite a lot of my 'suntan' goes down the drain with the soap suds".

Another rain squall at 0900 provides the fresh water for a laundry session. Fantastically bright rainbows arch amongst the dark clouds, including the smallest I've ever seen, which starts at the bow, and ends at the stern.

In the light winds, I add "Studding sails" to the main sails. The fore has my storm jib triced under its boom, and the main has the ex-boat cover, a bright blue light tarpaulin, tied along its boom to increase the sail area.

Thursday, 1900. a big black cloud in the South is being watched with a wary eye, two very wary eyes in fact. it appears to have a black line attaching it to the sea – a waterspout?? Alarm bells ring, dusk is approaching. As we close, the "waterspout" becomes a smoke-belching ship. I call her up on V.H.F. and hold a halting conversation with the Greek Skipper of the "Anna". He is full of "Bravos" for my sailing on my own to Cape Town, and promises to "Report me to Lloyds".

Sunday, 25th August. It looks as though we are in for a bit heavy weather. All along the Eastern horizon are dark purple clouds piling high into the sky, at their base, just above the sea, is a black line with lightning flashing in its dark maw. From the dark continent of Africa it approaches, blotting out the sun, cooling the atmosphere already. I disconnect the battery and the radio in case we should get struck. The black line approaches. I am naked in the cockpit, with soap and washing all ready. I reef down both sails, batten down all hatches. The wind approaches ahead of the squall, brilliant white horses stand out against the blackness of the pit of the clouds, a cold blast gives me goose pimples. The wind arrives and Roamer tears off into the approaching rain, which arrives as a solid grey wall, beating down the waves, making me gasp with the cold and the pain of the large drops – I slip a shirt on. The wind eases in the rain and the torrential downpour continues for an hour, lightning flashing all around, but not much thunder. I have a lovely bath, do all my washing, and – get cold. The cold becomes too much and, despite the torrent of the rain pouring off the forward end of the main boom onto the sliding hatch, I open it and slide my dripping body down the companionway ladder. It is quiet below, I dry myself for warmth, towel round the neck, waterproof coat on and back to the cockpit. I don't like to be below when there are squalls about. The storm passes and leaves us with a West wind, which wafts us Southwards, with steaming decks.

So we "wriggle and squirm" to the South on any little breeze We get. We are averaging 50 m.p.d. which of course is poor, but better then being stopped.

I use the these quiet times to carry out maintenance work aboard, some painting on the upper deck, grease the steering sheaves and wires. I lower the sails one at a time, check over the stitching, smear tallow at chafing points, check shackles and blocks.

I mount a major campaign to re-site the L.V.M. Wind Generator. I can't live with the thought of the mainsheets tangling with the blades in the strong winds of the South. So I rig down the whole assembly and move it from the starboard forward corner of the pushpit, to the port aft corner, about 3 feet immediately aft of the mainsheets blocks. Here it is fairly safe from the sheets, but too close to the Levanter wind vane, so I have to lower the L.V.M.'s mounting board to get the blades below the vane. The job is done though, and is a great relief to me.

I sort out my tools in the workshop and notice what a nice cool draught comes under the heads door. I look at the door with a critical eye. It is a nuisance, in the way, blanking off the ventilation. It is only there to give privacy to anyone using the Racasan bucket, and privacy isn't really required at present. I attack its hinges with a screwdriver, remove it and lash it to the ship's side over the sail bin. Whilst sweating in the workshop, I re-stow the folding dinghy, oars, scrubbers, spare timber, etc., and lash it all down more securely for "The South".

Thursday, 29th August, 2100. Ship's Log; "What a sight I have just witnessed! Laying out my bed on the fore deck, I hear the familiar snort of porpoise coming up for air. From the bow there is the moving and wonderful sight of a dozen or so of these lovely creatures swimming leisurely directly below, not ten feet away. Illuminated by the full moon, they glisten green and grey, swimming in perfect Line abreast, sometimes they all surface and blow together, just six feet below, the fishy smell of their breath wafting up. For half an hour this entrancing entertainment continues as they swim contentedly below, shining in the moonlight, their conversational whistling perfectly audible. Then, as at a signal, they veer off to the starboard in perfect order, and are gone."

Friday, 20th August, I'm having a little trouble with getting a Meridian Altitude sun shot at this time as I am almost directly under the sun. that is, my Latitude is equal to the sun's declination. The sextant angle is nearly 90 degrees and trying to get it to rest on the horizon would require the use of a swivel chair, as it circles overhead. I have to give up Mer. Alt. sights for a few days.

Keeping myself busy, I start my garden" in the workshop, a plastic tray screwed to the worktop, containing smaller trays with seeds of Mung Beans, Alfalfa, and Fenugreek. The Mung Beans grow prolifically, the other two, not so good. I make and paint some spare wind vanes for the Levanter Gear.

Saturday31[st] August, 1630. Ship's Log; "I'm almost afraid to say this, but I must – we appear to be out of the Doldrums!! At 7 - 40'N., 23 - 10'W., after 10 days and 530 miles, The Southern horizon yesterday evening took on an ominous appearance. High dark cumulus clouds, with sheet lightning flashing under them, lay all along the sea. There was hardly a breath of wind, but I had a "feeling". I checked all round the ship, secured all gear in case of a blow. I slept in short naps, but had to wait until 0430 for my wind, it arrived in the usual form of a rain squall, which was moderate and didn't call for a reefing. It passed and left a lull, another black rainstorm washed over us – and – this one left a Sou'westerly breeze, Force 5, on which we romped off to the Southeast. It has held all day. What a relief to be bounding over the waves at 5 or 6 knots in a fresh cool breeze, making good progress at last.

We run off the bottom of the "Lisbon to Freetown" chart, an have to change to the smaller scale, "North Atlantic, Eastern Portion", which has a scale of one to ten million.

We are heading for a spot in the ocean which I have designated the "Magic Roundabout". This is at 5N., 18W., where "Ocean Passengers" says I may alter course to the South West, towards South America and the South Atlantic. These different courses are necessary to work our way across the prevailing Southerly winds in this Equatorial region and to take advantage of the currents which flow. The Guinea current, which I'm in now, runs Southeast, and then East, following the Africa coast. As we move South, we run into the Equatorial current which flows West along the Equator towards Brazil, where it divides. North of Recife going N.W.

towards the West Indies, South of Recife, S.W. to become the Brazil current.

The boisterous Southwest winds become more Southerly and drive me to the East. I pass North of the "Roundabout", and at 0730 on the 5th of September, make my 90 degree turn at 4 - 30'N., 15 - 40'W., thus further South and East of where Ocean Passages recommends. I can only make a course of 250 which seems acceptable since I can expect the winds to gradually back to the Southeast, thus allowing me to make more Southerly course.

This is an empty piece of ocean for shipping, the main sea lane between the Cape Verde Islands and the Cape of Good Hope being further to the East. I don't mind this, an empty sea is a safe one for a singlehander.

There are plenty of flying fish about, squadrons of them "scramble" at my approach, a shimmering sparkling explosion of silver fish taking to the air. I'm not getting any on the deck during the nights now though as I did near the Cape Verdes, maybe they are better pilots down here!

Sunday, 8th September, 0900. Ship's Log; "There is a feeling of despondency aboard. Progress is poor and has been since we turned to the Southwest. The wind stays in the South, with even a little West in the air at times, barring my way to the Southwest.

Speed is poor in the Force 3 to 4 winds, with daily runs of around 60 to 70 m.p.d. Latitude today is 3 - 08'N., with only 23 miles of Southing made since yesterday. Robin Knox-Johnston made it to the Line in 43 days, Alec Rose in 41, and they romped across in boisterous South Easterlies.

I am being pushed relentlessly Westward by my course and now by the Equatorial current. There is nothing I can do about it, I must just plod on trying to make to the South to reach the Southeasterlies which blow South of the Equator. It's a hard struggle though, my Junk Rig, as mentioned before, doesn't go to the windward at all well, at the best of times, and in the choppy seas which I have here, it is painful. Business. I have to keep her on the wind, so speed is slow, because speed is slow, any series of extra steep or short waves will stop her dead in the water, then she will fall off to the West before picking up a little speed again.

Thursday, 12th September. 46 days at sea, the same number of days that "Debenham's" took to reach Cape Town in the 1977-78 Whitbread Race, and I'm not even at the Line yet!

Fed up with trying to drag a comb through my greasy, salt-laden hair, I attack it with my clippers and scissors. Quite a massacre! Heaps of hair in the heads, but when the job is done the result doesn't look too bad. It feels a lot better anyway, and I'm not going anywhere special for a while.

Friday the 13th of September. As we move West, the sun sets later then I like, so I put the clocks back an hour. I'm not superstitious, but take extra care today!

Sunday, 15th September, 0900. well, what a poor week this has been, my moods are absolutely dependent on progress and there has little enough of that. We are still not across the Line!! What a week – the wind stays stubbornly in the South or South by West, not allowing us to make better then 250, which is no good. The current pushes West, in Longitude 25W., we cannot afford to go further without making Southing or we won't make it past the bulge of Brazil before the current washes us to the Northwest.

What a week – I've been in despairing moods, nearly in tears of frustration at times, my poor bonny ship hard on the wind, pitching into short seas at 2 knots, 1½ knots and worse. My slow progress has allowed a considerable growth of goose barnacles to accumulate on the hull. I stopped the ship, and swam all round her scraping off all that I could, fearful all the time that a shark might appear on the scene. None did, but the barnacles grow further under the hull than I can reach, and it is difficult anyway as the sea isn't at all calm.

Sunday, 15th September, Ship's Log; "1600 – Crisis time. I really am in trouble now, having been in virtually the same position for 48 hours, despite my trying a tack to the East, motoring due South during a lull, and anything else I have tried. The basic fact is that I am pinioned by the wind, sea and current on 1'N., and cannot make to windward, that is, South. I daren't go any further to the West in search of Southeast winds. What a situation!

I am seriously considering a mad plan to turn West, sail up to 2 or 3 N., to get out of the current, and traverse the entire Atlantic, back to 10 W., and start again. It would be a desperate business, but I'm in a desperate situation. Nothing less than the possible failure to succeed in my project!"

Monday, 16th September. Ship's Log; 1900. "What a difference a day makes! Just as I was considering that mad plan, the Southeast winds, obviously tired of waiting for me to come South to them, reached over the Equator to get me. We are making a bonny course of 200(M), which, with variation, is due South on the chart. I can let her off the wind a little, and even let the sheets out somewhat. We are making 3 1/3 knots, a very good speed by recent standards. Noon Lat. Was 0 - 32'N., Long. 25 - 20'W. I'm hopeful of crossing the Line during the night – what a relief!

Tuesday, 17th September, 1800. Well, life hasn't been much fun recently, but, having crossed the Equator, though not until Noon today, and now being in the South Atlantic, I'm going to have a little party. I've "Crossed the Line" many a time and am a fully paid up member of the King Neptune's Empire. My bonny ship hasn't though, so, in gratitude for her struggles in getting us here, I write her out a "Crossing Line Certificate". All sorts of fun and games take place in ships on these occasions, with uninitiated crew and passengers undergoing certain penalties, which, in the Royal Navy in my time, consisted mainly of having your face plastered with a thick sticky paste being shaved "with a huge wooden razor, and then suffering a ducking in the swimming pool from King Neptune's "Bears".

Opening a 1lb. Tin of Ham specially saved for the occasion, I eat it all, with French Mustard, and Branston Pickle. It is washed down with a few cans of beer, the odd glass of Port, and I finish this splendid repast in the cockpit as the sun sets beautifully, feeling very mellow with a glass of Brandy and Port in my hand, listening to Wolfgang Amadeus Mozart's soothing music.

We are in the South Atlantic!

Chapter Nine

The Voyage – The Equator to South Africa

A ship went sailing over the Bar,
Way down Rio,
They've pointed her bow for the Southern Star...
("The Rio Grande")

Wednesday the 18th of September. "After the Ball is over", it's back to reality. The wind has wandered back to the South a little and we are struggling on the wind again, course 230/240, speed 3 knots, just.

Surprisingly, the sunsights put us nearly a whole degree South at 1 - 30'S., and 27 W. This is a pleasant surprise and cheers me no end. I wonder if there is a wayward current around here setting South or Southwest, as the sea is very lumpy. We plunge and pitch into it. I spend many hours in the cockpit, willing my bonny babe through the choppy seas, encouraging her, and myself, with the expectation that it surely can't be many days before the wind hauls to the East and we can be set free from this on-the-wind bondage that we have suffered for so long.

Sunday, 22nd September, 1830. Journal, "In honour of the quietness of the evening and the fact that today is the first of the Southern Spring, I write this in the cockpit. Facing to Starboard, I'm having my daily treat of watching the sun move towards its setting. From behind small puffy cumulus clouds golden sunrays beam down to the horizon. There is a light and friendly breeze from the East, not strong enough for my liking, but it's all I have. It ambles us along at 3 knots to the South. All is quiet save for the rustle of the sea alongside. My world is the peaceful one I have long sought and on this, my 57th evening alone at sea, I am perfectly content. My world consists of a great circle of sea to the clear horizon all round, broken only by the occasional wave top. No man-made object has broken that horizon for so long now that I can't recall when I last saw a ship, but I don't mind at all."

We progress steadily but still slowly, at 1300 we are at 4 - 38'S., 28 - 50'W., still being pushed to the West at 40 to 50 miles a day, but approaching what I regard as the safety of 8 South, where the West current should start curving off to the South West.

I busy myself with the Sunday tasks. It being quiet weather today I give the engine a run and, happily, the battery starts it. This is a great relief; maybe I don't have a battery problem after all. Fill up ready-use containers of Paraffin, Meths, Coffee, Muesli and Ovaltine.

I hang over the Starboard side and attack the barnacles with the long-handled stiff broom. Where we have been on the Port tack for so long and heeled to Starboard, the beasts have been growing up the side, high up on the black topsides. They come off fairly easily there, but another attack on them on the rudder isn't so successful. I can't get into a close enough position and anyway, they have grown mostly around the nut and bolt heads of the rudder and trim-tab hangings and I can't shift them.

A tasty supper this evening of corned beef, tomatoes and rice. I am beginning to economise on the food, as the voyage is taking somewhat longer than I had planned. That tin of corned beef was lunch as well, and will be tomorrow's lunch too, and tomorrow's supper, padded out with soup and tinned vegetables.

1900. taking an R.D.F. bearing, the island of Fernando De Noronha comes up where it ought to, on the starboard beam. Noronha is 220 miles distant, Brazil 400. Our next "Waypoint", Ilha Da Trindade, is 950 miles to the South. Now that I have transferred to the South Atlantic chart, the project looks more possible. I have marked in my preferred track as far as 200 miles North of Tristan Da Cunha.

Wednesday, 25th September.

Not a good day for me. The weather has been squally, we were reefed down all night and being blown off to the West. I shook out the reefs just after 0800, then, while I was below writing and typing, the wind came on strong and fast. I was late to reef her, and the lower batten on the foresail was broken, my first serious damage.

Then at lunchtime, while looking in the forward bilge for some rope, I notice that my "6,000 mile" Stilton Cheese, which is stowed there too, smells rather strongly. I cut it open, on the grounds that if it is going off, it is better to eat some of it at 5,000 miles, rather than none of it at 6,000. Huh! Look at that – I'm not going to eat any – it's all brown, dry, and cracked right through. Damn and blast. Taking no chances with my stomach out here, over the side it goes. Sad blow that, it was the last "Luxury".

There's a lot of huntin' and killing going on in the sea, as I have been adopted by a pack of Dorado. There are about a dozen of them, bluey-green, about 4 feet long, with a pair of small horizontal fins just abaft their heads, and a swallow-tail fin aft. Some swim alongside, others range out ahead to Port and Starboard, like a pack of killer submarines. Their voracity and hunting skills are impressive – they literally bound across the sea after flying fish on the wing, keep up, and grab them as they return to the sea. Terrific speeds they attain.

Our Latitude is 8 - 32'S., just South of Recife's, and I'm presuming that we are out of the danger of being washed to the Northwest. Maybe I was a bit neurotic about it, but it's easy to say that with hindsight. At the time, when we were "trapped" 1 degree North of the Equator, it was a very real danger.

Recife's radio stations are very lively, with fast-talking D.J.'s and Brazilian music, unspoiled by Western pop music I'm glad to say. I find them a little too lively though, in my state of peacefulness, and usually switch off after about half an hour.

Thursday, 26th September. At 10 South, I have made up a survey of our dismal progress thus far.

Portion	Miles	Days	M.P.D.	Speed
Penzance to C. Verdes (End of Trades)	2480	23	106	4.4
C. Verdes to End of Doldrums	550	11	50	2.1
Doldrums to Magic Roundabout	467	6	78	3.25
Roundabout to Equator	870	12	72.5	3.0
Equator to 10 S	707	8	88	3.6

Thing can only get better. Can't they?

Thursday, 2015. Damn and Blast – again. Just had my first ship for 11 days pass not half a mile to Port, and I couldn't raise him. Just a mutter on the radio and he drove off over the horizon to the South. That's a pity, I'm keen to get a message out so that the folks can see that I'm going to be late getting to Cape Town. I don't expect to be seeing many ships from now on...

Friday, 27th September. I am 45½ today!

The days blend into a routine of sunrise, breakfast, couple of hours bookwork, a.m. sight, lunch, noon sight, read and sleep, supper, sunset, read and sleep, sunrise... The wind stays on the Port beam and we amble steadily South.

Saturday, 28th September. The Whitbread Race started at noon, the leaders are expected at Cape Town from the 5th November. Ridiculously, if I don't get a move on, they'll be there before me!! I had hoped to get clear of Cape Town without getting too involved with the racers, I remember what the Royal Cape Yacht Club was like 8 years ago.

For the first time for a long time, we are heading East of South! Not a lot, but it's encouraging. At 12 - 36'S., 31 - 50'W. 5,240 logged, 3,300 to go.

Sunday, 29th Sept. I repair the broken batten with Resorcinol glue, turn over the engine and prop shaft, good check in bilges, tap down mast wedges etc. Am preparing

Lone sailor on course

Lone sailor Bob Burns is on course to make his first stop in Cape Town after leaving Britain two months ago on a round-the-world voyage in his 30ft crusing yacht Roamer.

His brother Terry, who lives in Brighton, has received a message via Lloyds that Bob was off the east coast of Africa west of The Gambia.

After a stop in Cape Town, Bob will be heading for Sydney and the Falkland Islands before returning home next Spring after completing 27,000 miles.

Evening Argus
27th September 1985

for worse weather to come in the South by improving stowage, extra lashings here and there, jamming the books tightly in their shelves etc.

Monday 30th Sept. "Boo, I suffered a very sad loss today. I had hauled in the log line to check it for barnacles, which would slow its turning. There were quite a few on the line so I got my knife and scraped them off no bother. Having finished the job, I dropped my knife into the scuppers "for safety", and it skidded and jumped its way out of the nearest drain port in the toe rail. I was mighty sick with myself for doing such a stupid thing, it was my very favourite knife, which I'd had since I was a Boy Seaman on H.M.S. Adamant in 1956, a good old-fashioned Navy rigging knife. Damn Damn Damn!!!"

The wind continues light, and progress slow. I rig my studding sails again, the storm jib under the fore boom, the ex boat cover under the main. I tie out the lazy jacks to stop them rubbing on the sails, and other anti-chafe measures.

Later – "What a beautiful evening! I go up into the pulpit and stand savouring the pleasures of gliding along almost silently, rising and falling gently on the swell, the cool evening breeze wafting across my bonny ship. Looking at the sky, I'm sure I can see subtle differences in it as we proceed South. It looks higher and paler, and out to the West, as sunset approaches, it's a lovely shade of green. Ah, this is a fine place to be alright."

Later still –

"Having seen no aircraft or flying objects all the voyage, there are two lights moving across the sky, one Eastwards, one Southwards, I'm sure they must be satellites, there are no bright flashing lights that aircraft have, just slow-moving white spots, very eerie."

Tuesday, 1st October, Journal 0900 "Had two flying fish aboard last night, one I found lying on deck I put in a bucket to keep it fresh. The other, although I heard it come aboard and flop about, I never found until this morning, when I went to the washplace for my daily splash, and trod on it!

It had come in the fore-hatch – treading on it didn't make it look too appetising, so over the side it went to my veracious escort – I gave them the other one as well:

Log "Do we get there this month?" During the 24 hrs to 1300 we make 89 miles on the log, but 102 on the chart, no cheating. This takes us to 16 - 21'S., 31 - 20'W., on course for Trindade, 265 miles away.

The weather looked ominous earlier with high-piled cumulus clouds to windward, but they dispersed to nothing.

Friday 4th Oct. 1930. it seems that we won't be seeing our first piece of land since the Canaries. We have arrived at the Latitude of Trindade but 50 miles West of it, which is a pity. I should have liked to have used it as a check on my navigation, but we shall have to proceed on theory only.

I doubt if we'll see any land now till Table Mountain looms out of the East. When will that be? Who knows ? we still have 2,800 miles to go, 28 days at 100 m.p.d., and we haven't made 100 miles very often lately.

Sunday 6th Oct. Journal. "I was going to do a review of the situation, as we move into our 11th week, but am not in the mood, feeling sick and frustrated at continued poor progress. 50 miles yesterday, 48 today, absolutely hopeless". "I'm really fed up, this plod has been going on for too long". – Later – "Ah, my blues never last too long. I throw a "Leaving the Tropics" party, as we sail, slowly, under (or over?) Latitude22 1/2 South, leaving the Tropical Zone and moving into the Southern Atlantic. Having no food luxuries, this has to be a drinks party so I have a couple of cans of beer, finish off the last (there were only ever two) bottle of Port, and toss a few Brandies into it. The menu was a bag of Planters peanuts with the Port, and a Mars bar, King Size! for sweet." I went to sleep not to awaken until 0400, with a slight hangover!

Monday 7th Oct. 70 day review? Well, the situation is poor, we still have 2,600 miles to go, and it'll take a strong-wind miracle to get us there before the end of the month. Morale goes up and down depending on progress, but is basically good. Roamer and I are both in good health with no problems. Stores, water, and equipment are O.K. "I can't get round this progress problem though. We are actually sailing down this vast Atlantic Ocean at walking speed, about 3 -3 1/2 m.p.h. This is no damn good, but what can I do?

Am keeping myself busy with jobs as ever. I put a rope serving on the steering wheel, which makes it look nicer, plus it will be warmer on the hands when the weather turns colder soon. The midships spoke is marked with two Turk's heads in nylon. Am making up "Baggy-wrinkle" to hang on the lazy jacks. Baggy-wrinkle is a soft pad of small pieces of spare rope, which, when tied to a part of the rigging such as the lazy jacks, will prevent the lines chafing away the stitching on the sails.

The Master Compass, the Sestrel-Moore, has been stowed below for safety, and am using the Concept, mounted on the mast, as a steering compass. It may sound dramatic, but if we roll right over and the masts break oft as they almost certainly will, the Concept would go, and possibly the Moore too, leaving me with no compass to steer my Jury Rig by. Dramatic maybe, but these are dramatic waters. Commander Bill King, in his Junk Rigged Galway Blazer, was rolled over and dismasted not so far South of here in October 1968.

The Wendy House floor has been cleared, it had become a home for the typewriter (I am actually writing and typing this as we go – absolutely Veritas!)

Briefcase, books and papers.

We are now Latitude 23 - 50'S., Longitude 26 - 50'W., which is the same Latitude as Rio De Janeiro, 900 miles to the West.

Tuesday 8th October.

I am extra busy today. I do a big job about which I've been thinking for some time. Reading Moitessier's "The Long Way", which I often do, I came across the part where, in this area, he had a grand clear out of equipment to reduce weight in the ends of his boat for very good seamanlike reasons. He dumped 375 lbs of food, paraffin, rope etc., I can't afford to do anything drastic like that, neither do I have enough of anything to want to. I have been worried that she is heavy forward though, which would increase the chances of "Pitch-poling" that is, somersaulting stern over bows in the monster seas further South. So – from right aft I move out the 720ft of Manila "Southern Ocean Brake" rope to the deck and coil it down on the Engine Room hatch. After a pause to do some reefing, I then make a raid on the workshop compartment and move aft all the heavy items, spare metal, two drawers of tools, full paint cans, grease cans, coils of rope and wire etc. These are stowed right aft where the rope had been and must lift the bows a little. I won't know until we get into port and I can see the waterline.

We pass 6,000 miles today, 2,500 to do?

Wednesday, 9th October. Our first blow in the Southern having been pleading for wind recently, today it arrives. I'd had a difficult night reefing up and down and trying to steer in the desired direction, "Difficult to stand up, let alone do anything", the Log says. I am up on deck to get the routine log reading for 1000, when the wind increases from Force 7 to 9 in ten minutes, giving me some more reefing, in a rush. I shut her down to one panel and the top triangle of each sail. There is quite a blow for an hour, the wind whipping the surface of the sea into a white foam, hurling wave tops across the deck. Having got her reefed down, I nip below and put on my "Heavy Gear", the Henri-Lloyd "Ocean" set of waterproofs, big green welly boots, safety harness, and back up top to study this first Southern Ocean blow.

After this first hour, the wind eases to Force 8., but I leave her shut down, quite willing to watch and learn. I am very conscious of being a "new boy" down here. Safety First is the word. Just as well too, for after I grab a quick bite of lunch, she blows up again, hard, backing from Nor'East to North, and then, in a series of violent rain squalls and a Force 10 wind, backs swiftly right round to West. I have been on the Port tack during this time, and find myself heading North, not quite what I want, so in a lull, I gybe her and head South. Having been on the Port tack since North of the

Equator, the masts creak at the unusualness of this. But – at 1500, we are heading Southeast at 4 knots, in clearing weather, the wind, now at W.S.W. Force 6, having backed 180 degrees in 5 hours. We run S.E. for a while, but the wind continues its wanderings, right round to South and during the night increases to gale force again. I have to reef her right down again at 0300 and head East, to ride it out on the best course I can make. All this in 25 S., what's it like at 35?

Thursday, 10 Oct. 75 days at sea. This is the day I gave my E.T.A. at Cape Town. From today anyone worrying for my safety will be doing so – increasingly. Nothing I can do about it I'm afraid.

All day we make to the East well reefed down on the strong S.S.E. wind. A Meridian Altitude sight and a p.m. sight through a break in the cloud, gives unwelcome but not unexpected news that we have slipped North of the position at noon yesterday, to 24 - 30'S., and 24 - 00'W.

Later the wind continues to back, forcing us to N.E., and then by 2300 to N.N.E. This is too much to bear and I gybe her round to the Port tack and try to make to the South. Can only make 220/230 (M). What a game!!

Friday 11 Oct. Awaken at 0330, we are making slow speed just West of South. I suffer a black fit of depression, throwing things about, cursing and shouting. I hurt my knuckles, which depresses me further. Bemoaning my ill-fortune, plans flood through my mind of giving up this long and bitter struggle at Cape Town and either sailing gently home for early Spring, via St. Helena and Ascension Islands, or finding a job in South Africa, putting a "proper" rig on the boat, and finishing the voyage next year. "There have been too many entries in this log." I tell myself, "talking of pain, hurt, frustration, agony, and purgatory etc. It was never supposed to be like this." 0500 is a bad time to feel sorry for myself.

At first light, 0530, I hoist a little more sail and immediately feel better. As the day goes on I shake off the blues and do some jobs. I change out the L.V.M. to the high speed, small vane assembly, hook it up and get it changing – it works well. I tighten the steering wires which have stretched a little. There is a "nasty" on the foresail, some stitching has pulled out at the aft end of the lower batten pocket. During yesterday's storm the sail, lashing about, has torn more stitching and the sail material, allowing the batten to poke through the batten pocket end. I could do nothing about it at the time, but now, during a lull in the wind, I do a lash-up job from the batten end to the cringle eye and the sheet tab. It looks O.K. and will allow me to set full sail if and when the wind decreases.

The position at 1230 is the expected disaster, 24 - 52'S, 24 - 00'W. just 22 miles South in 24 hours is the result of our running back and forth across this wind.

By nightfall the wind is up to 7-8 again and I have to shut her down to two panels and the top triangles. We labour in the general direction of South.

During the night I suffer a small disaster. Awakened at 0100 by excessive rolling and banging, there is then a loud bang as though something has fallen on to the deck. It is teeming with rain and I dress as fast as possible. Outside, in full oillies and harness with my big flashlight, I find the wind has dropped completely, the ship rolls like crazy and the sails hurtle from one side to the other. I haul in the sheets tight, but too late to prevent the down-hauls of the main breaking off the Concept compass from the mast. The compass lies in the cockpit well. Its bracket broken but itself seemingly O.K. Damn and Blast, but it could have been worse.

I await developments, stand through a violent downpour, the wind returns, fast and within 2 minutes is blowing at 7 again from the previous direction – back to bed.

There is a little good news about. I am visited by my first albatross, a great big beauty, soaring on the wind flap of those huge wings, he has a quick look at me and glides off down-wind.

More good news on the radio. Four Arabs had hi-jacked an Italian cruise ship, shot a 72-year-old American in a wheel chair! and thrown him over the side. Then they gave themselves up to the Egyptians, who let them go! Good news is that the Yanks intercepted the plane in which these Arabs were making off to Tunis, forced it down in Sicily and the Italians have them in custody.

A little more good news! At last I have found Cape Town on the radio, on 4833 Khz. It will be good to listen in as we approach and they give out a comprehensive sea area weather forecast for out to 50 miles. Not much use to me at present, at 2,300 miles away, and not getting any closer.

Saturday, 12th Oct. Same situation, Gale 8 from E.S.E., Busy myself checking bilges and forespeak for water, but all dry. Battery meter shows it fully charged and over-charging, so I shut it down. Writing various books and articles, nowt to be done about the wind. I have a new motto. "It could be worse – couldn't it ?"

Sunday, 13th Oct. Still heading for Antarctica!

The wind stays steady at E.S.E. As is normal with me, after a short period of anger and frustration at a set – back I soon accept the situation and become surprisingly cheerful. I also try to make the best of a bad situation. Take this one now, here we are heading South instead of Southeast, bad news, but as Julie Andrews used to sing, "A spoonful of sugar makes the medicine go down". I look for my spoonful of sugar, and it could be there, 800 miles S.E. of us, an island called Tristan, Tristan Da Cunha as most people know it. The name and its remote position have long fascinated me, and here I am, not far away and being pushed closer all the time, by this otherwise unfavourable wind. Without this East Sou'easter I would have passed 400 miles North of Tristan and couldn't have justified the diversion, but now...? We'll see. I could probably get a message to Cape Town and maybe even the U.K. to stop the folks worrying, which is my main concern. I'm O.K. but they don't know it.

The new compass plinth is occupying most of my time at the moment, I'm making it out of mahogany, some 3" x 2" lengths of which I just happen to have. It is "interesting" working forward in the workshop in the violent motion.

Monday, 14th Oct. Good News!

The wind has backed to North of East and I am heading for Tristan on course of 160 (MW).

Tuesday, 15th Oct. After being up and watchful most of the night, I am able to hoist full sail for the first time for a week, in moderate rain. My lash-up job on the fore's lower batten looks O.K.. I treat myself to a hot breakfast, a rare treat. Suddenly my day becomes a good one. I pop my head up the hatch for a routine peep around and to check the course, and – on the Starboard quarter, looming out of the mist and rain is a great big beautiful ship!! I rush below, leap into waterproofs, grab the radio and back to the cockpit. "Calling on Channel 16, Call on Channel 16, calling the ship, this is the small sailing craft on your Port bow, do you receive me, over?"

"Hello the yacht, hello the yacht, this is Sanchos Topaz, Sanchos Topaz, do you hear me, over?" A Chinese voice comes across the sea, my first contact for many weeks. This good chap on the Topaz and I have a good chat and although I have a little difficulty making myself clear to him he accepts my ZD2 message to Lloyds and promises to send it off. My luck certainly was in to see him, the general visibility was only a mile and I just happened to take a look as he came through a break in the murk I feel very elated at having got a message home. They will wonder what I am doing 2,300 miles from Cape Town, but at least they will know I'm still a going concern and can work out their own E.T.A.

Topaz disappears into the mist, though shortly after, it blew away and I saw him again a long way off on the horizon, on his way to Taiwan. He has a long haul.

The day improves further, the Noon position puts us at 29 - 24'S., 22 - 45'W., a 100 mile run, and they are always nice. The wind hauls to the N.E. Force 5 - 6 and we speed along at 5 knots. It's a glorious day, and I wash some socks, a very special occasion, and do some odd jobs.

2030. Ship's Log; "Absolutely stunning night sky, millions of stars Low down on the horizon. Stellar clouds cast a positive glow on the sea to the West. Wind is down to F. 4, sea is very moderate and we glide along quietly under this awe-inspiring canopy. Where else but alone at sea can be better for considering the enormity of the Universe, and for feeling tiny and humble, (and vulnerable) under it."

Wednesday, 16th Oct. Another beautiful day. A run of 108 miles takes us to 30 - 13'S., 21 - 05'W. The ship's clocks are advanced to G.M.T. which makes sun-set at more reasonable time of 1930. It sets, like a great golden egg, straight into the sea, leaving behind a stunning orange and green sky, and the thinnest of one-day-old crescent moons.

Having crossed Latitude 30 South, I mark the occasion by transferring to the chart, "South Atlantic Ocean – Eastern Part". And can now see my destination. It doesn't look far until I measure across that Ocean and see that Cape Town is still 2,000 "distant".

The weather is fine but I am still distrustful of it. At nightfall I close and clip both deck hatches and put the lower washboard in the hatchway entrance. I'm well aware of where I am. I have a strange feeing of menace around me.

Thursday, 17th Oct. Plugging on toward Tristan, though the wind is pushing me off more to the East then I like. Am making preparation for Tristan. I have a chart of the Island, one of the lovely old-type "Soundings in Fathoms; black-and-white versions, which seems to have so much more feeling than the modern Metric charts, full of information though those are. The chart tells me that there is 16 fathoms of water at the Anchorage, which is a little way off the shore to clear the kelp beds. As I only have 80 metres of anchor chain, which is not enough for that depth of water, I shall have to use my 14mm nylon anchor ropes, so I splice a thimble eye in one of them, serve it, seize the eye in tight and prepare joining shackles etc.

After supper I am standing in the cockpit, gazing aft, leaning on my "Southern Ocean Brake", when a small bird I call Petrel, lands on the coil of rope not two feet from my nose. He's a pretty little thing, white, with grey wings and a powerful black beak a good inch long. We gaze at each other and I talk quietly to him. Perhaps he's never seen a human before and doesn't know that some of them would kill him for no reason at all. "You're quite safe with me old chap." I tell him. He rests there for some time but flies off during the night in a rising wind.

Sunday, 20th Oct. Busy days for long sailors. Southern Ocean weather has claimed me with a vengeance. Since I last wrote, the wind, after dithering across the stem from N.E. to N.W. a few times, settled in the N.W. and blew a full gale and more for a day. Then it backed to the West and increased to a Force 9 and is blowing that now. I have one panel and the top triangle of each sail up which is quite enough. We are making about 4 knots, (it's hard to tell), on course of 165 for Tristan which by 1300 should only be 200 miles away.

Having got the sails snugged down, I do most of my observing from the relative comfort of the viewdome from where I can see that the masts and sails are O.K., the Levanter and the L.V.M. (which is shut down), I can of course also observe the wind and sea state, and see the Setrel-Moore compass and listen to nice music while I'm doing it.

The seas are not mountainous, but are certainly hilly, and it's interesting to look "uphill" to the oncoming wave, especially if it has a breaking crest thundering down towards us. My bonny babe rises to it though. Sometimes the breaker hits us with a loud bang, spray and sometimes green water surge over the foredeck and the dome. I can't help ducking and blinking as they hit.

What a boon that dome is for safety and for keeping me warm and healthy, few things are so dispiriting as long hours in a cold, wet, and windy cockpit. It is cold now, and the movement is violent, so – the order of the day is, "Hold Tight".

Monday, 21st Oct. "Trafalgar Day." After a squally night in wild seas, the sky clears enough for the sun to tell me I am at 34 - 46'S., 14 - 40'W., a poor run of 70 miles. I'm not doing too well in making for Tristan and am tempted to run off towards Cape Town which is only 1600 miles to the East. Tristan is still 180 miles away.

Journal, later; "Today is Trafalgar Day and I am holding a small party, to celebrate Lord Nelson's Victory over the thrice-accursed French and Spanish, frogs and onions incorporated, in 1805. I have broached Jack and Betty's bottle of "British Navy Pusser's Rum" which I had said wouldn't be opened till Cape Horn. However, I'm sure J & B won't object, as we have shared many a tot of "wood's" on past Oct. 21st's. So – I have a glass of Pusser's, a bottle of same, a bottle of lime, can of Foster's, and a bag of peanuts stowed all round me, the bottles very carefully wedged in amongst my pillows, it's still rough outside.

A Toast! "Cheers to Jack and Betty, all my friends at the Roundhill Tavern, and the late Ron Presland of the Park Crescent Inn, and, of course, to Admiral Lord Nelson."

Quite apart from the rum, I am extra warm tonight. In honour of it being the beginning of the second month of Spring, I have donned my Damart Thermal underwear, vest and long-johns, extra shirt and socks, and my favourite roll-neck, oiled-wool fisherman's jersey. I need it all, it's cold and windy out there. Out there maybe, but here in the cabin it's real cosy, paraffin lamp warmly glowing, nice music, rum, beer, nuts, who could ask for more ? It's cold and dark down here in the Southern Ocean."

Tuesday, 22nd Oct. Journal 2000 "After last night's party, "It's all gone wrong". I had a busy night looking after my babe as at 0330 the end dropped right off and she rolled about madly in the swell. This calm lasted until 0800, then a light wind came in from the Nor'east, by 0900 it was a F. 7 from the East and by 1200 I was double-reefed down. At 1400, triple-reefed, I grabbed a quick nap and was just up in time at 1530 to reef her right down to the top triangles as the wind backed to N.N.E. and blew like a fury, a full Force 10. During the evening the seas built up enormously, but we were well snugged down, sails reefed and tightly lashed down, Levanter shut down and the wind-vans stowed below, L.V.M. lashed down, all deck gear secured. The split washboards are in and bolted, and the sliding hatch shut and securely wedged with a strong teak batten, so let her blow. We are still on course for Tristan, and I'm glad the island isn't closer, as visibility is only half a mile."

During the night though, things didn't go too well. While I slept in the rough and tumble madhouse which is a Force Ten down here, the wind backed right round to the S.W., and morning finds us plodding N.W. (!) in truly impressive seas. A full Force Ten blows from the S.W. in the greatest ocean of them all, great smoking greybeards, up the leading face of which we climb, teeter on the crest, and slide down their long straight backs. It is fascinating to me and I spend some time in the viewdome gauging the situation. I dress fully in all my rough-weather gear and clamber out into the wild and windy cockpit. Choosing my moment, I gybe her round in what I think is a relatively smooth patch in the hills and valleys which pass as seas down here.

The course is determined by wind and sea now, I have little say in the matter, and, having gybed her, can only head E.S.E., and admit to myself that I won't be visiting Tristan after all. All day Wednesday she blew strong from the S.W., but eased during the night. The barometer rose from the 984 mb it had descended to, and the storm was over.

By 1000 on Thursday the 24th I am becalmed! Rolling wildly in the heave of the after-gale swell, a horrible situation to be in, hating to have the sails up, slatting and banging themselves about, yet not daring to lower them, or the boat will roll itself gunnels under. I have to suffer this all day, a bitter fill to join the equally bitter one of having been thwarted in my hopes of visiting Tristen. I am not a happy man. Then the pain of the knife in me of these painful times is given a sharp twist when a ship passes just a few miles to the North of me, but I can't raise him on the radio. I even let off a white flare to attract his attention, but he just drives off to the East. He'll be at the Cape in a few days and could have given them a message for me.

I try to cheer myself by having a hot-water wash-down, shave my itchy, hairy neck, and powder myself with nice-smelling foo-foo (talcum powder to you), and this does make me feel better. Progress is what counts though, and we are barely moving in a light Southerly breeze, the glass is up to 1022 mb and doesn't look good for more wind.

Friday, 25th Oct. Journal; 0800 "still pretty much becalmed and have been all night. At present have both ghosters up, (after a half-hour struggle with the fore Port halyard wrapped around the lazy jack's shackle), and am headed North! The breeze, what little of it there is, has obligingly gone to the East! I am in a sad state of depression, slumped in the cabin surrounded by enemies I had always thought of at least neutral if not actually friends. The wind and the sea have turned from me and I don't know why. Everything is about as bad as it can be. Just over the horizon to the S.W. lies Tristan, only 100 miles or so, still in my mind. I see the anchorage, and Roamer lying at anchor, off the village of Edinburgh, grassy slopes in front of it, rocky heights behind, and I am very bitter. I swear if this wind hardens from the East I'll run back to the island and to hell with everything. Any other breeze or wind and I'd better make my way to the East. I plan to shake myself out of this slump and see if I can repair the foresail while it's stowed."

This job I do, in very trying conditions, not much wind, ship rolling, sails slatting, etc., but I manage to improve the batten pocket and put some extra stitching in damaged places. Later in the evening we get a S.E. breeze on which I can only make 050 (M), 025 on the chart – hopeless!! I treat myself to a couple of beers and brandies, for no particular reason, and read Bruce Chatwin's "In Patagonia".

Staurday, 26th Oct. 0745. Journal; "Well, I said I would, 'if the wind blows strong from the East I'll run back to Tristan!', the wind is, and I am. 'Twas the last straw of the last straws to get a wind blowing exactly from 120 (M), exactly from Cape Town. So – I am now headed for Tristan Da Cunha, sailing at 5 knots, on a sunny day, and my spirits high. I had to justify this action to myself but it didn't take a lot of doing.

"Look", I said, "You went to do it – then do it, the barometer is at 1028 mb, this wind could blow for days, look at the state of you, all bitter and twisted, there's more to life than days and miles – so go."

All day we bound Southwest, enjoying the best sailing I've had for ages. Worrying like mad lest the wind should drop, but it doesn't, I try to stop myself worrying by "Positive Thinking", thinking of all the good things I will get by going to Tristan. Radio message to Cape Town and maybe the U.K., a walk ashore, photographs for magazine articles? All these against the miserable on-the-wind slog I would be having if I hadn't turned back. "As it is," I say, "You'll be straining your eyes on the horizon this time tomorrow looking for a 6,700 ft volcano!!"

Sunday, 27th. 0730. having breakfasted on a big bowl of porridge, with coffee and biscuits, I take a walk to the bows, "Just for a token look", I tell myself. We're still 55 miles away.

But – what's that there? On the Port Bow, can it be?

Yes it can, a great big beautiful snow-capped mountain looming above the clouds, its peak glistening in the morning sunlight, what a moving and wonderful sight, right out here in the middle of the ocean. It is my first sight of land since Ilha Da Palma, in the Canary Islands, 76 days and 6,100 miles ago, and what a sight!

Luckily I am able to see the island, take a bearing and alter course towards it, for the peak disappears into cloud and haze soon after and I only get the odd tantalising glimpse as we approach.

The wind increases as we closer, so I steer to stay upwind. There won't be time to get near Edinburgh settlement before dark so my plan is to stand off upwind, hold my position overnight and run down in the morning.

At 2100 I am in position. I can see only the dark bulk of the island, its East and West extremities as they drop into the sea from the cloud base, and a huddle of orange lights at Edinburgh. They are a delight to my eyes, the first lights I've seen since Penzance, 92 days back!.

After that, it all goes wrong – again. The wind rises more during the night, rain comes in, visibility falls and I have a cold wet busy night reefing down, gibing on and off the dark bulk of the land, trying to hold my position. At first light, at 0530, I run towards the island, the wind now gale force, visibility down to one mile or less. I see the gloom of high land, then a black vertical cliff rising out of the sea into the cloud base. A swirl of wind parts the mist, giving me a tantalising glimpse of green slopes above low cliffs These must be the "Potato Patches" just to the West of Edinburgh. Damn, I've been blown downwind of the settlement. Nothing I can do about that, and no chance of working back up this wind, it is fierce. All I can do is try to hold my position and hope conditions improve. All day I do this, in terrible weather, ferocious wind, teeming rain, steep breaking seas. I stand on and off having to run in close to the land, where the wind is at its fiercest, to identify my position. I daren't get lost, Inaccessible and Nightingale Islands lie to the Southwest, now down-wind as it has backed to the Northeast. At 1730 I have my last peep of a murky cliff which I reckon to be Cave Point on the S.W. of the island, and set off on a 6 hour leg to the N.W., to what I think is a safe area. At 2300, after a short snooze, I look out of the viewdome, can see nothing, and check the course with the flashlight.

At midnight I am due to gybe and start the run back, to find Tristan at daybreak. The night is dark and foul, even though there is a full moon above the clouds.

AT 2345 I EMERGE THROUGH THE HATCH FULLY DRESSED FOR THE STORMY NIGHT AND — OH NO!! RIGHT IN FRONT OF ME IS A BLACK CLIFF, NOT 100 YARDS AWAY, CRASHING SURF AT ITS BASE, ITS TOP DISAPPEARING INTO THE CLOUDS!! MY HEART THUNDERS, MY MOUTH AND THROAT GO DRY. BLOODY HELL!! FOR HALF A MINUTE I CAN ONLY STARE – STUNNED!!

Then – Action – Gybe her, quick, unlash the helm, hard a-port, the foresail gybes O.K., the main doesn't want to go, the boat is rolling madly, we are so close to the cliffs there is hardly any wind here! I manage to push the main over and we now lie parallel to the cliffs, not much wind, but the heave of the waves pushes us closer – we are in mortal danger. I am very frightened.

I talk to myself loudly and firmly, "Keep calm Robbie-boy, Think, Engine, Pronto". Luckily the engine throttle control lever is rigged for Tristan. Into neutral, three-quarter revs. Down below – Fast. I order myself; "KEEP CALM – Read the Engine Start Check List, Open Exhaust Seacock, O.K., Open Cooling Water Seacock, right, Check Oil and Water levels, no time, Is the fuel on?? – Yes." Right then, take it easy, Don't Panic. Turn the key, ten long seconds of heater, will she go?? Start – She Goes!!, I almost sob with relief; my Lovely Lovely Polly Perkins!, Up top quick, the cliffs look closer, waterfalls rain down out of the cloud, I am looking UP at them!!

Into Forward Gear, easy now, "AAGH! Is the log line clear?" Yes it's O.K., some forward revs, not too many now, stall her and you're doomed. We move ahead, turn to Port away from those dreadful cliffs, looking for rocks ahead in the black heaving water – WE CREEP AWAY FROM DEATH.

Death it would have been to have hit those cliffs, the black vertical cliffs of Inaccessible Island, which is where I must be, must have been set down to the S.W. from my N.W. course. I can hardly believe it, but we move away and are out of immediate danger. As we move away, the wind returns, in force. I realise that it was those awful cliffs which actually saved me. So high and vertical are they that the wind swept over them, leaving a windless zone close in which prevented my being blown on. Shutting the engine down, I creep away from the island under the storm triangles. The gale blows hard from the N.E., Inaccessible is now to my N.W., a dark mass in the mist with an eerie glow atop, cast by the full moon.

I am still in some peril, amidst the unlit islands in the storm. Inaccessible's neighbour, Nightingale Island, lies only ten miles to the S.E. It has offlying rocks and islets, I won't be as lucky again. The wind has reached its previous ferocity, the seas are large and steep, with roaring breaking crests, I reef down and stow the mainsail. Leaving her settled on S.E., I go below to scan the chart.

"Get this right boy, or you won't see this night out", I tell myself. Nightingale is indeed ten miles to the S.E., O.K., the plan, run towards it for 5 miles, to get me midway between the two islands, then a 90 degree turn to Starboard, and head S.W. till dawn, which will give us about 6 miles in that direction, clearing Nightingale, then off to safety in the S.E. again in daylight. Never has the old adage been so true, "A sailor is safe at sea, only near land is he in danger".

All through that terrible night I run before the storm, first S.E., then a dangerous gybe in those great waves, unable to look for a relatively calm patch, I just have to helm over and hope nothing big hits us as we go round. The fore lashes across to Port and we are round, running clear to the S.W., waves sweeping the deck, the unceasing torrent of rain making it difficult to think, let alone see!

Through the cold and cruel early hours I steer her through the storm, dawn doesn't break, the sky gradually becomes grey instead of black, the seas look more monstrous, visibility is no better. I check the log reading, have another quick look at the chart, (how different it is below, warm, dry, quiet), and decide it is safe to gybe again to the S.E.

We run on till 0900 the wind eases, and stops, in ten minutes – from storm to not a breath! No wind maybe, but the sea, released from the pressure of the wind, becomes chaotic, waves pile up pyramidically, fall off and over each other, breakers cascade in all directions. I can only lash the helm of the sail bundles, wedge myself in a corner of the cockpit, and bear out this further agony. The rain pours down in increased torrents, which turns out to be an advantage. So heavy is this downpour, that it actually beats the worst of the sea flat, leaving only the large swells to throw us about. I judge I can go below, put the stove on and pour cup after cup of coffee down me, the first with a large slug of Brandy in it. I make a pot of thick porridge and eat every last drop, running with honey, biscuits follow. I feel weak with cold and hunger, and from the reaction of last night's escape.

At 1200 the wind returns, calm to gale in ten minutes again, still from the N.E., and I make off to the S.E. with a little more sail up now. I am very keen to make as many miles from this turbulent area downwind of Tristan as I can before dark. I have been straining my eyes into the rain and mist, fearing to see Nightingale appear ahead of me, but as the miles slowly add up on the log, it becomes more and more likely that I have passed to the South of the island, until at 1800, I have 20 miles logged since I turned S.W., and must be past it – inexpressible relief. The wind has eased, the seas are not so bad, even the rain is letting up. I leave my bonny stalwart ship to herself and lie down fully-dressed on the bunk for a few much needed hours sleep. Up for a look at midnight, she is going along O.K., and I go back to bed and sleep till dawn.

Wednesday, 30th Oct. Dawn actually does break today, bright and clear, the sun rises early. The Sun!! The sea is still a confused one, with a big swell from the N.E., a lesser one from the N.W., and a Force 6 Northerly tumbling smaller waves over them both. I eat a large breakfast, dress up warmly and get on deck to hoist more sail. By 0900 I have 3 panels up on each mast and am making nearly 4 knots to the East.

I "mop up" after the storm, festooning the guardrails with floor cloths and rags, gloves and towels etc., which flap in the fresh breeze. I even open the hatches, risking a splash to get some air into her. Levanter is in charge of steering again, the L.V.M. is unlashed and charging, and we're back in business.

To the North, Tristan's peak rears into the sky, still looking beautiful, but not quite so attractive! She is 30 miles away I estimate, 30 miles, half hour by car, but to me, absolutely unattainable. "I'll save you for another day", I tell her. I am cured of "Tristanitis" for the time being, it is now 100% effort for Cape Town, I'm very late.

1600: On Reflection: I sit in my cosy cabin with a cup of tea, Beethoven's 3rd Piano Concerto on the stereo. A world so different from the past few days that it seems scarcely possible. The seas have settled down now, the sun has shone all day. I have my position on chart, we make 4 knots to the East.

I review the events of the past few days – how now my decision to visit Tristan?

I regret nothing, (Edith Piaf's "je ne regrette rien"), it was a good idea, since I was baulked by Easterlies, which, had it come off, with a visit to Edinburgh Settlement, would have been wonderful. As it turned out, I didn't manage such a visit, or even make radio contact, due to atrocious weather not allowing me to present myself to be seen from shore. I wouldn't expect that Tristan keeps any sort of listening watch.

In the foul weather, which I now believe was caused by the mountain itself, I had to try to keep close contact or have no idea of my position. The storm was ferocious. I have never known one for the literal ferocity of the wind or the incessant heaviness of the rain. As to very nearly coming to grief at Inaccessible, I can only assume that (a) my position at 1730 was further to the S.W. than I imagined, and (b) the storm just swept me sideways. (Mind you, at the time of writing this, 3 days after the event, I am becoming suspicious of the veracity of my compasses).

I was exceedingly lucky to survive that close call. Had the shore been low-lying or had off-shore rocks I would have been wrecked, only the fact that the cliff was so high that it actually caused a lee close in saved me. Had I slept for another half hour, or been ten minutes later on deck, had the engine not started… There is a saying in the Oil business, "Only people who do things make mistakes, those that don't try, don't get into trouble, BUT – to get on, you must survive your mistakes". I survived mine, just.

So – we head – East – I have 1,450 miles to go to Cape Town, and am hopeful of being there in around 14 days. There are alarming reports on the radio of civil unrest in the Port – it would be just my luck for the place to be burnt down by the time I arrive!!

Thursday, 31st Oct. Journal 0800. "My bonny ship headed East all Wednesday and through the night, while I caught up on sleep, and though I was up at 0400, when the wind fell light, I didn't mind. I'd slept, with one break for a look-see, from 2130. whilst watching her through a tricky period of fluky winds, by 0800 I have greased, oiled, and re-wrapped the anchor winch, greased the steering wires and their sheaves, checked and tapped down the mast wedges at deck and keel positions, and tightened L.V.M.'s grub screws."

The noon position is 36 - 59'S., 9 - 50'W., a pleasing run on the chart of 95 miles, course was too much to the North, but I wouldn't mind going back up to 35 so am not too much worried about that. Cape Town is 1,355 miles, 14 days or so, I hope.

In the afternoon the wind backs to the West and falls light, so I have to gybe to the Starboard tack and tack downwind. Can only make 150 (M), 124 on the chart, not so good. After a nap, I attack some loathsome-looking fat goose barnacles on the Starboard side, they come off fairly easily. I think the cold is killing them, I hope so.

Using the wood edge of my long-handled scrubber, I scrape as far under the bilge as I could reach, bring off lots of barnacles, which looked like large cockles. I fear the underwater hull is very foul after all this time, 96 days at sea today.

My food rations for this leg are consumed and though I have plenty of "Goodies" stowed in the after lockers, they are for the next stages. I am planning to live on rice and canned vegetables till Cape Town. There is plenty of brown rice, veg, porridge and biscuits, so I won't starve. I am fortunate in that I can eat almost anything at any time of the day. Water stocks are still good too, I have hardly touched the 65 gallon Starboard tank, and am still getting water from the Port tank which has been supplying all needs to the galley pump.

Thursday, 30, Journal 2100. "Damn! It's all gone wrong – again. A black bank of cloud came in from the West, looking evil and ominous. I dressed up in full oilies and harness ready to reef down and – nothing. It didn't bring wind. It stole it! We are now becalmed – what's to become of us??"

Friday, 1st November. A new month brings no wind and flat seas. But – "It's an ill calm that brings nobody any good!" I used the calm forenoon to make urgently needed repairs to the sails. Their luffs, above each batten, which ought to have localised strengthening, have none, and the cloth is tearing!! I stitch on emergency strapping, out of spare car seat belt material I have. Four hours is spent on this during a complete calm, and finished just as a breeze comes in, from the Southeast, of course!!

Journal; "Noon position was the expected disaster:- A run (?) of 20 miles to 37 02'S., 9 - 28'W. Absolute disaster! Surely things must, can only, get better?"

Monday 4th Nov. Day 100. One Hundred days at sea!!

It's getting a little ridiculous, I've been suspicious of the compasses lately, there being 20 degrees difference between them. I'd assumed that the Concept had suffered from its rough treatment when it was pulled from its bracket some time ago. This evening however, I check the bearing of the sun with both compasses at sunset, then extract the true bearing from the sight reduction tables. Surprise, Surprise, it's the Sestrel which is incorrect. Revelation! This could have, nay, must have been, a factor in the near-disaster at Inaccessible. I was using the Sestrel at that time. Having a compass 20 degrees out is bad news, knowing about it makes it less bad – but only just.

At noon on this 100th day we are at 36 - 25'S., 5 - 30'W. Almost due South of Falmouth, by 5,200 miles! We have run 7,900 to get here. The 24 hour run was 82 miles, but there was so much Northing in the track that only 40 of those miles counted towards Cape Town, which remains 1,130 miles away.

One hundred days! I can't get over it. I would never have believed it possible before departure that I could be so long at sea and still have 1,100 miles to go – but I am and have.

Here's a "100 day review".

Personal: Healthwise no problems. Morale is generally O.K. but obviously getting stale, mainly due to the progress problem. We only have to head East at a decent rate and I'm as happy as a pig in clover!

Food: Plenty aboard but stocks for this leg used up and am unwilling to break into reserves aft. So plan to live very basically on rice/canned veg/ Pot Noodles and rice. Food doesn't worry me a lot as to its variety, so long as I have something to eat. I eat 2 Vitamin C, 4 Calcium, 4 Brewer's Yeast, and one Halibut Oil pills per day.

Water: Plenty. Still some in Port tank, Starboard must be almost full, plus I have 20 gallons in containers around the ship.

Equipment: No problems except sails. These are showing signs of wear, particularly at their luffs above each batten.

I did valuable repairs in the recent calm but will be glad to get to Cape Town and get to work on them.

Progress: Absolutely terrible. Having had plenty of time to study and think about this one, I can see that my troubles began just over the Equator when we made slow progress against the Southerlies. Many days were spent in the warm waters of that area and allowed the goose barnacles to proliferate. I did scrape some off at that time but they obviously got a foothold then. Progress continued slow right down through the tropics allowing further growth and now the water is too cold for me to get into the water and attack them. The winds I've had since the Equator have hardly been favourable. Added to which the Junk Rig is hopeless "on the wind", where we have spent an amazing and completely unexpected amount of time. So I don't see much chance of improvement until I get to Cape Town and rid the bottom of the "Undergrowth".

Prospects: Not so good. E.T.A. Cape Town now after Mid-November. If I get away by 1st December, 2 months to get to Hobart, (rather than Sydney), makes it 1st February. After a short stop and to Cape Horn equals early April at the very earliest which is already rather late. Later than I'd like.

Weather: Very trying. So irregular, never blows from the same direction for more than 12 hours and not often for that long which makes for a confused sea through which we have great difficulty in making any useful speed with the foul bottom, so it's a bit of a vicious circle.

Plan: To make North while East winds blow. Try for contact with a ship or Whitbread yacht for a message to Cape Town.

Thoughts in general on this 100th evening none too happy due to being practically becalmed, with sails and battens banging on the mast, sheet blocks rattling, and rain beating on the hatch and viewdome. It's none too warm down here, I don't try to heat the boat, preferring to heat myself with Damart thermal underwear and plenty of clothes, and no silly ideas of taking too many of them off, for going to bed, for instance. It's my belief that "shore people" are so unhealthy because they shut themselves up in hot house/offices/shops etc., instead of turning the heat down and wearing more clothes. The same with this washing business, much overdone I believe, washing and showering away natural bodily oils and letting in the cold!!

Also thinking on my way of life at sea. It's very basic, being based on basic needs, food and sleep. Life revolves round the weather and looking after the ship. If wind or storm come along in the middle of the night then I'm up to attend to it, conversely, if all is quiet during the day, I have a sleep at any time. Life can be very uncomfortable and wearying in rough weather, having to plan every move, holding tight every step of the way, crawling around the deck like a monkey, every minute, with a sharp pain the penalty for inattention.

I think it's that I could most do with a break from – I look forward, in Cape Town, not so much a cold beer, or fish and chips, though those are high on my priority list, but mostly to being able to stand up without holding on, wedging myself in a corner to dress in waterproofs, to work at the gallery, or use the toilet. To be able to stand up straight, walk along the jetty, stretch my legs. Ah, it won't be long. Or will it?

Am getting precisely nowhere at the moment. Still, there's nowt to do but to press on, no one can help me, wind and sea rule, I shall persevere.

Thursday 7th Nov. Journal: "Good news and bad news time. Bad is that we have made next to no progress overnight. Wind blows exactly from 120, just where I want to go – it's uncanny. Good news is that I saw a light at 2100 last night, to the North. After expending two white flares to attract his attention plus a lot of Morse flashing of VHF on the masthead light, I made contact with the Russian Tanker, "General Grevas". Had quite a language problem with him although he was very helpful. I hope I got my message across for him to give my position and name to Cape Town Radio asking them to pass it on to the Royal Cape Yacht Club with an E.T.A. of the 20th. If that wasn't hard enough to get over I also tacked on a request for the R.C.Y.C. to phone brother Terry in Brighton. Quite wearing that conversation. The Russians were very friendly though, considering their reputation, they even offered to "Come to your ship", which I talked them out of. The last thing I want is a big ship close to me, especially at night. Anyway, Thanks, to my Russian friends. Ah, if only the world were run by Sailors?? What a thought!!"

Friday the 8th Nov. 1300. "We had a quicky of a Force Ten Storm last night. The wind was built up on Thursday afternoon and by Midnight I was reefed down to top triangles in very hairy weather just holding on tight. The wind eased by morning and then did a quick tour of the compass, causing terrifically confused seas. By the time the wind had blown furiously from the Northeast for 12 hours and then backed in 2 hours to the Southwest, I had waves coming from the Southwest climbing over an enormous swell from the Northeast which had its crest blown off by the Southwest wind! Not a nice piece of ocean at all down here. But at least the blow gave me some miles. 92 in the 24 hours to noon, bringing Cape Town to below 1,000 only 990!

I have plenty of company in the way of seabirds, from the age-old grave albatross, to the little white fluttering terns. They show off their impressive flying skills, but surprise me by appearing only to do that, fly around. They never seem to be trying to catch any fish, not like the birds up in the tropics.

Saturday the 9th Nov. I calculate that we shall cross the Greenwich Meridian this evening, so must be due South of Brighton, 5,200 miles due South. Ship's clocks are advanced one hour, the sun rose at 0450 today, a little too early, even for me.

Monday the 11th. Oh Dear. It's a pretty depressing scene, here I am stuck on this persistent East wind, making only a little East of South. Am feeling very badly treated by the elements.

Contacted another ship last night. My 6th sense, E.S.P., works well. I was reading below, but felt this urge to take a peep out of the dome, an urge I never ignore. Up I pop and there is a ship, to the South, which is

Relief as lone sailor radios

A BRIGHTON family today breathed a huge sigh of relief after receiving news that lone sailor Bob Burns is safe and well.

Brother Terry admitted he was beginning to fear the worse after a 14-week silence and reports of severe conditions in the South Atlantic.

But today Terry received a message via the Cape Town base of the Whitbread Round the World Race that bachelor Bob, 45, had radioed in.

Worried

"I must admit we were getting rather worried for his safety but it is a tremendous relief to know that he is still afloat," said Terry, of Uplands Road, Hollingdean.

Bob, who left Brighton Marina at the beginning of July on his round-the-world voyage, should have reached Cape Town during the first two weeks of October.

But his latest message to South Africa puts him off course heading towards the Tristan Du Cunha Islands. "Obviously there have been some problems," added Terry.

Evening Argus
12th November 1985

unusual. Made contact with a friendly South African voice who turns out to be aboard the "Causeway Salvo", a converted tug taking supplies to Tristan! Had a good chat and he promised to pass another message on to Cape Town for me.

Tuesday the 12th. Still trying to get East against light and contrary winds. Today's position:- 36 - 40'S., 1 - 35'E. 840 miles to Cape Town. We have made 105 miles in the right direction in 4 days!! Heart-breaking.

I make up a barnacle scraper, attack the beasts along the waterline, and get quite a few off, great fat things about 3 inches long. During the operation, I get my best view of the bottom, and am horrified by the state of it. In places, it looks like a half-tide rock, absolutely covered with growth, and the horrible things festooned all along the bottom of the keel, no wonder I'm going so slowly. The water is very cold and no way am I going into it. I don't like going into, let alone under, the sea at the best of times, and a cold sea, definitely not.

Going slowly East in the sun this afternoon it was so warm in the cockpit that I strip off and give the body an airing. My hard-earned tropical sun tan is wearing off (and no doubt will disappear when I take to the shower!), and the body feels thin. Changed my undies and socks, and washed them later.

Wednesday the 13th. "Did some good work on my "writing". Edited the article I've written about the Tristan events, and retyped some of it. I've done quite a lot of this writing, and hope to raise some much-needed cash in Cape Town."

Friday the 15th Nov. After a lovely run of 98 miles yesterday in a brisk Northerly, it's back to light airs and calms today, damned frustrating. A big swell rolls in from the West, long and low. It throws out what little wind is in the sails. The sound of the sails and battens banging on the mast is the most horrible one. It's painful to listen to, means I am not making any progress, and wears and strains the sails.

Several schools of porpoise, or dolphin, are playing round the bows, the first I've seen the Southern Hemisphere.

Life is becoming a bit of a drag. Latest pain is that my "Freshness" water filter has become clogged, and I've had to throw it out. I don't have a spare. I thought they were supposed to be good for 1,000 gallons or so. The water now tastes horrible.

Tea and Coffee taste awful unless very strong and dosed with lots of honey, and I'm short of that. Am reduced to drinking hot lemon squash,

Lone sailor is safe

FEARS for the safety of yachtsman Bob Burns, sailing alone around the world, ended this week when he made radio contact for the first time in more than three months.

But relatives in Brighton believe his yacht could have been severely damaged in Atlantic storms that have hampered the progress of much larger yachts in the Whitbread Round the World race.

"We were worried sick," said his brother Terry. "We could not help thinking that something dreadful had happened to him, but all we could do was sit and wait in hope."

Bob, 45, failed to arrive in Cape Town in early October as planned. And yachtsmen in the Whitbread race — who followed a similar route — reported that they had not seen or heard from him.

But this week Bob contacted Cape Town. According to a message, relayed to Terry by Whitbread, he is some 1,200 miles west of Cape Town, heading for the island of Tristan da Cunha, which is in the opposite direction.

A puzzled Terry said: "We can only guess that Bob's yacht is damaged or he is running out of supplies.

Bob sold his flat in Ditchling Road, Brighton, to help pay for his adventure. He set out from Brighton Marina in July, stopping in Falmouth to collect equipment and provisions before attempting to cross the Atlantic.

Bob planned to call at the Falkland Islands for a pint of beer at the Upland Goose pub in Port Stanley.

Brighton & Hove Leader 16th November 1985

which is not quite the same. The beer is almost gone, all Syd's Brandy has gone, Port went long ago, Mars Bars and Planter's peanuts looking thin, Oooh Deear, things not so good.

I had my first headache of the voyage today. It went on till midnight when I drove it away with a couple of Phensics, but I don't like taking pills, except my vitamins. The headache could have been caused by an unused-to dose of the sun, my nose got quite painfully sunburnt, it never gets used to the sun.

Saturday the 16th We get our bonny Northerly breeze back and make 90 miles on track to 35 - 30'S., 7- 20'E. Only 555 miles to go. Thoughts leaping ahead to being in by next weekend, it hardly seems possible I shall be in a harbour soon after so long. This is day 112!

I have a bit of a Spring Clean this morning. Give myself a good hot wash and a neck shave, do all the washing up, then a good clean out in the heads, workshop, and the saloon. Makes me and my bonny babe look, feel and smell somewhat better!!

I'm doing a lot of reading and writing in these quiet times, and the eyes aren't too good. I'm sure my diet isn't helping me to be healthy. Pot Noodles and Beanfeasts are O.K. for the odd snack but not to live on! Too much Monosodium Glutamate!

I promise myself one can each of my goodies from aft, Corned Beef, Tuna, Pilchards, etc., to improve my menu and morale.

Log 1800. "We toddle on – this lovely little Northerly breeze keeps me going at 3 knots and is the difference between joy and despair. Sky is blue, sea is calm, a sharp horizon, high white cirrus. Quietness."

"This evening is the most beautifully starry one I've had since the tropics. Millions of stars right down to the horizon, a quarter moon to the West, the Southern Cross pointing to the South Pole, Orion the Hunter hauling himself out of the Eastern Sea."

2400. The Witching hour, the graveyard watch. Wind is very light, it's so quiet. We head slowly Northeast between the Pleiades to Port and Orion to Starboard. Mr. Moon has just set in the West, and Jupiter hangs brightly on the Port Quarter. Four sparkling torpedoes streak beneath us as the porpoise swim around in the fantastic phosphorescence. Isn't it marvellous?

Sunday the 17th Not much sleep for me but on such a night of wonders I don't mind. Abed at 0100, up at 0330. A new breeze comes in from the West and I gybe here at 0415 into the pink and green pre-dawn glow. The sun shows himself at 0511, and has hauled himself out of the sea two minutes later. I watch all this spell-bound, from the pulpit, I'm so glad to be out here to see such sights in such peace, even on Day 113!

Over a porridge breakfast at 0530, I tune through the radio waves. I decline the B.B.C.'s financial report, then manage five minutes of Saint Mary's Oyster Festival from Maryland, U.S.A., before the twangy American accents drive me away to some quiet Arab music. This lasts until I am surprised to hear "The Chimes of Big Ben for 0600". I have stumbled on another of Auntie's outlets, her Arab service. I switch off and sit in the peace of the cockpit with a coffee and a marmaladey biscuit.

Thoughts are now 500 miles ahead to shoreside in Cape Town. Nearly four months now I've been out here, although it doesn't seem like that – it feels as though I've <u>always</u> been out here! Looking forward to mail, fresh food, long walks, socializing in the Yacht Club. Will I know any of the Whitbread Racers? I've been talking to myself a lot lately to keep the voice in practice. I don't feel too strange but who am I to judge? It will be interesting to see how I behave in company, I will probably prattle on endlessly, especially after a few pints!!

Sunday the 17th Nov. Log 1730: "I need to be careful now that we're getting close that I don't get pushed North of Cape Town by the prevailing winds and by the Benguela Current. Wind S. - S.S.E. Force 5. Cape Town's weather forecast speak of strong S.E. winds! I am 101 miles South of Cape Town's latitude at Noon".

Monday the 18th. Log 1215: "Trouble with a capital T. We have been pushed North. An incredible 71 miles in 24 hours!" Trouble indeed but there is nothing I can do about it. Wind is S. to S.E. and the current is pushing me North. I have a problem.

Wed. the 20th. Having a bad time with calms and headwinds. Making no progress to the East. It's so calm I rig and launch the folding dinghy and row around the ship taking photographs.

Thursday the 21st. I contact my South African friend on "Causeway Salvo" and tell him of my poor progress. He is returning from Tristan Da Cunha and will tell Cape Town Radio and the Royal Cape Yacht Club I'm O.K. but going slow. Slow is the word –about 2 knots! 500 miles West of Cape Town, a long way at 2 knots.

By the 22nd of Nov. I am resigned to having to make for a port North of Cape Town, refresh myself and the ship, get the barnacles off the hull and then head South. But we are very late, and I think a lot about how late I am going to be at Horn.

This is a bad time for me – after 118 days at sea to be faced with a 500-mile struggle to the coast with no charts for the areas North of Cape Town is very depressing.

Sunday the 24th. Log 0600: "Clocks advanced one hour to G.M.T. plus 2 which is South African time. (In case I ever get there). Check out engine and top up lube oil, run engine for 2 hours. "Thar she blows", whales blowing on the starboard bow. Very little wind".

Thursday the 28th Nov. We have struggled and scraped to within 100 miles of the coast, about 50 miles North of Cape Columbine, 150 miles North of Cape Town!! There is a fly aboard, the first insect since England, checking on the R.D.F. Beacons, I have Cape Columbine clearly, and D.F. Malan, which is Cape Town airport, but no-one else. Hmmm, what next? Now, at 1900 I'm in thick fog, a real pea-souper, and I'm in the main shipping lane! I can hear several ships, hope they have their radar on, and are looking at it!! The ship is battened down, Xenon flasher on, lifejacket on – what a game!

The fog clears during the night, next day we plug on to the East a lively S.W. breeze until, at 1530, after a wee snooze, it's "LAND HO!!", on the Larboard bow. Africa – at last, high purple mountains to the N.E., I'm glad to see them!!

Doringbaai Light shows itself at 2030 so at least I know where I am. There are bright lights ahead where I believe a port called Lambert's Bay should be. (I get this information from the "Lights List", which contains details of every light from Brest to Cape Agulhas, all for £3.50!).

Saturday, the 30th of November. After a difficult night in fickle winds, we are, after 125 days at sea, and 9552 miles, in harbour. In Lambert's Bay, a small fishing port. We were quite a sensation on arrival, I believe I may be the first yacht they ever saw! Certainly the first foreign one, people of all races swarmed over Roamer, beer flowed, music played. Wow! What a feeling to be in harbour again.

By 1700 though everyone has gone, leaving me, it being a Saturday and no banks open, with no money, no beer, and nothing on the menu except the same old diet of the past 4 months. Depressed, I wander the streets looking for a telephone box to ring home and let them know I have arrived. The streets are wide and empty, curtains rustle as I pass, rain falls lightly. Then a car draws up alongside me, it is Jan Hunter, the fishing jetty manager. "Like to come to a barbeque at the Golf Club, Bob?" "Jan you have saved my life!!" So the evening is transformed, the beer flows again, though I blame my unsteady legs on 125 days at sea. I cause much amusement by eating all the lettuce and tomato trimmings of the barbeque, being starved of fresh veg. A great evening.

I spend a few days in this friendly fishing harbour, and do ring home. They are amazed to hear from me. (I'm sure they had all given me up for lost). But there's no chance of me getting on the slip for a bottom scrub so, on the following Tuesday I leave and head South for Cape Town. But it's the same old story of head winds again trying to get Roamer to windward. A shipping forecast tells me of 45 knots S.E. winds expected at Cape Colombus!! Charming. On receipt of this good news I head for shelter in the wide St. Helena Bay. I'm navigating by my Reader's Digest World Atlas now, South Africa is 200 miles to the inch! Another difficult night

Sailor Bob in great shape

LONE sailor Bob Burns has spoken to his brother in Brighton for the first time since leaving on a round-the-world voyage five months ago.

Bob, 45, telephoned Terry at the weekend from Lambrets Bay, near Cape Town, with the message that he is tired, but safe and well.

"It was a crystal clear line," said Terry, of Uplands Road, Hollingdean. "He said he and the boat are in great shape but they have been making very slow progress and are way behind schedule."

Bob, who left Brighton Marina at the beginning of July, was hoping to sail around Cape Horn but will now have to re-think his plans.

"He's planning to get to Cape Town and then decide what to do," explained Terry. "He's too late now for the Horn so he's not quite sure what he'll do."

Bob, who sold his Brighton flat to fund the adventure, is due back in England in about April but a new schedule could mean he will not arrive until at least September.

Evening Argus
2nd December 1985

passes with very light or non-existent winds. Early on Wednesday the 4th of December I photograph a stunning sunrise over the Picquetberg Mountains, and at full light I can see land to the East, South, and Southwest. In light winds I motor South heading for the Great Berg River, which my "Lights List" tells me has a harbour.

At 1000 on a hot windless morning I enter Laaiplek harbour, after some nervous navigating in shallow water outside. A young man in a small yacht I meet tells me there is plenty of water in the harbour entrance. Gingerly motoring in between the sizeable breakwaters, eyes glued to the echo-sounder, I tie up to jetty in a gap between fishing trawlers. A broad Yorkshire accent greets me!

"I sailed under the Red Ensign many a year, Lad. Ee, why don't you get y'self oop to Port Owen while the tide is high?"

"Why don't I?" Port Owen, it seems, is a new yacht marina a mile up river. More nervous motoring up the buoyed channel, eyes on the echo-sounder again, at one time I have 0.2 of a metre under the keel. Then I see yacht masts over the flat marshlands, a little further and the entrance beacons appear. As I motor between them a voice greets me from a guy with a megaphone.

"Good Morning Roamer, Welcome to Port Owen. Turn to Port at the end of the channel and we'll meet you on a jetty". I do so and see a crowd of people at the end of "India" jetty. I bring her alongside, tie up, and am then welcomed by the Yacht Club Commodore, the Marina Manager, their wives, and half the population of Port Owen.

I have arrived – In Paradise!!

Chapter Ten

South African Interlude

He Found Port Owen A Paradise

Bob and Roamer, one Saturday,
Came out of the fog, at Lambert's Bay.
After 125 days at sea,
They were glad to find South Africkee.

They enjoyed a few days of food and rest,
Then on to Cape Town, Bob thought was best.
But ran out of wind, and couldn't get goin',
So heading South, he found, Port Owen.

Although he thought Lambert's Bay was nice,
He found Port Owen a paradise.
In the Sun, cold beer a-swiggin',
Under a palm tree, with standing riggin'.

Bob Burns
South Africa, December, 1985

A Paradise indeed. From the warm reception accorded me by the Staff and
Residents, to a delicious breakfast next day given by John Little, the Marina's
Landscaping Engineer, who used to be Marketing Manager for Brighton
Marina. I relax very easily into the comfortable embrace of Port Owen.

After the struggles of the previous years to get the boat built, fitted out, and ready for the sea, and then the long and frustrating voyage down the Atlantic, now at last I reap the benefits, get a taste of "The Good Life". Roamer is safe and secure at the end of a wooden jetty in a clean and calm Marina 1½ miles from the sea, the hot sun shines from a clear blue sky. It takes very little to persuade me to "Stay on for the Christmas Party, Bob, you'll love it".

The people here are some of the friendliest I've ever met in my life. Everybody, from "The Boss", millionaire financier Owen Wiggins and his wife Shelia, Managing Director Paul Stuyck and his son Frankie, the Marine Manager, their wives, the Residents, Boat Owners, and the Staff, all these lovely people draw me into their circle, give me their warm friendship, and I love it.

Although, I would claim to be a shy character, I can be extrovert too, especially with a few beers inside me, and I make them laugh, teach them songs, tell jokes and become part of Port Owen's social scene. Two days after my arrival, at the Friday evening "Sundowners", I exchange Burgees with the Port Owen Yacht Club, make a speech, and enjoy a very social evening in the cosy clubhouse, never suspecting that within a few months I would be running it!

The Port Owen Project is "Under Development", and there is a lot of work taking place, and much to be done, but "Stage One", the present marina, is virtually complete. A dredged waterway, about half a mile long, has 8 wooden jetties on one side, each with a neat 4-point mooring system for about twelve boats. The tide range is slight, 1 metre at Neaps, 1½ at Springs. Around the waterway are plots of land, mostly sold, and, at this time, only a few houses are built. Great efforts are being made on the landscaping and grass-growing. The Marina is very quiet, no traffic, surrounded by a bird sanctuary. I just love it!

At the end of the waterway is the Clubhouse, the "Galley" Restaurant, workshop, 10-ton crane and slipway. At the other, toilets, showers and the "Braai area", children's swings, and part of the sanctuary, with a large population of Flamingo's, Egrets, Pelicans etc., a Paradise!!

A week later, after I've settled in, a young sailing couple give me a lift to Cape Town, 80 miles to the South down the West Coast Highway. At one point, Mike and Jill say, "Close your eyes Bob". The car stops. "Look now", and a breath-taking vista is spread before me. 40 miles away, across a huge and magnificent bay, stand Tafelberg, or "Table Mountain" to we

English. By whatever name, it is a wonderful sight from our high vantage point. "The Table" grows in my eyes as we drive South, becoming amazingly massive, its 3560ft top absolutely flat, the flanking mountains, Devil's Peak and Lion's Head enfolding the city of Cape Town. I've seen the Table before, of course, a long time ago from the deck of H.M.S. Newfoundland way back in 1959, and more recently when "Debenham's" stopped over during the Whitbread Race, but never from the North, and it's a stunning sight.

As we drive into the Northern suburb of "Table View", we have a laugh over their "robots", traffic lights to me, and another over my "sighting" of Milnerton Lighthouse, on the car's Starboard bow! Mike and Jill drop me at the "Tulbagh", a modest hotel, but clean and friendly, close to the city centre, and not far from the Royal Cape Yacht Club.

It's good to be back at the "Tavern of the Seas", but though I have an enjoyable time, the visit, as a useful project is a failure. I came down mainly to pick up my mail from the R.C.Y.C., and to try to sell articles about Roamer and the voyage to Yachting Magazines.

The good people of the Royal Cape have looked after the mail, a fat packet full of congratulations from friends and family, and a bonus, from Roggebai Parcels Office I collect the Jury Rig Jib, sent by AIR Mail by Jeckells. Good for them!

I'm not so lucky with the Magazines. There are only two, catering for the fairly small South African yachting and boating community. "S.A. Yachting" covers the whole world of water sports, surf boards to fishing boats, and "can't fit your stuff in, sorry". "Sailing" is a much more modest affair, selling for the equivalent of 50p. Its Cape Town Editor, John Fensham, visits me in the hotel, and though he shows a lot of interest, and takes my articles away for perusal, after several weeks he writes 'his own articles on Junk Rigs, and squeezes in a half-page piece by me, for which I receive the princely sum of 50 Rand, (£17). He and I "had words" over the matter, but became friends, of a sort, during later visits he makes to Port Owen.

Whilst in this hospitable and bustling city I look up friends and contacts and have a very interesting time. My old pal Syd Crocker is back in S.A. from England. Quite a character is Syd, a retired Simonstown Tug Skipper. He shows me around town, treats me to a magnificent lunch at the Metropole Hotel. They're big eaters here. We have New Zealand Mussels, Stalbras Fish & Salad, and, unusually for me, a sweet, Pecan Pie and ice Cream, all washed down with fruity Stellenbosch Wine. Cheers Syd!

Later in the week, he and I, plus his two young grandchildren Daren and Melanie, tour the wonderful scenery of the Cape Peninsula, with me driving!

Back in my hotel room though, I worry over the finances of the situation. My money ever seems to be thinly spread, and now it is very thin indeed. I had phoned Mum, and Terry & Brenda, and expected the hotel bill to be a bit fierce, but when I check out, it's horrendous!! Hotel 25%, Phone Bill 75%. I have to take a £200 cash advance on my Barclaycard just to clear the hotel!

I leave for Port Owen on the 5 p.m. Saldanha Bay bus, which I had been told makes a circuitous route. How circuitous I soon find out! It's like no bus I've ever been on, articulated, for a start, and, as an articulated lorry backs under its trailer, so a "tractor-unit" backs under the bus. Apartheid is in full force on long distance buses, though not on the City transport. I felt somewhat degraded by being in the "white section", 12 seats at the front, separate from the Blacks and Coloureds, who are crammed in the back. The bus even picks up at separate stations, all calm and orderly at the "White Station", all chaos and laughter at the "Black". Eventually we get away, and, roaring up the West Coast Highway at 100 km/hr, I'm hopeful it won't be long before we are back at Port Owen, for I feel rather weary. Then, the bus turns off the metalled highway, and bumps along gravelled roads to horrible pre-fabbed and litter-strewn Black townships, dropping off the happy, yet down-trodden natives. We "tour" half of South Africa, it seems to me, before the bus drops me off at the Marina entrance, and I have a long walk, with bag and Jury Jib, to the Clubhouse. My flagging spirits are soon revived by a friendly welcome, cold beers and a hot steak in "The Galley".

So, back at Port Owen and ten days to Christmas. I try to work on Roamer's Job List, but this is no place to get work done! Sometimes I manage to put in a few hours in the forenoon, but at lunchtime someone is sure to tempt me out for a beer, or lunch, or Port Owen's speciality, a Braai. Braai is Afrikaans for a Barbecue, and is a way of life here. Meat is cheap, there are fish in the Marina, and in the river. More fish out in the calm blue waters of St.Helena Bay, plus crayfish from the reefs there, we got fed up with eating! From the Journal: "This is a great country to get fat in!!" Once tempted out at lunchtime, the day's work is finished. "Oh, I'll do it tomorrow", always tomorrow.

And so I have a marvellous time, eating, drinking and swimming, promising myself that, "After Christmas I will do all my jobs, sail to Cape Town, and then on to Australia, so I will.

The Christmas Eve Party is a resounding success. We are a party of about twenty, including "The Boss", Shelia, and their three sons. We have

DIE WESLANDER 20 DECEMBER 1985

"Mad Englishman" finds a veritable paradise at Port Owen

EVEN at Velddrif's Port Owen marina, where the residents have grown used to interesting visitors from exotic ports, a lone Briton sailing single-handed around the world is bound to attract a fair amount of attention.

Good-naturedly dubbed "the mad Englishman" by the locals, Bob Burn's delightful sense of humour and love of chatting have made him a firm favourite with everybody here and he keeps getting invited to numerous parties and braais.

No wonder he describes this part of the world simply as "paradise"! Just the place for growing fat, he says. He doesn't mind that too much however, since he will soon be sweating off any excess weight on the arduous trip to Australia soon to be started.

Bob left England in June this year and reached South Africa's west coast only after 125 days. He is very sure about this figure; when you are alone on the wide ocean, you have plenty of time to count the days!

It took him so long to get here because he cannot sail against the wind with the type of sail he has on his boat, the so-called Chinese junk sail.

The 45 year old former oil-drilling operative designed the yacht himself. It was designed specifically for a one-man voyage, down to the last detail. This is also the reason why he uses the aforementioned type of sail. The sail, which rather looks like a Venetian blind, is very easily handled by a single person. All the lines come together in the steering-cabin and the entire 36 foot yacht can be steered from the safety of the cabin without putting a foot outside.

The resourceful Bob has found ingenious ways of coping with problems on his lonely voyage. One of his more colourful plans was to fasten the one end of a line to the decompression lever of the diesel engine and the other to his left leg. Using his hands to crank the engine into life, he needs only to give a good kick into the air to get it roaring.

It has always been Bob's life ambition to attempt a single-handed cruise around the world and he estimates that it will take him two years to complete. Bob hopes to leave Australia for Cape Horn at the south point of America in December next year in order to make the dangerous crossing when there is least danger of icebergs.

Although Cape Horn is notoriously dangerous, Bob wouldn't even consider going through the Panama Canal. No self-respecting adventurer would even dream of using the safe canal like any ordinary commercial vessel, says Bob. It would be an insult to the fine tradition of single-handed seamanship. Besides, if you want to become rich and famous, you have to go around Cape Horn, he says with a distinct twinkle in his eye.

On board, Bob keeps himself busy writing magazine articles and he is also working on a book.

Die Weslander 20th December 1985 (See photo overleaf)

a wonderful meal, sing carols and other songs. I recite my "Poem to Port Owen", in between verses of which Gideon Langart, the Advertising Manager, inserts his own verse of "No he ain't going, from Port Owen, not until the year is past". The black girls from the kitchen come out and sing, shyly but beautifully, carols of their own, and scuttle, giggling back to their domain.

Next day, not feeling wonderfully well, I played Father Christmas on a blistering hot day, in a plastic red suit, cotton wool beard, and seaboots, to

The "mad englishman" inside the cabin of his yacht "Roamer".

Die Weslander 20th December 1985 (See story on previous page)

the three youngsters on the yacht "Zanj". Afterwards, I tour the Marina, sweating into the seaboots, reminding the residents of the tradition of feeding and watering "The man in the red suit"! In the afternoon I recover on board Gideon's Motor Boat "Absolutely!"

From Boxing Day till New Year's Eve the Marina is packed out with 50 boats of the "West Coast Cooler Cruise" fleet, which of course is a never-ending round of parties and braais. Culmination of the festivities, after the Cooler fleet has gone, is "our" New Year's Eve Party, held in the open-air braai area, on a beautiful warm starry night, lots to eat and drink, singing and dancing under the bright night sky. It's hard to leave a place like this, but I recite again, the last verse of my poem.

Bob and Roamer would like to say,
Before they sail along their way,
A great big Thanks to all at Port Owen,
Goodbye, Good Luck, but we must be going.

And we do. As soon as we have recovered sufficiently from the festivities, with Gideon as crew, we make a cold and windy passage to Cape Town, to berth at the Royal Cape, right in front of the Clubhouse, on "Millionaire's Row".

"In Town" we're into another round of socialising and fun. Gideon helps me out over the finances, to a degree, but that's not the way I like to live, so under the fun, all the time, I'm worrying about money, or the lack of it. I have very little so if I go on to Aussie, how will I survive the 6 months or so I'll have to stay there, waiting for the right season to set off for Cape Horn? I know the Australian authorities are very strict on Immigration and Employment rules, chances of a job will be small. So, when Gideon tells me there is a job at Port Owen, on the 2nd stage of the construction plan, which would seem to fit in with my drilling rig experience, I say "Yes Please", and sail back by the 16th of January 1986.

At Port Owen I go to work for "Toffee" Turner, Engineer in charge of dredging and land reclamation work. I've been told, jokingly (?), that he is the worst Engineer in the business and has a certificate from Taiwan University to prove it. But he is friendly enough to me and I try to be a willing worker. I try to drill holes for buttress poles with a drilling machine with no muscle in it, I try to operate his drag-line bucket dredger, but it breaks down every other day, as does most of his machinery. His coloured mechanic spends all day repairing the run-down and poorly maintained machines. I end up as odd-job man and assistant to a young Afrikaaner who plays religious pop music on his car radio all day, until he goes off to become a prison warder. I leave too, Toffee's operation and I don't go together.

I have become very friendly with Gideon, the Advertising man, who is, in turn, very close to Owen, The Boss. Between the three of us we come up with the idea that I should become "Landlord of the Pub", and Entertainments Manager! The thinking is that the Marina has reached the stage where the leisure facilities require expansion, and the Yacht Club bar, The Pub, needs a boost. I am to do the expanding and boosting.

Entertainments are practically non-existent, and the Pub is open only on Friday evenings, 7 p.m. to 10.30 p.m. for "Sundowners", the weekly gathering of the Port Owen community, and for the same hours on Saturdays, which isn't very much patronized. The bar has been run by Danny de Villiers, a young and very extrovert coloured guy, of whom I heard it said, "It's a crying shame that Danny should be black", but that's South Africa, Black he is, and it makes all the difference. The Yacht Club drinkers aren't comfortable discussing their private affairs at the bar with Danny listening in. Then, he has the unfortunate habit of parking himself in front of the T.V. in between serving drinks, and has to be called every five minutes.

So, I replace Danny, I widen the drinks range from the basic Beer or White Wine of previously, introduce "Bob's Cocktail Bar" make "Specials" for the Ladies, provide bowls of cheese and biscuits, brighten up the walls with photos of Port Owen and yachts, and generally turn the Club into a cosy social centre. I give them plenty of chaff and chat, and they love it. "The Pub" becomes a success, and shows a profit for the first time ever. A "Sundowners Special" menu by Mandy in her Restaurant, is very popular. As time goes on, word gets around that "Bob closes the Pub when the last guy staggers home", and the Friday and Saturday sessions get to be rather late affairs when the younger Club members assemble for a booze-up and sing-song. This is Great Stuff! All my life I've been thrown out of pubs at closing time and now I have the say-so when "Time Gentlemen Please" will be!

So, "The Pub" is doing well, and we widen the Social Activities by introducing a Darts Board, Chess and Cards. A resident kindly donates a one-quarter size Snooker Table, and outside I mark out a Volleyball Court which becomes very popular with the youngsters. Sailing dinghies and a rowboat are made available, organised boat trips on the Great Berg River to view the teeming bird life, a whole new range of Activities and Entertainments are introduced.

In addition to running the Pub at weekends, and over-seeing the activities, I also take over the maintenance of the 3-boat-Charter-cum-Time-Sharing fleet of Beneteau yachts, checking their inventories, ensuring their equipment is in good shape. I take people out on "Jollies", and for Sailing Instruction. It's a very busy life, but very varied and enjoyable.

To help me with the yacht's maintenance, I have a "Boy", "Mr. Cat" is 62, and a very interesting character. A "Saint" from St. Helena Island, he

Long wait for lone sailor

Bob Burns with Roamer at Brighton Marina

LONE SAILOR Bob Burns' plans to sail round the world in a year have been dashed.

Storms followed by calm weather put him weeks behind schedule on the first leg of his trip to Cape Town.

Now the 45-year-old bachelor from Brighton has missed a period of good conditions in which to sail round Cape Horn and will have to wait a year.

Writing

Brother Terry, of Uplands Road, Hollingdean, Brighton, said Bob now planned to leave Cape Town, where he was trying to raise money by selling articles about his adventure, next month.

Bob would sail on to Australia and New Zealand on the second leg of the 27,000-mile voyage, which he now hopes to complete in two years.

He had planned to arrive at Cape Town in early October but, after falling behind schedule, made a detour near the island of Tristan da Cunha, about 1,000 miles from the port.

In a letter Bob tells how he narrowly escaped being shipwrecked and losing his life near the island.

During a storm, his 36ft. yacht Roamer was swept only yards from the foot of cliffs at the aptly-named Inaccessible Island.

He managed to steer to safety and later discovered his compass had an error of 20 degrees, which had led to him being off course.

Terry said he had been frantic when there was no news. "It was such a relief to hear from him. But basically it was because he was experiencing adverse weather conditions and currents.

Book

"Also, the bottom of his boat was fouled with weed and barnacles, which slowed him down."

Evening Argus
21st January 1986

has been all round the world on fishing boats, and we get on just fine. He isn't too "quick" but is willing enough, and he and I keep the boats up to scratch.

I make other friends in the Coloured Community of Port Owen, notably "My Good Friend" Francois Simerie, the Storekeeper, Gurt, the Workshop Foreman, Amos, the Engineer Foreman, Wilf, Mervyn, Boetie and many others, are all good friends of "Mr. Bob". They are all good guys, and damned good workers too. Then there are the ladies of "The Galley", working under Mandy's pretty eye, they too are happy and hard-working, I make them laugh with my attempts at speaking Afrikaans.

And so the Southern Autumn becomes Winter, the hot sun less hot as it moves North of the Equator, but at 32S., Port Owen's is still a very temperate climate. Occasionally we might get a few days of wet fog and chilly North winds off the sea, but I am often heard to say, "If this is Winter, we'd be glad to have it as Summer in England."

We have our little excitements as well. Port Owen is a Lifeboat Station, and the Rescue Boat would speed out into the bay now and then to pull a boat off a sandy shoal. But on April the 23rd, St. George's Day, I am having a cuppa in the "Galley" when Frankie calls. 'Zanj,' is on the beach at Dwarskersbos, want to come Bob?" Do I? Into the boat I jump, with Frankie and Oom Joey, the river-boat Skipper, and we roar off down the river at 30 knots.

At the harbour mouth we run straight into the fog which has caused "Zanj's" grounding. We creep through it, piloted by Oom Joey, a retired trawler skipper, who knows the coast like the back of his hand. Eventually, 10 miles up the coast, we find the yacht, a heavy wooden 40-footer, well aground, and on a falling tide, no chance of pulling her off at that time. Frankie takes off, for safety, Marlene and her three children, and puts me aboard to aid Chris, and his buxom girl crew, Jennie, in the rescue attempt on the next high water.

At Low Tide Zanj almost dries out, but Chris is so lucky in that the weather, and the sea, is calm, and he is on sand. At 0300, Port Owen's two boats and Zanj's anchor pull her off and by 0500 we are all safely back in the Marina.

Next evening of course, we hold a Party to celebrate the rescue, and I am called upon to recite a Poem about the event, written in 25 minutes over a cup of tea.

Drama on St. George's bay, Or,
The Account of an Occurrence
at Dwaskersbos on 23rd April 1986

'Twas all upon St. George's Day,
The signal it came in to say,
The good ship Zanj, it seems we lost,
On the coast, at Dwaskersbos.

Frankie and the rescue crew,
Along the coast in Kotie flew,
To find Zanjie, at all costs,
In the fog, at Dwaskersbos.

With Joey conning, Frankie steering,
Bob in the murk is peering,
There she is! Cries Frank the Boss,
On the beach, at Dwaskersbos.

Sterling efforts then were tried,
To pull her off on that high tide,
But too late they were, for hauling,
For the tide by now was falling.

The day is calm, the sea is flat,
We can be grateful for all that,
But should a storm come up,
She's lost On-the-Skeleton-coast, at Dwaskersbos.

Lawrence, Andrew, and Chamonie,
Three brave children there we see,
They depart the dangerous scene,
With their equally brave Mum Marlene.

Now waiting for the next High Water,
Bob and Chris and Jennie's - Mum's-daughter,
Are the apprehensive crew,
Sustained by Jennie's forty-five degree stew.

After such delightful eating,
And much groaning and a-creaking,
Up stands Zanj to meet the tide.
See, the big full moon doth ride.

The sea stays calm, the night is still,
We'll rescue thee, we will, we will,
The rescue boats come in the night,
To see that Zanj is treated right.

First Kotie and Frankie, their duty for to do,
With Ken and Fats, her sturdy crew,
Then Kingfisher, Oom Joey, and Old Cat,
No rescue crew cope hope to better that.

High Water, and Kotie's at full throttle,
Kingfisher to Starboard, Zanjie giving lots of 'bottle',
Some swells, some bumps, the anchor chain comes free,
And Zanj pulls clear,
Into the open sea.

And so we come to the end of this long Saga,
We all will take a nice long drink of lager,
And drink to Zanj, her crew, her boss,
May they never bump again, on the sands of Dwaskersbos.

Bob Burns Port Owen April 1986

My job gets busier as Owen, Gideon, and I come up with ever more ideas
to make the place more social and active. Maybe too much for the present
population, but we are planning for the future, for next Summer, when I
won't be here. Owen and Gideon try hard to get me to stay, they even
dangle the carrot of a franchise for the proposed Sailing Academy in front
of me, but I'm not biting. Much as I love it here, it is but a pleasant interlude,
I must carry on with the "Grand Project", the voyage.

I want Roamer out of the water, for a bottom clean and anti-fouling
paint job. Frankie has a crane, but it's not really man enough to pick up my
"big steel beastie", so I take her down the river to the trawler slip at

Laaiplek. It's a hairy business, hauling her out, for all of a sudden, she looks very small on the big slip, but all goes well, no problems underwater, and I do all the required work in two days.

At Port Owen, I give Paul and Frankie, with whom it has been a pleasure to work, plenty of notice of my finishing date, so that they can find a relief. I will quit on September the First, and sail on the 7th for Cape Town. Ten days or so there, and we'll be off to Sydney. At last it all seems possible, Roamer in good order, money in the pocket.

September arrives and I am "retired" again. I plan a hectic last week of Dinners, Lunches, Braais and the odd beer, with the good people of Port Owen.

Last Days Countdown, Thursday; A Braii with my black friends, a warm evening in the open-air. Lots to eat and drink, lots of laughter and singing.

Friday; My last "Sundowners", at which I appear in my celebrated White Tuxedo, complete with Red Carnation and best Trilby. I give them The Leaving of Port Owen", my very last poem. Frankie allows me the honour of being the first to vandalise part of the Club wall with a farewell message. "Tot Sens and Gesondheit," (Goodbye and Good Luck, my Afrikaans is quite good by now!) "From Bob and Roamer". Saturday; A monster Braai at the Clubhouse for white friends. I have bought a whole pig, which takes Frankie, Peter Flor and I all day to roast, a very thirsty business! A splendid evening is had by all, I think, but I can't be sure!

Sunday the 7th of September, 1986, Time to go time, and what a send-off!! Just about the entire population of Port Owen waves me off from the Marina, and a whole flotilla of boats follows Roamer down the river in a happy cavalcade. Paul Stuyck, Commodore of the Yacht Cab, skippers Roamer for me, which I very much appreciate, not only because I don't feel too marvellously well, but I have so many people to wave to as we motor down the river.

As we approach Laaiplek, the Fishing Fleet is preparing to go to sea, but delay their departure for us, and shout farewells. At the harbour mouth though, what a fantastic scene! The breakwater is completely crowded with people of all races, waving and calling goodbyes. Car horns blast a final farewell as we leave the harbour and steam out into the Bay. How wonderful of these good people to give me such a send-off.

"Hell, Paul", I say, "Did I really mean so much to them?"

"It would appear so," is all the Commodore replies.

My stay at Port Owen has been a marvellous time for me, I shall miss them all, but hope to return before many years pass.

Roamer, accompanied by "Blazin", and "Orca", sail 10 miles across the Bay to Sandy Point Harbour, where I pick up a mooring buoy for the night. I have no intention of going out to sea until I am somewhat fitter. Jeremy Mace and his daughter bring Blazin' alongside to Port, Harry and "Moosh" Anders lay Orca to Starboard, and we have a last drink. Then, off they sail, taking Paul, and I am alone.

For 36 hours Roamer and I lay on that quiet mooring, getting ourselves in a fit state for the 100 mile passage South to Cape Town. Around the other side of the Stompneus Peninsula is the Atlantic Ocean, and it is well that I took the time to prepare us both for the trip, for we have a rough time, beating into my usual headwinds and seas. At 0400 on the Wednesday morning we are almost run down by a freighter, with my proper Sailing Light's brightly lit, and in good visibility.

But, we make it to the ever-friendly Royal Cape, and spend 10 days on final preparations, clearing Customs, etc. There is of course, another round of the social circle to be survived, but survived it is. On the Friday, a last Farewell to Joan Fry, the Club's hospitable Secretary, to Bobby Cattemore the Berthing Manager, my friend Chris behind the Bar, the girls in the Office, Goodbye All you Lovely People, it's time for Bob and Roamer to be On Their Way".

The Leaving of Port Owen – (Which Has to Be)

It all begun, you may remember,
On a sunny Wednesday, the 4th day of December,
Bob and Roamer to Cape Town were going,
But ran out of wind, and found – Port Owen!

Just a few days, he said, I'll stay,
And then I must be on my way,
Huh! He said that last December,
And he's still here, and it's September!

On arrival Bob was quoted,
As a-saying that he voted,

South African Interlude

Port Owen was a Paradise,
And now all the people – very nice!

Now after more than 9 months here,
He'd like to make it very clear,
He hasn't changed his mind at all,
In fact he really had had – quite a ball!

Remember at the Christmas Party,
When Bob was very hale and hearty,
Beer and Wine was fast a-flowing,
And Gideon sez – No, he ain't going.

And so I settled down to working,
Don't think the Ocean I was shirking,
But the season was too late for Cape Horn,
And me finances were too well-worn!

So - the Entertainments Officer I become,
To give our visitors lots of fun,
Also Landlord of The Pub
Dispensing "Dops", here at the Club!

All through the cold, harsh days of Winter,
(You have the cheek to call that Winter?),
Your "Winter" weather would compare,
With a British Summer there!

But now my friends, 'tis time to end this long long saga,
And so I ask you all to take a dop of lager,
(which may just jog the memory of some of you – *Cos,*
I used that line in "The rescue of Zanj at Dwarskersbos")!

But No! This really is too much,
I'm going on and on in such,
A way that really is most reprehensible,
But then, this evening, I really don't feel sensible!

But now the time has come my friends,
To really try to make amends,
For throwing at you all this terrible verse,
But here I am now making it quite worse,
By making this,
The very, very, very, last verse,
Much longer than an ordinary verse,
Which really is inexcusable,
Because it makes this poem quite unusable,
So – an end to all this cuck I say,
I really must be goin' on my way,
A great big Bale Donkey I am owing,
To all my lekker friends here,
At Port Owen – Gesondheit – Tot Siens –
This time I really must, Be Goin'.

Bob Burns, Port Owen
6th September, 1986

Chapter Eleven

Leg 2 – Cape Town to Hobart
During which 'Roamer' is 'knocked down'

Heave away, You rolling Kings,
Heave away, Haul away,
Heave away you'll hear me sing,
For we're bound for South Australia.

(Sea Shanty, "South Australia")

Saturday, 20th September, 1986, 0745. Letting go the mooring ropes from the Royal Cape's jetty, I manoeuvre out of the Marina. No farewell party today. Goodbyes were said last evening in the club. Just one elderly chap sees me go.

"Going sailing?" he calls.

"Yes to Sydney".

"Oh have a nice day".

Have a nice day indeed, quite a few nice days will pass before we see Australia. We motor across the huge harbour and clear with Port Control on the radio. They are very pleasant and I thank them and South Africa for their hospitality.

An early morning sea mist has drifted in and visibility is not good as I pass out through the breakwaters and turn to the West past a misty Green Point lighthouse and the high-rise blocks of Sea Point. We continue motoring West until 1000, 10 miles clear of the land, clear of the local shipping movements. Stow ropes and fenders, pump out the Engine Room bilge, hoist sails, sit and roll in the swell. There are a lot of seals about, and a large Whale. I haul in the log spinner in case one of them should think it's a meal. Very little breeze, start the engine and motor till 1200, shut the engine down, all quiet, no wind, long oily swell. The sun burns away the mist, and the ever-amazing spectacle of Table Mountain is gradually revealed, its flat top first, then the great cliff, and, as the sun's heat grows, so the sparkling city, its skyscrapers, and its suburbs, emerge into the full light of the hot day. I have plenty of time to savour the view of the city, and of the 12 Apostles mountains running off to the South towards the Cape of Good Hope, for I am sat there all afternoon and evening, motoring now and then to relieve the frustration. As the sun sets, varied and beautiful colour changes play across the mountains, yellow, red, ochre, a stunning sight.

Not until Midnight is there a breeze, from the West, and we trickle South. By 0400 we are making 5 knots and reef in down. At 0600 I can see the Cape about 15 miles to the East, the wind increases all the time as we bound off Southwards, and the land disappears into the mist. What will be my next sight of land I wonder, and when?

I'm tired, but there's no sleep to be taken here in this busy shipping lane. I do see several ships, and have to alter course for a pair of trawlers working to the West across my bows. I give them plenty of clearance, passing well astern.

By 1400 the wind is a Force 9 Westerly and we make to the South at all speed to get clear of the dangerous Agulhas Bank which extends well South of the Continent. The warm Agulhas Current comes pouring down the coast from the North East at up to 5 knots and, if we should meet a strong South West wind, especially in the area of the Bank, such enormous seas are caused as can, and do break up big ships, and roll over yachts unfortunate enough to be caught in that situation. My plan is to get down to 40 degrees South, and then turn East.

My plan is foiled by the wind backing Southwest, then South forcing us Southeast, then East, in very rough seas, pushing us towards that dangerous Bank. I spend a weary and anxious night trying to make to the South, or at least Southeast, but am not able to in the violent seas. Unsure of my position, I'm a worried man. It's a bad situation to be in, so soon after leaving port, I feel weak and indecisive.

22nd September. "First Day of Spring", says the Log, but it's not very Spring like! The wind veers to West Sou'west and we make South again. During the day, the wind feels warm, which is unusual. I pick up a bucket of sea water, and it's warm too, very warm, and can only be from the Agulhas Current. This gives me hope that the current is pushing us South West and thus away from the Bank. So I plug on, South or South East, as best I can.

Conditions are very unpleasant, trying to stay close-hauled on the wind, into a confused and violent sea. By Tuesday the weather has moderated somewhat and I am able to concentrate on establishing our position with regard to the Agulhas Bank, which is still my big worry. Trouble is, and I have to admit it, I've forgotten how to do it!! After 10 months ashore, the routine has gone out of my head and I can't sort out the various positions that Dead Reckoning, Radio Direction Finder, and Sun Sights, give me. Rather miserable with depression over this, the weather doesn't help, turning squally from the Southwest, with lulls in the wind, followed by black line squalls which might, or might not, have a bag of wind in them. There's no way of knowing until the threatening dark clouds are overhead, bringing sometimes nothing, other times 45 knots of wind, rain and painful hailstones. This weather becomes the norm for the next two days as we work South and East, reefing down, reefing up, cold, wet, and tired. Springtime in the Southern Ocean. Still, by Thursday afternoon we have made 500 miles on the Log, got clear of the Agulhas Bank, I'm fairly sure, and are at approximately 38° South, 22° East, and making to the East. The barometer is very high at 1032 mb. Friday sees us heading due South in the face of an Easterly, not so good.

I throw overboard a "Message in a Bottle", a message saying who and where I am. The message is in the first "dead" bottle of Jeremy Mace's very delicious Port.

In the afternoon I'm pretty much in despair at this East wind, which is up to Force 7, and, worse, my inability to get the Navigation sums right – I just cannot work it all out. Log: "This is madness! I haven't really been sure of our position since I lost sight of the Cape, last Saturday! To give my mind a break from the problem I make up a job list; 1. Tallow on Batten Parrels. 2. Wrap up anchor winch. 3. Sew button on blue oilskin coat. 4. Repair big flashlight. 5. Repair snapped self-steering vane. 6. Uncover storm tow-rope? 7. Change out block on foresheet. 8. Check mast wedges. 9. Seal Port aft deck light. And people ask, "What do you do all day?"

Journal Friday 26th September. 1500. "Hmmm, I seem to have a few problems. Wind in the East, and High Pressure will keep it there. My

Astro-Nav is up the spout and I can't make any sense out of it. Oh Well, The East wind will change one day, and I will find out what I'm doing wrong on the Astro, soon, I hope. Mere 'Academic' problems, now that we are well away from the Agulhas Bank."

As I write those last words, my senses, always attuned to sails, and wind, tell me it's suspiciously quiet up top. I look up through the dome, the Main doesn't look quite right, up the hatch – Oh No!! But Oh Yes, the Main has fallen quietly into its Lazy Jacks, the Halyard swings wildly at the masthead. Oh No!! This is a problem, and not an "Academic" one either. On waterproofs, up top and view the situation. The stainless steel becket connecting the halyard shackle to the sail has broken, I only checked it at Port Owen, hoisted myself to the masthead on it in fact! Frightening thought. I have more frightening thoughts now, Damn, this is about the worst thing that can happen to a Junk Rig sailor, to lose his halyard up the mast. No way to get up there, can't have steps with a Junk Rig, no shrouds to climb up. Deep gloom comes over me, must I try to pull myself up that 38 ft shiny pole on the ghoster halyards? Must I make for port? Port Elizabeth? Durban? run to the East to the Nerguelen Islands?

A tide of dismal thoughts flood through my head as I survey the scene, must keep calm about it though. Looking up at the halyard block and its rope, swinging wildly as we roll, I wonder... could I? ... Would it be possible?... From the foredeck I fetch a boathook, which has a double-hook fitting, tie and tape it to the Port ghoster halyard, hook end up. I slowly hoist it and try to engage the hooks in the wildly flailing ropes. It's not easy, it never is. Roamer rolls, the boathook hurtles about, looking vertically I tend to over-balance all the time, but can't hang on, I need both hands for the ghoster halyard. Try and miss, try and miss, a dozen times, shoulders ache, I fell over the cockpit and coamings, but at last, I have it! Never was a halyard pulled down so gently, lower on the ghoster halyard, ease out the Main, little by little, down she comes – *GRAB!!* I have it!! Relief sweeps over me.

An hour later and I have it re-rigged and the sail flying , this time with the Peak Downhaul connected to the halyard <u>above</u> the sail, so if it should happen again... I lower the Foresail, check its shackle and becket, and rig its downhaul similarly. Hoist the Fore, get under way, flop below and take a large Brandy neat. I'm cold and exhausted from stumbling around the deck for the last two hours. More Brandy in a strong hot coffee, and a hot meal and I come together again, that was a lucky escape. Music!!

Beethoven's Triple Concerto very loudly, to banish all weak and evil spirits, a big pot of Spaghetti and Meatballs with Curry Powder and Fruit Chutney – a feast – a survival feast, that was the nearest thing to disaster since the "Inaccessible Escape!!"

We press on, the sea is very confused and Roamer's motion wildly violent. The masts, whose wedges have dried out during the South Africa period, creak and crack alarmingly. I attack them with hammer and podger, and quieten them somewhat.

Journal, 2000, "sitting on the sea-berth, mulling over the day's events – still worried about my 'Admin problems', the Astro-Nav, which doesn't literally add up. I'm doing something very basically wrong, I try again with the Meridian Altitude figuring. Meridian Passage 1151, 22 degrees East Longitude equals 88 minutes, 1151 plus 88 minutes is 1319, same as I made it before. Read Mary Blewitt again. Mer, Pass, MINUS 4 minutes for each degree of E. Long!! Not ADD you idiot. Mer, Pass, 1151 minus 88 minutes is 1023 G.M.T. – adjust for the time difference on G.M.T. and I have it!! Oh! What an idiot, I did it hundreds of times coming down the Atlantic, must have had a mental block – a mental block head!

I treat myself to a can of Castle lager for being such a clever chap. E.S.P. says take a peep out of the dome, I do, and, there's a ship. I see her Steaming Lights and Port Light, and we are on a possible collision course. Below quick, switch on Masthead Lights, dress in full waterproofs, grab radio, up into cockpit. Ah, relief, while I was below the good chap has altered course and I now see his Starboard Light. I call him up anyway.

"Calling on Channel 16, calling the ship, calling the ship. I am the light on your Starboard Bow, I am a small yacht, do you receive me, over?"

"Hello the yacht, a sing-song Scandinavian voice, You are the light on my Starboard Bow?"

"Affirmative, thank you for altering course, very much appreciated."

"You are welcome, it can't be much fun for you this evening."

It isn't, but I'm glad to speak with this friendly chap who gives me a position check, 36° - 54'5., 23° - 00E, He asks me who I am, where I'm bound, for his Log I imagine. I tell him, wish him Bon Voyage, and he steams away to the East. I reflect on the safety and comfort embodied in his ship, and the danger and insecurity in mine, and then thrust such thoughts away. 36° - 54'! I thought I was much further South than that, lucky I spoke with him. A High at 40°S., just my luck, a High down here in the early Spring! Oh well, let's hope it moves soon.

One-Week-Out-Review. <u>For Us</u>: 1. We are 670 miles on the way. 2. Astro-Nav problems solved. 3. We have cleared the Agulhas Bank and are moving away from the notorious Cape of Good Hope weather. 4. Roamer is terrific in a storm, and she <u>will go</u> fast. 5. We survived the Main Halyard business. <u>Against Us</u>: 1. We have a leak in the Port Water tank, but it's at the top. 2. We have a big high in our way, but it'll move. So – Pros 5, Cons 2. Things is O.K. On we go.

Journal, Saturday the 27th; "I'm 46½today, Happy half-B'day to me! I am surprised to come across the Soccer Results on the B.B.C. Ranging through the radio waves, I come across "Radio Bop", Radio Pophuthatswana that is, its jingle? "Radio Bop Bop Bop Bop, the Station with a mind of its own". The DJs are hilarious though I don't think they are trying to be, it's lots of fun! Pophuthatswana is one of the "Native Homelands" the South African Government has set up. There are plenty of albatrosses about, big, ancient and beautiful. Chart work shows 7,400 miles to Sydney, long trip. The Sestrel-Moore compass is pretty useless at present, very sluggish, and, in rough conditions, the card goes 'walkabout' inside its housing. The "Concept" compass I have stowed away till we return to more Northerly latitudes, it developed so much "Southerly bip", as to be of no use.

I'm eating my way through the "Port Owen Goodies Boxes", a very welcome supply of grub from the Good Ladies of the Marina. Two boxes of Rusks from Gail Stuyck, (They're still crunchy, Gail) A box of cookies and a cake from Pam Tremlett, Home-made Marmalade from Jenny Sear. Thanks Ladies, very much appreciated.

Monday the 29th, 1615. Big News of the Day is that we are South of 40 degrees South and glad to be so. Noon Position; 40°- 01'.4S., 26° 15' E. Wind in the N.N.E. allowing us to make almost East. An eerie experience this afternoon, I awaken from a nap to violent motion and loud creaking of the masts. Up top expecting a squall, but no, we are in an area of turbulent, tumbling water, all confused, Roamer punching her way through, throwing spray in all directions, "shipping it green" over the bows. The atmosphere is humid, yet cold, fog seems imminent. Yellowy-grey clouds to the South West look ominous. All in all, a worrying set of conditions. A spray of water over my face feels cold, cold? I feel the sea, and it certainly is cold, and I take this as a sign we are to the South of the Agulhas Current and into the cold waters of the Southern Ocean. Then the sea becomes relatively calm again, it must have been an area of current convergence. Hopefully we may now pick up some of the East – going Southern Ocean Current of 0.5 to 1 knot indicated on the chart.

By Noon on Tuesday the 30th September I am able to write, "First 1,000 miles logged", it's always a pleasure to be well on the way, and this 1,000 m coming in 10 days of course gives me an average of over a hundred, 101.9 actually. I need to keep above the 100 m.p.d. average if I'm to make a decent passage. Am now plotting progress on the chart "Indian Ocean, Southern Portion", which is pretty much a large sheet of white paper, with South Africa on the left edge, and Western Australia on the right, with just a few islands dotted around in the centre and lower regions.

A 1½ inch vertical tear has appeared in the Foresail lower panel near the leach, I've no idea how that happened. It's too rough at the moment in the boisterous North wind and sea to do anything about it, will fix it soonest.

At 0900 on the First of October I advance the ship's clocks to G.M.T. + 3 as we move East. 8 hours to go to Australian Time, seems a long way – it is.

During the night a cold wind passes through non-violently, and turns my nice North wind into a Sou'westerly, the seas turn as if by magic, from easy ten-footers, to magnificent thirty-foot Southern Ocean rollers. The Sou'west swell is always there, lying low under all the waves, but just as soon as the wind goes to the Sou'west, up he comes. The awe-inspiring Southern Ocean swells sparkle in the sunshine as they cruise everlastingly to the East. Log: "Lots of bird-life about, albatrosses, smaller black albatrosses, terns, Cape pigeons etc., they all still mystify me in that they appear to just fly around all day with no attempt to catch food. I have never seen an albatross eat anything."

The Sou'west wind builds up into a Force 9 with impressive seas to match. Reefed down to one panel we make 5 knots to the E.S.E. Then the squalls come marching up on the wind. They come on the 'back end' of a depression after the Low has passed to the South. The S.W. wind blows at its hardest during this phase, then eases a little sometimes, but not every time. This is when the squalls arrive. During the day they are easy to see, great black masses of cloud and rain, looking ominous in the extreme. The problem is, they're not all full of wind, some bring a blast, some don't, the trick of sailing safely through them is in deciding which do and which don't. Some have the wind ahead of the rain, a shrieking blast, 10 to 20 knots above the normal wind speed, followed by a grey wall of torrential rain, of hail, which flattens the waves and numbs the senses. Some have the wind after the rain, so just when you think the squall is over in comes the blast. All in all, I believe it's best to reef down further in the face of an oncoming squall, as a safety factor to protect sails and masts, for it's too late to try to reef down once the squall arrives, the only thing to be done then is to run her off and hope nothing breaks. At night of course, without a moon they won't be seen coming, and if the lone sailor is sleeping, he will awake to the noise and action of the squall already upon him, and if he has a viewdome and inside steering wheel as I do, he will be glad of it, for there will be no time to wake fully, dress and get out into the cockpit.

Come the weekend, my well known and feared enemy is back. High Pressure, at 1032 millibars. The wind has gone light and to the Southeast, the sea is lumpy and horrible and we make poor progress. How is it possible for me to get a 2nd High at 40°S. in the early Spring?? As is usual when I am frustrated like this, I do odd jobs aboard to take my mind of it. Today I re-stow gear in the workshop, improve (I hope), the wedging system at the masts' feet, stow boathooks from the foredeck to the workshop, clean out the toilet bucket, do the washing up and sew a hanger on my red oilskins.

There's a nasty knock coming from the rudder, this is a new one. I investigate fully, but can't see anything amiss. The lower batten on the Main has poked out of its pocket at the leach. Jobs, jobs, jobs, it's hard to do anything in the violent rolling though.

The East wind continues, Saturday the 4th of October is a lovely day weatherwise, but we make 165°(T) (true bearing), not a course that'll get us to Australia very quickly.

Sorting through the fresh vegetables, I throw out some carrots, the onions and potatoes are O.K., grapefruits fine, satsuma's drying up. I put in a rather neat "Herring-bone" stitch job on the Foresail tear and fix the lower batten pocket on the Main. On a quiet evening I enjoy a couple of glasses of Jeremy's Port, a generous slice of Pam's cake, and a fun session of Radio Bop, (The station with a mind of its own, remember?).

By the Monday we are being forced S.S.E. by a persistent N.E. wind, up to Force 9 at times. I'm becoming worried and despondent, 43°S. is further than I want to be this early in the season, and is bringing me too close for comfort to the "Iceberg Line". A "Winds Survey" tell me that in the 17 days of the voyage, we have had 9 days S.E. to N.E., 5 days S.W. to N.W., 1 North, 1 South and one day calm. 75% have been F.6 to F.9. Seems a pretty unfair bunch of winds for the "Roaring Forties" in early Spring.

It's not all bad news though. I am glad to write in the Journal, "All is quiet and warm below. I am very fortunate in having a strong, steel, dry boat to live in, compared with, in their books, stories by Robin Knox-Johnston and Alec Rose, of leaky boats, wet gear, full bilges etc. The dome continues to be a major comfort and safety factor." Nevertheless, this plaguey N.E. gale continues to drive us S.E. I worry more about the iceberg problem. "Ocean Passages" charts put the "Extreme limit of ice" at 42S I have a short and quickly rejected thought that I should dig out the life-jacket in case we hit something, but no lifejacket or raft is going to do any good in the rough and icy seas down here. Roamer is both of those, and everything else.

I lie in my cosy berth in a warm sleeping bag but my thoughts are far from comforting. The wind moans across the deck, rain spatters on the dome, grey light filters in through the portholes as she rolls and pitches endlessly. "How long can I continue to the S.E.? Where am I? after 3 days with no sun sights. Where are the Marion Islands? Worrying times indeed, I feel as miserable as the conditions outside. Miserable thoughts creep in at times like this. When will I get to Australia? I'm well behind schedule now, 18 days out I should have nearly 2,000 miles logged but only have 1,700, and I doubt 1,2000 of those are "Good miles to Aussie". I can't face the idea of getting to Sydney so late that I couldn't make the Horn this season! "Tis a sad and disillusioned man who sits alone with such thoughts as these."

By Wednesday the 8th Of October, reckoning myself to be at 44° - 20'S., 39°- 20' E., I dare not go any further South for fear of meeting ice, and the possible proximity of Marion and Prince Edward Islands. I gybe and head North on Starboard tack in the face of this awful East wind, fog, drizzle and turbulent sea. A bad business, but I feel happier heading away from the dangers of the South, at least till I get to see Mr. Sun and fix our position.

A wind comes in from the S.S.E. in the afternoon, on which we make to the E.N.E., in a world of swirling fog banks and eerie cloud formations in all of which I see land and black rocks, but the fog clears and – no Islands. At least that's a relief.

Log: 0900 10th Oct. "Day 21. Well, if ever my saying of 'What a difference a day makes' applies, it is to yesterday and today. Yesterday Hell, Today Heaven!! Here I am, AT LAST, sailing downwind, downswell, down the Southern Ocean waves and isn't it marvellous!!!"

At last too, got a fix from the sun, which put us 100 miles S.W. of my D.R. Position!, at 45° - 48'S., 41° - 22 E. Back tracking courses and distances, this position would have put us within 20 miles of Prince Edward Island 2 days ago! Too close for comfort. But - to survive is everything - spirits zoom, we head East and all is well. Banish all thoughts of giving up and going North to the sun, Eastward we go!!

An omen? Picked up Radio Australia on 15.395 Mhz.

Sunday the 12th Oct. We work our way to the East, though it's quite a struggle most of the time with light airs, a lumpy' sea; and constantly changing winds. I even fly the Ghosters at one stage, Ghosters!!, in the Southern Ocean at 45°S. in the Roaring Forties!! On the 14th we get smack bang on the nose East wind against which I can only make North or South, so North it has to be as the Crozet Islands are not far off to the South. Progress hopeless again, in 24 days we've made 2,138 miles at 89 miles per day!

Tuesday, 14th. Journal:"... I'm beginning to get into a strange mood, seemingly finding nothing unusual in being in a very dangerous part of the world's oceans, hundreds of miles from anyone, making very little progress. I am, apart from the slow going and throwing the odd frustrated tantrum, having quite a cosy time, with plenty to eat and drink, warm and comfy below most of the time, getting lots of sleep and really just whiling away the time – but what can I do? In the face of these damned Highs and contrary winds, very little is the answer, except hope."

Thursday, 16th. Journal: "Making 5½ knots E.S.E. Sea is calm and light green, sky is blue and almost cloudless. We are 140 miles to the North of the Crozets, the Kerguelens are a long way S.E., so I don't have any Island problems. Nothing between me and Tasmania, 4,200 miles away. Due to our poor progress, my thoughts have been turning to a plan of going to Hobart rather than Sydney. Hobart is "On track" for Cape Horn whereas Sydney is 600 miles to the North, plus obviously, the same distance back down. All my arrangements are for Sydney though, mail, berth at the Cruising Yacht Club of Australia, meeting the Bradley's and Merv Palmer, full set of charts. Oh Well, lets see how we go.

At Noon on Friday the 17th, I have a lovely 135 mile run to record in the Log, on E.N.E. too, always very cheering the long runs, long for us, anyway. I'm hopeful we have got away from the area of High pressure and light winds, certainly we have a bagful of breeze today. N.W. Force 7-8 and making East at 5½ knots – Lovely. By 2000 the wind is up to F.9 with big seas and plenty of reefing practice. I stay on deck till 0100 hoping to observe a total eclipse of the Moon, but am foiled by thick cloud cover, which clears soon after. The night certainly went darker at eclipse time though.

By Saturday the 18th October '86 we have worked our way up to 43°S. at 56°E. and appear to be finding more wind, not less. At 1430 I have to perform a quick-quick reefing session, being nearly fooled by the blue sky and sunshine into thinking that the wind was only 6-7- N.W.'ly, but it's a gale alright. We tear East at 6 knots, this is the best time, with plenty of wind, but the sea not having had time to get up, it will soon. I have a feeling we are in for a blow tonight so lash down the L.V.M., rig down and lock the self-steering, uncover the "Storm Tow Rope."

Log: 1800, "Well, what I have here now is a real Stormin' ,Blowin' Southern Ocean Gale, N.W. 9-10 and it certainly looks like there's a rough night in store." There is, bludgeons of wind and sea hit us, but Roamer weathers it well, the sails shut down to the Storm Triangles. The storm's cold front passes through at 0330. I wake to the changed sea state and distinctly feel the lowering of temperature, even from inside my sleeping bag. The Storm Force 10 backs quickly from N.W. to S.W., the seas monstrous and chaotic. Our course becomes North, but I'll have to live with that for a while, for in the mad conditions, it's not safe for me or Roamer to attempt a gybe until the seas have settled a little into their S.W. phase.

Log 0830, 19th Oct. "The deed is done, await a squall, let it pass, then out fully dressed for battle. The wind nearly takes my breath away, but, awaiting a "calm" patch in the enormous seas, Gybe - 0, and we head East at 4 knots with the Storm and really impressive seas and swells on the Starboard quarter. The biggest waves are 40 feet or so, white foam streaks down their approaching faces, tumbling breakers fall from their crests, but very little hits us, just the occasional heavy lop of a wave on deck, or a flying crest bursts right over us. It's very impressive, and enjoyable, this is what I came down here for, not to fly Ghosters!".

The S.W. phase of the Storm continues with a series of violent black squalls bringing sheets of rain and hailstones, a shrieking wind before them, but Roamer, well reefed down, takes it easily, she's wonderful in a storm, slow and steady, strong and dry. Down below, I view it all very calmly from the comfort of the dome, even sitting on the "driving seat" occasionally, though this is not too comfortable in the violent movement which sometimes occurs, I fear I may be thrown off it.

All day Sunday she blows a F.9 from the S.W. with F. 10 squalls to keep life interesting, but we have no problems. During the night the wind "puffed and lulled" from F.5 to 8, with the barometer fairly steady at 1010 mb, rather high for a blow, but, stranger still, it rises to 1021 in the evening and blows stronger, to W.N.W. F.8.

On passing 60° E., I advance clocks again, to G.M.T. + 5.

Tuesday the 21st of October. "Trafalgar Day". All Honour to Lord Nelson.

I have a quiet night with a good sleep from 2100 to 0330 then it's up top to reef at first light as the wind gets up to N.W. F. 9. Looks like another storm a-coming. Barometer 1012 and falling. "Storm Procedure" is put into effect, that is shut down L.V.M., shut down Levanter, check all sail lashings, retire below, batten down the main hatch, and Bingo, one storm-proof ship.

Looking at the "Storm Rig", I'm very glad that I designed-out the Yard and Angled Batten. If I hadn't, those heavy spars, with no sheets to them, would be hanging out to leeward now, out of control and a potential menace.

We have now had strong Westerly winds since the 15th., and made 650 miles to the East in the 6 days. Not exactly record-breaking, but still satisfactory.

In the evening I drink a Rum toast to the memory of Lord Nelson, to the Health of Jack and Betty of the Roundhill Tavern, who donated the rum, and to the late Ron Presland, a good friend of the Park Crescent Inn. It's no night for a party though, for it's very rough with this N.W. F.9 and big seas.

Wednesday the 22nd. The storm continues, the wind wanders from N.W. to 5.W., blasts me with icy squalls, wanders back to N.W., another cold front and chaotic seas, but I'm getting used to the routine now after 7 days. But, it is rather wearying in the violent motion of the boat, hanging on tight all the time, not exactly survival time, but damned hard work for all that.

Thursday the 23rd October '86. All of a sudden, it is survival time. At 1030 I'm up on deck reefing the Main down to its triangle, when a cold front comes whistling through, a front like I've never seen before. Busy reefing in the cloudy weather and heavy rain, I never saw it coming, but, in five minutes, all cloud is blasted away from the sky by an absolute tempest of a wind, no way I can put a number to it, just a fury of shrieking hurricane, which backs in that five minutes, from N.W. to S.W., and the sea becomes a turmoil of boiling waves falling in all directions. In this turmoil, Roamer charges off into the old N.W. seas, half burying herself in the wild waves. I shut the Main down altogether and helm her through the worst of this chaos. About half an hour later, when the ferocious new seas from the S.W. have overcome the old ones from the N.W., and have settled to something a little less than utter chaos, I gybe her, an "exciting" operation in these seas, but we get round alright, and head East again. Log 1600: "For the first time ever, in 20,000 miles of sailing Roamer, we are under bare poles, having decided that not even my 10-ounce "Bullet-Proof" storm sails would last the night in that wind."

The barometer has dropped to 990 mb, and we are being swept by enormous breaking seas. Then, we are pooped by a 20 ft vertical wave, from my dangerous but thrilling position in the cockpit, I am, able to see exactly how this happens, from close range! I had seen a big wave break earlier, 50 yards to Port, watched as its leading face became vertical and higher, then, surging forward, it jetted at terrific speed and broke with a great roar. "Blimey", I thought, "What happens if one of those hits us?". I'm about to find out! I watch it happen. A wave like that is the product of two waves colliding, and, by a million to one chance, the collision takes place 10 yards dead astern of us. I watch, half in fascination, half in horror, as the waves meet, join forces, soar up to a vertically-faced pyramid, then jet forward onto my little ship and I, cowering before it. I grab a steel handrail and hang on, literally, for my life. Thundering tons of water fall on us, pressing me down into the cockpit well, a painful weight on my shoulders for a few seconds. Then, all is green water cascading off the decks, and emptying out of the cockpit drains. Thanks to my aft cabin roof, which bore the brunt of the falling tons of water, and the push that the wave gave to the stern, not so much fell on me. I am half-surprised to see the self-steering gear and the L.V.M. Generator still there! Bonny Ship! For the umpteenth time I am so glad I have a steel ship, and a centre cockpit. Imagine that wave falling into an aft cockpit, landing directly on the helmsman, smashing in doors or hatches – that's how yachts are lost.

Log 2000: "Spent a while in the cockpit, wild place man, blowing a general S.W. Force 9 to 10, but when these black squalls come through, the wind is just fantastic. The sea surface is whipped completely white, wave tops torn off and hurled to leeward. As the black clouds arrive, sheets of rain, snow or hailstones, like the proverbial machine-gun bullets, sweep the decks. It's an eerie sight to look through the dark tunnel of an overhead squall to the bright sunset sky."

Friday the 24th October 0530, Barometer 955, Wind S.W. Force 10. The seas are tremendous , great rolling hills, with foaming roaring breakers tumbling down their steep, foam-streaked fronts. Log 0730: "The lone sailor skulks below, writing and waiting. The ship rolls and plunges, thrown around like a toy boat in a bath. Surely it must ease soon? At least I'm warm and dry. I keep watch from the dome, and, seeing the mountainous waves roar past, I'm surprised that not more of them fall on us. Even though I am cosy inside, the violent motion is very wearying, especially after 8 days of it now. 8 days of holding on tight every step I take, on deck or below, only one limb moves at once, the other three hold and brace. A sharp blow and pain is the penalty for a second's inattention. Nothing can be left standing unwedged, not even for a millisecond. Very tiring. 1200, still she blows a tempest".

1255. I am cooking lunch, soup and a pot of noodles and veggies, when a louder roar than usual surrounds me. My 13 ton ship is picked up by one of the monster waves, flung on her Port side and hurled down a great slope of water. Lunch flies off the cooker and rolls up the Port side woodwork, I am thrown in a heap into the cosy chair as we lay over. "This is it!", I think, "She's going right over." Icy cold sea jets in through the closed and battened hatch, not a lot, but thin powerful jets hose over the galley and put out the burner, and soak my left side. With the roaring of the water all around me, is the added roar and rumble of all the ship's stores moving in their lockers. A huge hand presses the ship down into the sea, the same pressure keeps me in a heap in the Port seat, no way can I get up out of it. All this probably only lasts about ten seconds, but it sure seems longer.

As I lay there I try to work out how the water is getting in the hatch. Then the 4 tons of lead at the bottom of the keel does its job, levers the masts out of the sea, and we roll back upright. More rumbling of the stores as they tumble back. Rolling out of the seat, I remember to turn off the paraffin to the cooker, then leap up to the dome. The masts, are they still there? They are, bless 'em, sails and battens too. In fact, everything looks O.K., Oh, the Port lifebuoy ring has gone, and taken the lower guardrail rope with it.

I do a quick circuit round the ship below, to see if we are damaged or leaking, but no, all is well. All my early planning, for small lockers and cupboards, all with spring loaded catches, has paid off. Though the stores have fallen around in their stowage's, nothing has got free, not even one can! The wardrobe hasn't been so lucky, oily water from the engine bilge sump has been thrown over my shirts and coats, a small problem in the circumstances! Up forward in the workshop all is secure. Half a bucket of "pee" has been thrown out of its bucket, and a little evil-smelling fluid has escaped from the toilet bucket, but nothing worse, as I had the lid tied down! I lost my lunch, but on the whole we seem to have come through the knock-down pretty well. Later I discover that the bright-light flasher unit on the very top of the foremast, is bent over 30 degrees, and the radar reflector, near the foremasthead, has had its fittings cracked, so that masthead must have been well into the sea. Hurrah for a steel ship yet again, and for that 4 tons of expensive lead.

Later that afternoon, a slight reduction in the wind strength, to maybe a Force 11! I decide that these are the conditions to try out the "Storm Tow-rope", 600 feet of 2-inch circumference hemp rope, carried for a long time, for just this eventuality. Towed astern, it would, according to some schools of thought, hold the stern up to the wind, slow the ship and prevent her pitch-poling stern over bows, and calm the seas astern. I have a fairly open mind on the theories, and now is the time to find out. In the midst of the constant tempest, with occasional squalls of hail and snow, I stream 450 feet of the rope, and observe its effect.

Before streaming the rope, Roamer has laid, with no sail up and wheel amidships, with the wind 45 degrees on the Starboard quarter, making 2 or 3 knots headway. With the rope out, she still lies quarter to the wind, but almost stopped in the water, lying there like a waterlogged tree trunk. With no speed, the rope sinks and has no calming effect on the waves. We have no steerage way, Roamer feels like a sluggish log, lying stopped, fair game for any marauding breaking sea. Hating the feeling I take my big knife and chop the rope, which sinks quickly. Roamer springs away from her bonds, alive and lively again, like a boxer, bobbing and weaving, keeping on the move. No more tow ropes for me!! The seas by now are really big and dangerous, too dangerous I decide, for me to be on deck at all, plus I'm half frozen and am glad to retreat into my steel cocoon and batten myself below. My, how cosy it is below!! From the safety of the dome I watch the enormous seas, many of them now with cliff-like fronts. For the first time I see waves like those in the photographs in Adlard Coles's classic book, "Heavy Weather Sailing", waves of such a size and shape that I'd hoped I'd never see. The text reads "...It is difficult to see how a small ship might survive such seas, let alone a yacht". Maybe, but Roamer does, though I help her by steering from inside till it's too dark to see the monsters any more. Then I put her on a "safety" Port tack, and leave her to fend for herself, and me. Bonny ship, she does.

Saturday the 25th October 0800, after the storm, the calm wind is down to Force 4 at 0500. We roll abominably in huge swells and confused seas. I hoist two panels of sail to steady her. Later we are moving again under sail for the first time for 48 hours. 1500, Barometer 1003, wind North F.6. Going well. 1800, barometer 993, wind North F.8 - 9. I reef down to storm triangles. Oh No!! Not again?

Sunday the 26th: Log, 0330. "Sundays begin early here. Up at 0215 when a heavy breaker laid her over to Starboard and gybed us. Up on deck to remedy the situation I find the wind still in the North.

I am much alarmed to read the barometer at 982. Highly suspicious, and not a little afraid, I stand by in the dark night and moderate rain." The wind returns at 0430, N.W. F.8. 0900, N.W.F. 9. The barometer remains at 982 despite vigorous tapping and strongly worded advice for it to rise.

At 1230 a cold front passes through surprisingly quietly considering the low pressure. The wind goes to S.W. F. 8 with squalls up to F. 10. 1800, barometer up to 988, wind up to F. 9 with F. 11 squalls. "Will it never end?" I spend a long, cold, weary night in this latest gale but at last it is to be the end of my 10 days of gales and storms. In the morning, with barometer up to 998, and the sky not looking too threatening, we make off to the East at 5 knots with two panels of sail up. The water boils for hot, strong, black coffee, and I am, as ever, hopeful and optimistic, you have to be, in this game!!

After 5 days with no position fix, I only have a vague idea of our position, but I don't think it is a problem. I've drawn a dead reckoning course on the chart with lots of N.E. in it, and that course still puts us 120 miles South of St. Paul Island. We move to the Eastern half of the Indian Ocean chart today, with Australia on its right edge. Good to know we are progressing, even if not very fast in these endless storms.

I have to take serious action over the lazy-jack rigging. We spend so much time under storm canvas that the lazy jacks are chafing the stitching badly on the top triangle, so I take the forward lazy jack off the boom and tie it out to the guardrail stanchions. It still works O.K. but has stopped the worst of the chafe.

Down below I do a job I wish I'd done a long time ago. I drop a "Bilge Bib" into the engine bilge sump. This is a bag which soaks up oil into itself leaving clean water only, in the bilge. Very clever. Maybe too late, having ruined most of my shirts, but better late than never, I'm hoping we won't be laid over again, but who knows?

Monday the 27ᵗʰ October. Is it over? The barometer is up to 1002, we have a W.S.W. breeze of F. 5 and make gently to the East in small seas, it feels fantastic not to have the noise and violence of the past 10 days. Log, 0830 "Well, things are fairly moderate for a change. I actually have 2 panels of each sail up, Levanter in charge of steering and we're making to the East!"

I am amazed to see the time is only 0830 when I come in, for already I have: - 1. Emptied and scrubbed the toilet bucket, 2. Cleared the floor of the workshop, stowed fenders and ropes, hung out boat cover to dry, 3. Moved the remainder of the "Storm Tow Rope" to the foredeck, coiled it round the Fisherman anchor and lashed it down, 4. Lashed the surviving lifebuoy ring to the tow rope, and 5. Rigged a "Hanging Rope" across the aft doghouse roof for tying my reefing pendants, etc., to. I treat myself to a coffee and a chocolate bar for doing all that.

Later in the day when I get some sun sights, I find my D.R. position, after 5 days with no Fix, is 70 miles too far East, and 110 miles too far North! So much for D.R.!!

Obviously the storm didn't blast us to the N.E. as much as I estimated, which is interesting information for future reference.

Friday the 31ˢᵗ of October 1986. The last day of the month arrives as we lurch and bustle to the East at a poor average of 91 m.p.d. Things not so good for me, 42 days out, and only 3,730 miles logged.

It gets worse – Log, 0930. "It's said that we have "On" days, and "Offs." I'd better watch it today then for I seem very "Off." Whilst on deck a little earlier, with a lumpy sea and a F.7 Southeaster, I decided to rig down the Levanter vane, as I don't need it with the wind abeam, so, I undid the safety line and, while reaching up to unplug the vane, Roamer lurched, I grabbed for a hold, and the vane and its safety line fell off into the sea!! I felt sick!! How do I do such stupid things? Then, when back down below, I pulled at a metal saddle which used to hold the bilge pump hose, behind the companionway ladder, it came free with a rush, and split the skin on one of my knuckles, which will give me a hard time for many days, out here where nothing dries up in the damp salty atmosphere."

End of the month sort-out of fruit and vegetables reveals only one grapefruit, a dozen lemons, a dozen potatoes, and two dozen onions which are rapidly going off.

Sunday the 2^(nd) of November. Journal 1330: "Here I sit at the chart table, all hatches open, the sun wandering around the saloon, Handel's Messiah on the player. Quite a pleasant day obviously. Keeping myself busy as ever. Earlier I made up another mid-size wind vane, cleaned out the after tool locker drawer, and just as well I did, for some water had got in and some of the tools were rusting. Did a repair job on the blue waterproof trousers. Good reception of Radio Australia, lots of Chinese music too. Auntie Beeb not so good in this area, but the American W.W.V. Station very good for Time Signals for the Navigation Watch."

Tuesday the 4^(th) November. Enjoying watching my "Resident Flock" of Shearwaters, not a beautiful bird, more like a sea-going crow, black with an orange beak. I have about 20 which have been with me for hundreds of miles. They are good fliers and amusing landers, coming in with wings up high, feet pushed out as brakes, tail feathers splayed out. They sit around on the sea twittering and chattering like a crowd of small black ducks."

1730: "90 degrees East Party Starts Here." Yes, arrival at 90 degrees East is the signal for relaxation. At last I am one quarter the way round the World from Greenwich. I put the clocks on to G.M.T. + 7. It being pretty quiet outside, and Roamer making E.S.E. at 4 knots, I close the hatch, light the cooker and on with the first course, a simple one, strong hot black coffee laced with Brandy and Syrup. Music Maestro please, and on with one of my favourites, Andrew Lloyd Webber's "Variations on a Theme by Paganini."

To reach a quarter the way round the World we have so far sailed 14,062 miles! Rather a long way for a quarter, but we zigzag a lot! Whilst awaiting the kettle boiling for the 2^(nd) course, French Onion Soup a la Roamer, I stand in the viewdome, listening to the music, watching the sea and the clouds. This particular "Variation" suits exactly the easy rolling and moderate speed we are making. The sea is as calm as I've seen it for a long time, a long, low swell rolls in from the S., the Starboard quarter, with small wavelets curling and breaking. Roamer rolls gently along, the music swirls and rolls with her - I am giddy with ecstasy, it is so beautiful – but – the kettle whistles shrilly! Soup time. And delicious it is, only a packet soup, but with Chef's addition of Soy Sauce, a touch of Bovril, dash of pepper, drop of vinegar – Mmmmm, <u>Very</u> tasty.

And now, for something completely different, (different that is from the variation of Meat stews, Fish stews, Spaghetti and Meat Balls with spuds and onions which has been on the Menu for the past 6 weeks!),

"Salade de 90 Degrees East." Nicely laid out in a clean white bowl! some Beetroot slices, Creamed Sweetcorn, a savoury Chutney and a goodly portion of nuts and raisins. This tasty dish is consumed to the last part of Webber's Variations, with nutty South African biscuits to munch on. I fancy some wine, but the gentle rolling isn't that gentle to allow bottles and glasses to be stood on the chart table, so the wine will have to wait until later. A quick pop up to the viewdome to check sea, sky, sails and course, all is fine, what a blessing that dome is. With the barometer at 1020 mb, not a lot of nasties are going to attack us tonight. Ah!, the Wine Waiter has brought supplies from the "Cellar", the cool aft cabin. He pours me a glass for my approval, I sniff it delicately, it is a fairly cheap Blanc de Noir from Cape Town of which a case, for 30 Rand, about £8, = 75p a bottle! Very acceptable I find it. Wine music is J.S. Bach's Concerto in D Minor for 2 violins.

'Tis a hard life for a Lone Sailor in the wilds of the Southern Ocean. But remember last week! The 90 degree party ends with a cup of Milo, the Southern Ocean is no place for excess alcohol, it can change too quickly, but it was very enjoyable.

Saturday the 8th of November. We bustle and toddle East at no great speed. Noon Position 42° - 15'S., 98° - 55'E. "Had a quiet night though I didn't sleep very well. Head full of thoughts and scenarios, weird dreams too, Go-Go girls on a beach, secret agents prowling around houses and moors, old ladies in a house. Very detailed too with faces from my past." I had drunk the last quarter of Jeremy Mace's last bottle of Port. Any connection?

During the day I notice the Firdell Slipper Radar Reflector on the foremast wobbling about, its fittings must have got a clout when the mast went under the sea in "The Big Gale", which also bent the Xenon flasher over. Nowt to be done about it, must just hope it holds out to Hobart, or, if it should fall, may it do so when I'm aft and can maybe rescue it, there's £75's worth there.

Unusually for me, I'm eating lots of meat, having found out in Cape Town that the Aussie authorities allow no canned meat into the country, so, must eat all the Spaghetti and Meat Balls, and the Veg. Curry with Minced Beef. It'll just about work out at a can a day, not so good for my planned vegetarianism though.

Sunday the 9th of November. I listen to a very moving Remembrance Service on the B.B.C. World Service. Two minutes silence is very silent aboard, followed by the Service made more poignant for me by my isolation. The low moan of the wind and rustle of the sea, bugle calls and well – remembered military music. I once played the Reveille and Last Post at the Cenotaph in Castle Square, Brighton. Thoughts fill me of what a civilized country Britain is where Royalty, Heads of all political parties, and leader of so many different countries can stand together to honour their fallen heroes.

I'm reading David Lewis's "Ice Bird." Now there's a tale of suffering for you, how he sailed in a 32ft steel boat around the Antarctic, was capsized three times and suffered frost-bite and thirst. Not sure I could do that sort of adventure, it's a bit too cold down there!

Thursday the 13th of November. Yesterday was pretty rough, with a N.W. blow, then a cold front and S.W. winds of Force 9. Nothing really wild came out of the squalls though, till 2330. Log: "Up to check out 'lull' rolling and find bright moonlight all round, except for upwind where there's the blackest squall I ever saw. I'm in the dome, and have no time to dress and get out to reef down, only time to get wedged in the 'Wendy House' steering position and ride her through it. I have to steer by the wind vane, trying to keep it upright in the ferocious squalls. I'm sure it was blowing F.10 or 11. Huge foaming breakers roar past, some break on deck and over the dome, fantastic scenes of black clouds, torrential rain, bright moonlight. I see a rainbow by moonlight, first time I ever saw one of those, no colours in it, just an arch of varying shades of white and grey.

I stay in the steering position till 0830 riding out squall after squall and am damned glad when at last the windward horizon clears and I can climb down and brew some coffee. Imagine my position without the dome though, I'd have either frozen to death out there, or abandoned her to look after herself!

Saturday the 15th. I seem to be back in the windy area again, having had Force 8 or 9's since the Moonlight Squall Ride, and have a N.W. F.10 today. The only unusual feature is that I have been warned about it! Yes, by Perth Radio, 600 miles to the North. Cape Leeuwin has a reputation for being a windy place – its reputation is secure. Though 450 miles North, it has given me a rough time. Cape Leeuwin is the second of the "Five Great Capes" which I must pass to the South of, to complete a "Classic" circumnavigation. The others are, the Cape of Good Hope, South West Cape, Tasmania, South West Cape, Stewart Island, New Zealand and of course, old Cape Grim himself, Cape Horn.

It gives me much pleasure to start plotting our positions on the chart "South Australia", which at a scale I; 3,500,000, makes our progress appear much more impressive than the I; 10,000,000 of the Indian Ocean. This new chart takes us across to Tasmania, but has only part of that Island on it which is a pity, seems to me it would have been simple to get it all on.

The last time I was in these waters (with John Ridgway we were down nearly at 60°S.!), was in 1958 as a young A.B. aboard H.M.S. Newfoundland, a 6-inch gun cruiser. We had come down from Trincomalee, Ceylon, (Sri Lanka now), for a ten week tour of Australia and New Zealand, a dream voyage for a young sailor! But – after a great visit to Freemantle and Perth, we were on our way to Melbourne when we received a recall and hammered our way back across the Great Australian Bight into a Force 10, stored ship in Freemantle and spent a horrible 6 weeks up the Persian Gulf in horrific heat riding shotgun on Colonel Nasser. I've never been too keen on Arabs since!!

Wednesday the19[th] of November Day 60. Position 42° - 24'S., 122°- 15' E. We struggle across the Bight, getting a mixture of calms and blows, with 1100 miles to go to Hobart, having decided that I won't have time to go to Sydney, not in Roamer anyway. Strange sensations today! I'm warm, I'm calm!! Actually able to walk around without holding on every foot of the way!

The wind is from the North where there is a 1027 mb High. The Aussie Weather announcers call it a 1027 Hecto-Pascoule High!! Fantastic, the names these scientists think up. Some of the announcers have very twangy Oz accents, others are North Country British, Scottish, and there's even a very precisely-spoken Irishman, who pronounces 'decimal' as 'daycimal', exactly as it should be, on the radio. One of the Australians is a real killer, with a knife edged voice, and so friendly to the ships he speaks to. I get plenty of weather information, 3 or 4 times a day, from Adelaide and Melbourne.

My shearwaters have departed for cooler climes, but still have the occasional albatross, some Mollymawks, two tiny Cape Robins and one Pintado with beautifully painted wings, plump like a wood pigeon. Strange sky and clouds in the S.W. today. The sky is a White-yellowy-grey with tiny clouds of silver, all of which, small and separate, and peaked-up in their centres, like miniature Mount Fujiyamas.

We plod on across the Bight through calms and puffs. 21st, 35 miles, 22nd, 115, 23rd, 72. I hear Hobart Radio for the first time, from 830 miles. It makes me feel close to hear the coastal report for Maatsuyker Island, where I am planning a landfall.

Tuesday the 25ᵗʰ. Day 67. 595 miles to Hobart. Hard edged black clouds on the East horizon look very like Tasmanian mountains! Hope they're not, or my Navigation is way out! They dissolve in the sun. Hobart Radio Operator today is a nice-sounding lady, it's lovely to hear the fair sex's voice.

In the evening it's quite blowy and I'm dubious about leaving two panels up, but, I need the miles, so I do. Murphy's Law prevails and as soon as it's dark in come strong squalls and I have to dash out to reef down in a bitter cold wind from the South. I'm rewarded though, by a wonderful sighting of the Aurora Australis. All along the South horizon, up to a 45 degree height, the sky is lit by sheets of shimmering white light, curtains of writhing luminosity. I am thrilled once more to be sailing alone, able to view such wonders in complete silence.

Saturday the 29ᵗʰ of November. Day 71. Ah – the trials of the long-distance sailor! Today I make an elemental mistake and invoke the full wrath of Murphy's Law. In preparation for making Port, I stream the log for better D.R., uncover the anchor winch and rig the chain, prepare flags, test navigation lights etc. Mr. Wind, seeing all these preparations, goes to the East! This is very painful, to be virtually on Hobart's doorstep and have the door slammed in my face. I get full weather info 3 times a day, it tells me things I know and don't want to know. Another of my friendly Highs has tracked South of me and gives Easterlies, which will turn North East. Damn! Just what I don't want.

It's a hard life after 71 days at sea, but I keep calm, write letters and try to hold my position, but we are gradually driven S.W. by wind and currents. By Tuesday evening, the 2ⁿᵈ of December, we are 130 miles S.W. of Maatsuyker and have almost given up that island as a landfall. The rocks of Pedra Branca are now my aim.

Wednesday the 3ʳᵈ. The wind has just about died, and a feared of being washed to the East by the current, I motor Northwards for 7 hours, in 3 sessions.

Thursday the 4ᵗʰ. "What a difference a day makes – again." Yesterday motoring and hating it, today a bonny Westerly which has us bounding North, my heart bounding too. It takes very little to send my spirits flying high. I spend lots of hours in the bows seeing "mountains" in the clouds ahead, fantastically high. Surely even Tasmania isn't that mountainous, although the "Pilot" describes it as, "Probably the most truly mountainous island in the World."

No, the mountains aren't that high, I'm seeing things in the clouds. I force myself to take an afternoon nap, creep up on deck at 1600, and, is there? Yes, there is!! Whoopee, Land Ho! South East Cape on the Port bow, Pedro Branca's guano-covered cliffs to Starboard, a perfect landfall. Pedro Branca, which, unlit and 14 miles offshore, I have been fearing, turns out to be a perfect position-giver, otherwise I wouldn't have been sure which part of the coast I had found.

We run down the brisk West wind, leaving Pedra Branca 3 miles to Starboard, and gradually identify the coast with the aid of chart and Pilot. I am most grateful for having the Pilot, (Admiralty Sailing Directions), packed full as it is, with information, thanks to that zany trio, Cliff, Neil and Gazzy of the Roundhill Tavern.

At dusk we cruise gently along the coast in a calming sea as it shoals. Tasman Head looms to Port dimly black in the starlight, a thin crescent Moon hangs in the West. Tired as I am there is no sleeping now. Giving Tasman Head and its attendant rocks a wide berth, I alter course 90 degrees and head North into a calm Storm Bay.

Friday the 5th of December, Day 76. A pink and rosy dawn finds us becalmed on a flat and quiet Storm Bay, with the delights of green hills to feast my eyes on. I have breakfast, clean up the ship, and myself, stow the sails, start the motor and head towards the Derwent River. It's a long run, 25 miles across the Bay, past Adventure Bay, Queen Elizabeth Point, Iron Pot Light, and I'm in the enclosed waters of the Derwent. As I move into the harbour it gets warmer and I progressively shed layers of "Deep Sea Clothes." A pile grows on the cockpit seat, I throw it all below and change into shore gear.

It feels wonderful to be dressed in light clothing, to be able to stand up straight and walk around.

1100: Arrive at the John Garrow light and Hobart is spread before me, under 4,000 foot Mount Wellington. I stop the motor, drift in the breeze, out radio, sit in pulpit.

"Hobart Port Control, this is yacht Roamer, do you receive me, over."

"Yacht Roamer, this is Hobart Harbour."

Hooray, I've arrived.

"Roamer, are you healthy?"

I make them laugh, "After 76 days at sea, <u>very</u> healthy!!"

"You may proceed to the Royal Yacht Club of Tasmania." I do, clear a very friendly Customs and Immigration, the Health Inspector goes through my stores looking for cans of meat. "I ate them all" I tell him, but he stills looks.

At 1200, one Alan McKissick befriends me, treats me to beers at the Club. We look at Roamer berthed just outside the window, she has a layer of salt spray a foot high all along the side above the waterline. She looks well-travelled, many people look at her with wondering eyes. My Bonny Ship, she has brought me safely through the storms to Australia. 7,050 miles in 76 days; quite a trip!

Bramble, the ex-ambulance

The hull has been built. Bob shows keen interest!

Transporting Roamer to Brighton Marina

Cap'n Bob and Roamer
at the Brighton Marina

Roamer anchored on
the River Yealm

Sea trials

High and dry at Falmouth

The voyage begins.
Departure from
Brighton Marina.
June 1985

Roamer becalmed 500 miles west of Cape Town

Hobart, Tasmania,
December 1986

Bob as Father Christmas, Port Owen, December 1985

The good ship Roamer off the Cabana Jetties, Port Owen

Roamer rounding Cape Horn

The Falklands Disaster:
The foremast sawn off
by the Coastel's anchor
chain, March 1987

Safely moored in Brighton Marina, Jury Rig in position, November 1987

The Junk Rig
Sail System.
Falmouth 1987

Chapter Twelve

Australian Interlude : The Friendly Country

Ah! Ashore again, the pleasures and the temptations, the problems. Always problems, time and money, shortage of both, but I'd probably have them if I'd have stayed at home!

Forget the problems for a few days, it's the weekend in Hobart, the sun shines and the Terra Firma is very firm – I love it.

Alan drives me into the local township of Sandy Bay where I change some traveller's cheques and send telegrams to Terry with news of my arrival.

In the evening more beers in the Club and Alan introduces me all round. Cold beer, hot steak and chips, just lovely! Frank Bennett is the half owner of an antique shop...

"Would you like to see it ? It's a bit of a walk, and a few beers afterwards?"

"Yeah, sure Frank." We take quite a long walk, from Sandy Bay into Hobart Town. We find De Witts Antiques and I am immediately impressed for there right in the front of the display is a perfectly preserved 1940's Ford Prefect! Open the door and inside it smells just like cars should – leather and wood. The antiques too are impressive but not quite my scene. In a room at the back of the shop Frank rigs up a video unit and we watch a 20 minute film about square-rigged sailing ships! Storms, reefing and big waves across the decks – I pretend to Mal-de-Mer! Ha Ha, after 76 days and 7,000 miles HE shows ME a stormy sea film!!

Into town we go and, despite my having been awake for some 48 hours we 'do' the town-hotels, clubs, pubs with plenty of music and singing, finally ending up in a pub close to the Yacht Club at 0530! Phew, way past my bedtime. Back aboard I go to bed until lunchtime, up for a few more beers and a snack, then it's abed in the afternoon and I sleep right through till 0530 Sunday!

I do some typing on the "Ten Day Storm" articles I have written, then take a walk into town to check out "Constitution Dock", where it is planned I am to take Roamer tomorrow, there being no room for me at the Yacht Club Marina. A pleasant walk through the quiet streets, very English, a quiet Sunday morning, people wash their cars, water their gardens. I find the Docks and the Harbour Board office and arrange to come down in the morning at 10. I walk slowly back to the Yacht Club savouring the quiet, even though the legs are rather tired, as is usual after a long sea voyage.

Monday the 8th of December 1986

After a short trip across the harbour, I present Roamer in front of the Harbour Control office and toot a couple of times as instructed, get a cheery wave, and shortly the Swing Bridge traffic lights flash, the bridge swings up, I get the Green Light and enter Constitution Dock. I berth in just about the only vacant spot, and soon find out why it is vacant! The dock is ideal for town, two minutes from Banks, Shops, Post Office etc. BUT, where I berth is also five seconds from a 6-lane road, which is the main highway into town, and all day and most of the night, is frantic with pre-Christmas traffic. Right alongside is a set of traffic lights, so every few minutes all the traffic stops, then restarts like the Monte Carlo Rally getting underway!

Never mind, it is an excellent place to be berthed, despite the traffic, the Museum is just across the road, as is the Customs House, there are Sea Food Restaurants and Take-Aways afloat in the dock, two very cosy pubs. Stan from Kidderminster looks after me in the "Red Lion", and young Tasmanian Tim feeds me the local Cascade Lager, chillingly, in the "Telegraph". The dock is full of interesting yachts and fishing boats, in fact, the whole waterfront area is a living Maritime Museum, a splendid place.

Half of the population of Hobart walks by Roamer and shows great interest in her. This is gratifying and I do a lot of chatting, but it's poor for getting work done, and work I must if I'm to get away before Christmas.

First thing is to organise my visit to Sydney, even though it'll cost me. All my mail is as Rushcutter's Bay Yacht Club and plus I promised to visit the Bradleys, and so I shall I splash out 200 Aus. Dollars on a flight to the big city for Wednesday, hoping to recoup the cost by selling magazine articles. I wander round the pleasant but busy town of Hobart and send off the usual pile of postcards.

Tuesday the 9th of December I do an hour's interview for the "Mercury" the local newspaper, do quite a lot of my jobs, and have an early night, which is surprising, surrounded as I am by pubs and restaurants. I'm amazed at just how many of these there are, plus, in their dozens, cafes and many different kinds of eateries.

Banks and Finance Houses also proliferate. The best memories I have of Hobart though, are the open spaces, parks, children's' playgrounds and fountains - altogether a splendid town.

Wednesday the 10th of December. 0700, I secure Roamer, shut all the sea-cocks, and hope she will be alright. I have to leave her for a week and I'm not happy about it, but local friends and the good guys in the Control office have promised to look after her.

1050. The Air New South Wales jet zooms off from the airport, up into thick cloud for the first leg, which is a short one to Devonport in the North of the Island. A short stop and zoom again, the clouds clear as we fly over the Bass Strait at 25,000 feet. The sea is calm and blue, the Oil Rigs and Islands stand out clearly. Amazing how fast these planes go, 1320 and we land in Sydney, into hustle and bustle, and isn't it hot and humid ? Onto a town bus, and my intro to Sydney traffic and bus drivers. The former horrendous, the latter laconic and friendly. The first driver drops me off at Kings Cross, 10 yards to a bus stop, a short ride to Rushcutter's Bay, a 10 minute walk through a park, and at 1430 I'm at the Cruising Association of Australia, which is very busy with the fleet of yachts in for the Sydney/ Hobart Race. Still, the people are very friendly and give me a large bundle of mail.

I read some of it in the park, but am thwarted by another devil of Sydney, its flies! Tenacious and ferocious indeed they are, but after making my leisurely way back into town, my eyes are full of interest in this big, busy city. I phone Jan Bradley, get directions for the buses, and miraculously by 1730 I am enjoying a welcome cup of tea in the cool lounge of their suburban house at Rozelle. An amazing day, I'm grateful for a quiet evening and early night. Pete and Jan are the Organisers of the Australian Branch of the Junk Rig Association. They put out a newsletter too.

Pete and Jan the friendliest of hosts, busy working people, they give me a key and run of their house. Their telephone is at my disposal too, and I make full use of it to organise my 3 days in Sydney. It's a very big place, but with the aid of the phone, bus timetable, and a map, I am able to make good use of my time. I travel as far as the 20 miles to Avalon Beach to see Mark Davidson, Editor of the "Cruising Skipper" magazine and sell him 600 dollars worth of my articles. I visit the B.O.C. Singlehanders Race Office at Birkenhead Pier Marina to see Robin Knox-Johnston who is chairman of the race committee, to tell him of my plans, and to get information on the racers' Radio Skeds.

It's hot though, and the flies!! And the mosquitoes!! But what a friendly place too. In the middle of the City, in George Street, the shopping centres packed with people in the hot sun, with buskers playing on every corner. Two youngsters play a violin and a trumpet, a bagpiper, and a one-man band. In a pub I ask, "don't the police chase them away?". "No way mate, they're encouraged, makes the place happy". What a difference of attitude to gloomy grey England. "Makes the place happy indeed!"

The bus drivers too, in frantic traffic, with packed buses, have time to answer questions from this hot middle-aged Pom, and put him off where he asks. Big, husky drivers, with shorts and hairy legs, swinging their huge vehicles through the rush hour. Again and again, I'm most impressed with Oz.

Friday the 12th of December. After a busy hot day, Pete takes me sailing in the evening. We slip from his mooring on a brisk breeze and scud down the harbour, under the magnificent Sydney Bridge and out to the famous Heads. We just poke our heads out on principle, so that I can say, "I've sailed through Sydney Heads. We beat our way back up the huge and busy harbour as dusk falls. Boats of all kinds are on the water, floating discos, party boats, floating restaurants, motor cruisers and sailing boats. There are literally hundreds!

Approaching the lovely, floodlit Opera House, we are regaled by Christmas carols sung by children over the loudspeaker system, and a firework display is fantastic! "Good of Sydney to lay all this on for me, Pete". "Ha Ha", he says, "drink this". Coffee and Southern Comfort! A new one on me, but delicious. We make our way back to the mooring, but its almost until midnight, under the stars, at the quiet end of the harbour. A marvellous and memorable evening, Thanks Pete. Thanks Jan.

Saturday the 13th of December.

Train to Canberra, which is an unimpressive journey. The train is fairly clean, but is not a luxury puffer. It takes an age to clear the Sydney suburbs, but after "Liverpool" we are in a big country of wide open fields, cattle, and stunted trees. 1530, Bungendore, " it feels high up, air clear, sky very pale blue". 1615, arrive Canberra, and I'm met by Merv Palmer.

I became acquainted with Merv when he was organising a sailing event as part of the Australian Bi-Centenary Celebrations. I planned to take part, but unfortunately the sponsors dropped out and the event fell through. He shows me around Canberra, the "Capital Territory", and tells me it was built out here in the country to settle the argument between Sydney and Melbourne as to which was to be the Capital. Canberra is a beautiful city, well planned and laid out, with wide roads, parks and lakes – a lovely place. People in Sydney had spoken disparagingly of it, but as 60% of the population of Canberra works for the Government, maybe that's why.

I spend a pleasant 26 hours with Mery and his wife Elizabeth, but have to move on. Before I leave, Merv presents me with a star finder, his for over 40 years from his days at sea. I am most touched by this generous gift.

I ride the overnight coach to Melbourne but don't enjoy it, I can never sleep on a coach and arrive in the Southern City washed out. Into the city centre on the spotlessly clean Underground Railway, a big breakfast and lots of coffee and I feel much better. After an interesting day looking around, I board the "Abel Tasman", the Bass Strait Ferry, quite a big ship, and it's full as the holiday approaches. She carries hundreds of us across a calm sea to Devonport. Off the ferry, onto another bus bound for Hobart, and I'm now weary of travelling.

The bus journey is enlivened for me by Miss Louisa Kley, aged about 9, travelling with her mother Joan. Louisa and I make friends, play games, and we enjoy an otherwise unexciting journey across the Island. It's like being in England, we pass through Launceston, Brighton (a small village incidentally), Swansea, and here we are back in Hobart. Half the bus cheers as we pass Constitution Dock and I can see that Roamer is still there and all is O.K.

Tuesday the 16th of December.

Back aboard, and it's work time. Must get organised for sailing in one week.

Wednesday the 17th of December.

Have arranged for slipping tomorrow, and found a chandlers for food and drink supplies.

Thursday the 18th of December.

To the Harbour Board's "Domain Slip", out of the water and find an amazing number of goose barnacles on her, they're horrible big fat slugs.

Blast them off with a water jet. The rudder knock is found to have a worn bushing on the lower gudgeon. On my own and by previous planning, I rig a block and tackle and remove the entire rudder then renew the bushing plus one other, then reassemble. Putting the rudder back on isn't so easy due to the tightness of the new bushings, and I much appreciate the help of Dave Harrison, the Slip Foreman. I miss the tide though, and have to stay on the slip overnight, but it's an ill wind etc., and I can visit the "Red Lion" for supper, which is just down the road.

Friday the 19th of December.

Back in the water by 0830, back in the friendly dock by 0900, sorting out paperwork and letters. John Day of the Junk Rig Association visits me, and later he and his wife Jill treat me to a massive Curry and Veggies Supper at their home high in the hills overlooking Hobart.

Friday the 20th of December.

Working on the sails mostly, which is difficult, not because of the actual work, which I enjoy, but because of the number of passers-by who want to chat. This is fine, but counter-productive, and also because of the wind which gusts and eddies around the tall buildings across the road.

Sunday the 21st of December.

Mid Summer's Day. Vic Reynolds of the Junk Rig Association comes to visit, then takes me to lunch at a very pleasant restaurant. In the afternoon, more paperwork, typing "The Book" and writing letters. Letters, cards – writing becomes a real drag at times but I persevere and write to the many people who write to me and who I am sure are interested in my exploits. Many of <u>them,</u> but only one of me, that's the trouble. I fill the water tanks and bottles, thanks to the loan of a hose with the correct fittings from Gregg, of the Yacht "Mistra", who has just returned from the Queensland, having been wrecked on a coral reef for three weeks, but he got her off and repaired the damage.

Monday the 22nd of December.

Problem, money, I run out at last. Barclaycard won't let me have any more. Curses on these worldwide computers! Have to prune the stores list, again, I should be much slimmer by Stanley! In the evening John Day calls and takes my mind off work. Along the docks to "Knopwood's Retreat", for a few halves of Draught Guinness. Whoopee!

Tuesday the 23rd of December.

My stores arrive and are stowed. Customs officers, one male, one female, stand and observe the loading of the "bonded stores". Not a great deal, 96 "tubes" of Foster's lager, 4 litres of Port, 4 bottles of Rum, 4 of Brandy. The food stocks don't look huge and disappear easily into the lockers. I take the bus to Sandy Bay and have my laundry done at a launderette while I have a beer with fish and chips. In the afternoon I manage a snooze, and later in the evening it's a Christmas Dinner with Frank Bennett and his elderly American neighbour Bea at the Prince of Wales pub up on Battery Point. Back to the docks early, and in the office where friendly Geoff Gore gives me the latest weather information, and it all looks good to "Go" tomorrow. Geoff also gives me a sailing book with a piece of very creditable poetry in it from him. Back aboard and find a Christmas present from Joan and Louisa Kley, and I'm sorry I missed them. Earlier John Day had given me two big pots of honey – lovely people all, I shall miss them.

Wednesday the 24th of December. Christmas Eve, Sailing Day. Up early and stow all gear for sea. Tony the Customs Officer is aboard at 0840 to give me my clearance. Into town and post last letters home and spend last dollars and cents on bread and cheese. Back aboard, start engine, let go, and extricate Roamer from a tight corner, and then AWAY! The swing bridge is up for me and I motor out through the narrow gap from friendly Constitution Dock. Farewells to the Control staff and few onlookers, and then out into the harbour. One more job – round to the "Diving Board" at the cattle jetty. I moor Roamer under the Board which is a perfect height for me to lash tightly the Blipper reflector and Xenon flasher, both of which have broken fittings. No time for fancy repairs, just a tight lash up with 6mm rope, and hope for the best.

Goodbye Hobart, Tasmania and Australia. It was good to visit – "The Friendly Country".

Chapter Thirteen

Leg 3 – Hobart to Stanley

My ship lies rigged and waiting in the Harbour,
Tomorrow for Old England we sail…

Roger Whitaker

December the 24th, 1987: Motoring South down the Derwent River, we pass a red yacht with lots of people aboard who wave vigorously. They have obviously read the "Mercury" story about the Lone Pom Sailor who plans to set off to sail round Cape Horn on Christmas Eve! (It takes a hard man to do that, but I must be on my way.) At the Iron Pot Light, the wind is in the South, Force 6, and making a very lumpy sea on the ebb tide, it's wet and bumpy already, and I'm not even at sea yet! Nearing Cape Queen Elizabeth it gets worse, wind up to S.W. 7, the seas quite large and surging round the Cape.

I raise a couple of panels of sail to steady her, and motor-sail S.E. across Storm Bay, which is living up to its name today, unlike on my arrival. The ebb helps us to the South, with Cape Raoul 40 degrees on the Port bow, Tasman Island opens beyond it, confirming that we are clearing the land. At 1600 I estimate we are going clear of Tasman Island, shut down the engine and secure it for sea. The wind has settled at S.W. F. 6 and we make S.E. at 4 knots.

The grandeur of the coastline is stunning, high, rugged cliffs, Cape Raoul a jagged sharp headland. Between Raoul and Tasman Island lies Port Arthur, the notorious penal colony of earlier days, which figured largely in the book and film, "For The Term Of His Natural Life". Tasman Island is a high rectangular block, its light perched atop at 905 ft. "Frequently obscured by fog and cloud," says the Pilot.

We scud off to sea on this brisk Sou'wester and soon leave the land well astern heading for the Snares Islands, 120 miles South of New Zealand, 800 miles to the S.E. In deeper water, the seas become more regular and I can leave Roamer to steer herself and fix myself a supper of soup and cheese sandwiches. I'm not feeling at my best, have a heavy cold, sore throat, and not 100% energetic.

Christmas Day, 0100. I awaken from a snooze to adjust the steering and sheets, as the wind has fallen light. Tasman Island light is "dipping" astern, which puts us about 30 miles away. Log: "Sea loppy, Sky half-cloudy, Me half-dopey with Phensics, Lem-Sips, etc. I have a cold, headache, sore throat, diarrhoea, nice Christmas Day! The day improves little except that the seas calm some. I feel awful, dizzy and very weak, just as well there is no wind, I doubt I could do much sail-handling. We get a N.E. breeze in the evening and toddle off to the S.E. I have another bad night unable to sleep for a running nose and fever, but am feeling a little better on Boxing Day.

Journal: "Festive Greetings to All Family and Friends. My health gradually improves, and at Noon we have 182 miles logged, in two days, and to the S.E. too, which is just where I want to go. The sea turns light green in the afternoon, and on checking the chart, I see that we have crossed the 4,000 metre depth line – interesting!

Saturday the 27th. Heading S.E. and going well. Picked up Awarua Radio, which is at Invercargill, New Zealand, and now have their weather information. Invercargill is just North of Bluff, where I worked for 5 months for an Oil Company after leaving John Ridgway in the 77/78 Whitbread Race. That's another bunch of friendly people I'd like to revisit, but not this time I'm afraid. Am just about getting over my illness, and very glad to see it go.

Christmas messages from Hobart. From Louisa Kley and Mum Joan, a box of home-bakes with the message, We hope they will warm the cockles of your heart on your journey. Thank you for making our journey on the bus from Devonport a happier time".

From Geoff Gore, of Hobart Harbour Control, a sailing book, and a poem:

May the breeze that fills your battened sails,
And speeds your homeward run,
May the waves that kiss your gleaming hull,
Be like diamonds in the sun....

...Till the shores of England greet you,
Where 'ere your landfall be,
And know the thrill of conquest,
From our heritage, the sea.

From John and Jill Day, two big pots of honey. Thanks Folks.

The W.S.W. wind is causing our course to be more Southerly than I would like. But against that, it's good to be making Southing into the big wide open Southern Ocean. There are some nasty rocks up around the Snares, like the Traps, Boomerang Rock, etc. I'll be quite happy to get to 49°S., and "run my Easting down".

Sunday the 28th. A good day, feeling almost 100% fit now. 1800, having a pleasant "Happy Hour", Can of beer, 2 glasses of Port, bowl of dry muesli, Tchaikovsky's Nutcracker Suite, all hatches open, making S.E. at 4 knots, all A - O.K. Going along very nicely, she slips through the water well, and I'm glad I took the trouble to slip her and clean off those pesky goose barnacles. Another "goodie" from that operation is that we no longer have a worrying knock from the rudder hangings.

Monday the 29th. Log, 1245. "Noon Fix Result, Whoopee! A 135 mile run to 49°S, 155E. Terrific Eh?" Always nice, these long runs, I love 'em, especially in the right direction.

2000. Rolling down the big swells magnificently at 5 knots. She's terrific in these conditions, off the wind, with plenty of it, she sails like a square-rigger."

I finish the Hobart bread, no more toast till Stanley!

Tuesday the 30th. Advance clocks 1 hour to *G.M.T.* + 12, I really am about half-way now, right round the globe from Sunny England. I hold a "12 hours from Greenwich/50°S. Party", Foster's Lager and Lime, Brandy and Port, Beethoven, Mozart. Barometer is high, nothing can go wrong! Toasts all round, to absent Family and Friends. Beethoven's Triple Concerto allows me to demonstrate my formidable conducting powers. Pity the Orchestra that came under my baton! Maybe I'd better stick to the Southern Ocean Orchestra. Am feeling immoderately happy, Bob Burns and the good ship Roamer at 50°S., free as the wind, if only we had some, but it'll come, or I'll run South to the Antarctic, only 600 miles to the South, till I do get some! I have some lovely company, two beautiful albatrosses, one big brown one, at least 1,000 years old, and a smaller, more attractive one, white and brown, an Alberta-ross? They don't like these no-wind conditions anymore than I do, they fly a little, land ahead of me, pass by like huge rubber bath ducks, then catch up later. I feel they will be with me for some time.

It's very much a time of parties aboard Roamer and ashore in New Zealand. The Southern part of South Island is very Scottish and I listen with great humour to the Aberdeen-type parties and celebrations on the radio. I have no feelings of loneliness, down here in the near- ntarctic seas, a long way from anyone, I'm quite happy.

We continue to make good runs, and, due to the wind I get, am heading to pass South of Auckland Island, which is rather a detour, but I don't have a lot of choice, and I have to go South at some stage, so why not now? At 51°S., it doesn't really get dark at night, I have the twilight glow of the sun all along the Southern Horizon, plus more Aurora Australis, it's a beautiful place down here.

Friday, 2nd January 1987. 1500. "Land Ho". Auckland Island broad on the Port bow. It's surprisingly large and high, I'm 15 miles South of it and very glad to pass by before the short night. Islands down here don't have lighthouses or R.D.F. beacons! There's a lot of marine life about, schools of porpoises, seals, and many birds, albatross of course, pintados, petrels, and many others.

There's no land due East now until Tierra Del Fuego, 5,000 miles distant! Just a few Islands North and South of my planned course along 50°S.

Saturday the 3rd Fog! Thick, cold, wet fog. My am I glad we got past Auckland Island before this lot came in? The fog swirls around us for the next 4 days, making life cold, damp, and worrying. Fog and calms I really do dislike, storms I can fight, but calm weather, and not knowing my position, even if there's no land close, I don't like.

Tuesday the 6th.

I'm still enjoying Radio New Zealand, or Enzed as we used to call it. Enzed or Godzone, *(God's* Own). More English than the English, more Scottish than the Scots, a great country. Radio Dunedin entertains me as I sail past to the South. I really would like to go there again, I had a smashing time working in Bluff, living in the New Eagle Inn, working just across the road in the docks. I had time to take a hire car tour right round the South Island, up the West Coast, past the glaciers sliding down from Mt. Cook, on up the coast to Westport, a coal-mining town, across the mountains to the East Coast, and back to the South across the vast green plains. It's a beautiful country alright, the same size as England, and only 2 million people live there. Back at sea, the wind goes into the West, which might sound good for someone heading East, but in my case this is not so. Winds dead astern are difficult for me to handle as she just won't go dead down-wind unless I'm on the helm, so I have to "tack down-wind". Here I have another problem. Visibility is still poor, I have Antipodes Island to the N.E., and the "Iceberg Line" to the South. This is a pecked line on the chart which informs me that "Icebergs and loose ice may be now, in mid-Summer, is when the big bergs will be breaking off the Antarctic Continent, only 600 miles South of me, and drifting N.E. I have to zig-zag as best I can, along a line I hope is between the two devils, Antipodes and Icebergs. The chart track looks ridiculous, zig-zagging along the bottom of the world. Maybe, but in my position, I do what I have to do.

On Thursday the 8th, at 0330, (it gets light early here), having been in the bows most of the night looking for an island I'm 90% sure is 40 miles to the North, I am fairly sure we are now safely clear of Antipodes, and, ...tired but exhilarated, I run to 30 miles South of the Iceberg Line, then gybe to the N.E. again, happy that there is now nothing between me and Tierra Del Fuego!!

At 1400 on Thursday the 8th of January, I achieve something I never did in all my previous travels, and cross the I.D.L. The International Date Line, that is, which, mostly on Longitude 180 degrees, with a few diversions to avoid splitting some Island groups, divides those countries "West of Greenwich", from those to its East. "Crossing The I.D.L." is always a big day for Circumnavigators, especially loners in small boats, and even more especially, those from the U.K., as this really is "Halfway Point" , and from now on, every mile is "Downhill". "Crossing the Line" also allows us to play with the clocks degree to which we may never again be able to. Travelling to the East, we get back the 12 hours we have lost, one at a time, when we put the clocks on, and we get an advance of the 12 hours we will lose between here and home. We get these 24 hours all in one lump and, therefore gain a whole day. So, today is Thursday the 8th of January, and so is tomorrow. Does this make me one day older than all the people who stayed at home? I wonder, it gets too complicated for me!

Sailor Bob is ale and hearty

LONE SAILOR Bob Burns looks likely to fulfil a strange ambition and sink a pint of bitter at the famous Upland Goose Hotel in the Falkland Islands.

Brighton-born Bob, 47, has left Australia on the latest leg in his solo voyage around the world and aims to clear Cape Horn and arrive in the Falklands by early March.

Bob, who sold his flat in Ditchling Road to fund his adventure, is almost a year behind schedule.

He originally planned to complete the journey in 12 months after leaving Brighton Marina in July 1985, but his voyage has been hampered by appalling weather.

Bob Burns

Letter

He had to stop in South Africa for months until better conditions allowed him to carry on to Australia.

Storms caused further delays between Cape Town and Hobart, a 7,000-mile trip which took 77 days to complete.

In the latest letter to his brother Terry in Brighton, Bob says he hopes to complete the long haul home, up the Atlantic from the Falklands, by May or early June.

He reveals that a "monster wave" had sent his yacht sprawling on to its side, with icy water forcing its way through the battened hatch of his cabin.

"We were only over for about ten seconds, but it seemed a long time, not knowing if she was going to go right over or not," Bob writes.

"It was pretty scary and brought home to me what a wild and dangerous place I was in."

Evening Argus
8th January 1987

Anyway, it's a good reason (or excuse?) for a 180 degree party and much philosophical thinking about being Homeward Bound, is it all worth the effort? can and will everything go O.K. on this, The Leg, for this is it the time when all the dreaming and planning stops and reality stares us in the face. For now, it's, Round The Horn – Or Bust.

By Sunday the 11th, 20 days out, we have 2,000 miles logged, 2,105 to be exact, an average of 105.25 m.p.d., very satisfying and we continue making this good progress at 50°S., but moving North or South depending on the wind, trying to keep a safe 60 miles North of Ice-berg Line. It's rather cool at this latitude, not to say darn cold, but making good progress keeps me warm. Further North is warmer, but has less wind and it is more variable.

Down below, Roamer is her usual cosy quiet self, dry and comfortable for coming down to even if it is cold, wet and windy up top. I'm eating and drinking well and feeling fine. The only real disappointment I have is in the Australian Corned Beef, it's more like Spam!

Sunday the 18th January. Journal: "B.0.C. Racers start today". Yes, the 20 or so contestants in the Round the World Singlehanders Race set out from Sydney, and seeing the amazing speeds these guys achieve these days, I reckon they will be overtaking me in just a few weeks time. I'd visited Robin Knox-Johnston, as Chairman of the Race Committee in Sydney, to tell him my probable course and speed, and my likely whereabouts when they do get to passing me. I'm not sure who would come off worse in a collision, my steel beastie, or a 60 ft G.R.P. racer, I hope not to find out.

I have some busy fun during the afternoon watch. Having collected two buckets of rain this morning, I change my undies and socks, and start to do the laundry, in the cockpit, in a bucket. Mr. Wind sees his chance for some fun and increases quickly. I have to drop the washing, and drop the sails, quick, quick, and it's all very "exciting", wind and waves, ropes everywhere, plus buckets of soapy water sliding around the cockpit. Then, having reefed to this N.W. F. 7- 8, I feel duty-bound to finish the washing, (or dhobeying, as we ex-R.N. sailors would say), so, in full oilskins, with sheets of spray flying across the ship, there I am, arms in a frothy bucket of water, a storm-swept laundry wallah!

In the evening we're fully back to Storm Routine, everything lashed down double, frequent checks on bilges and seacocks, hatch battened shut, and eating Corned Beef Hash supper securely wedged between the cooker and the companionway ladder. Again I am glad to have the viewdome and inside steering wheel, they really are saviours in this sort of weather for checking the rig and adjusting the course without going out into the wet and cold.

It's a mixture of Weather down here though, I often have cause to remember Alec Rose's lament of his Southern Ocean crossing, "Storms and calms". On Tuesday the 20th, after a windy few days, I write, "2100, becalmed again! Consoling myself with Port and Brandies, Mozart and Beethoven, and Gavin Young's "Slow Boats Home", one of the most interesting and fascinating books I've ever read".

"2300, in my quiet frustration I drink 4 large Port and Brandies, eat a whole packet of chocolate biscuits, then go up top and find it so calm I can stroll around the aft doghouse roof to reef the Main to save wear and tear. It's so quiet! Not a sound. A dark orange post-sunset sky to the South and Southwest, a mackerel sky. Barometer at 1000 and rising. All very nice for holidaymakers, not so good for sailors keen to press on. Is that a breeze I feel? Ever optimistic". Looking around the ship, up top and down below, checking stores etc., it occurred to me that I'd been plundering the biscuits a bit lately, so I do a store check, with alarming results. At 28 days out, and probably 40 to go, I only have 17 packets of "useful" biscuits, plus 11 packets of "sweeties". Raspberry shortcakes and chocolates. Not so good, I decide that I must ration myself to one packet every 2½ days. I check and restow lockers down below, throw out some rusting coat hangers. My eyes are always looking for anything which doesn't justify itself for being aboard, if it doesn't, it gets the "float test".

Thursday the 22nd, 0900. "Half-way house! 3,000 miles logged, 3,000 to go to The Horn".

By Sunday the 25th, at 49° - 02'5., 139° 20'W., I am able to transfer the chartwork to "South Pacific Ocean – Eastern Sheet".

An exciting moment, for, although there's not much on it, just the odd reef and Easter Island right at the top, over there on the extreme right, Aha!, the South American Continent and Cape Horn a long way down at the bottom. It all becomes reality, I really am heading across the Southern Pacific for the biggest Cape of all, in many ways. Thursday the 29th• Bad news – we've been pushed North by wind and current to nearly 47°! Not so good, and, it's no warmer up here. Out on deck to do some late night reefing, I'm wearing Damart Thermal vest and pants, Thermal long-johns, a quilted jacket and trousers, and full "Cape Horn" insulated waterproofs, 2 pairs of gloves, thermal and heavy rubber ones, 2 pairs of socks, sea boots, and my quilted fur-lined, ear-flapped hat. It's cold!!

I have a leak on the cooker's paraffin tank and have to resort to "old-time" methods to find it. When I was a rigger for the Civil Aviation Authority, a big part of my job was curing leaks in the dry-air system of helical membrane aerial cables. To find the leaks we then we used a fluid called "Spotleak", but it was only soapy water really, so I make up a little washing-up liquid and water, and with a small paint brush, dab around the joints till I find the leak, then cure it with pipe-jointing compound.

I've been trying on the radio for news of the B.O.C. racers, but have heard nothing on the frequencies that Robin K-J gave me. Surely they must be in radio range by now? Reading the book of the last (and first) Race, "The Ultimate Challenge" by Barry Pickthall, it seems that the mad racers will stay South of 50°S., to reduce the mileage. I hope they do, I don't want any company.

"Lone Sailor's Lunchtime Routine". I fancy a hot toddy today, so, on with the cooker and boil some water, into a glass with a generous tot of "The Famous Bundaberg Rum" from Australia. A high standard of acrobatics is called for during this operation, and for all other operations come to that, for Roamer is, today, a leader in the Bucking Bronco competition. Into the glass of Rum, a spoon of syrup, then a drop of Roses Lime Juice, Oops! Too much lime, need a dose more Rum, it'll be a good toddy today! Kettle boils, water onto Rum, stir well, toddy into saucepan, (a special one for hot drinks), and almost boil it. Into glass, glass into thermal can-holder, equals one strong hot Rum/Lime/Syrup toddy. On with lunch, which is last night's supper left-overs of Potatoes/Onions/Spinach/Runner Beans, into which I throw a packet of soup, Lentil & Lamb today. Heat it and eat it, out of the saucepan, sat at the bottom of the ladder, well wedged in with legs splayed to steady me. One biscuit with soup, kettle on again for a cup of coffee and one more biscuit and peanut butter.

Time for the Meridian Altitude sunsight, so fully dressed in waterproofs, up top and get it, another acrobatic feat to balance myself on the boat, and the sun on the horizon. Zero the log, and back down below with the sextant reading chanting through my mind, 59° 56'.8 Work it out, plot it on the chart, and feel good, having made 120 miles on 105°(T), and 110 miles to the East. Write up Log, Journal, various graphs and tables, relax and read, check the course, and have an afternoon nap. Easy life eh?

Friday the 30th. Am listening to the America's Cup Race Series from Freemantle, on Radio Australia. The Finals are about to commence. 4,000 miles run, 2,100 to Cape Horn. We're having good runs, but the sea is very rough and the motion wearying. Still, we made 357 miles in 3 days out of the last blow.

I have a few problems though. Journal, 31st January. "Am concerned about the colour of the water from the hull tank, it's very murky indeed. Makes me wonder if it is the cause of pins and needles in my hands and feet." I decide to start using the Emergency Water from various bottles and containers stowed around the ship, there should be enough in those to get me to Stanley if I economise, use the tank water for cooking and dilute it with sea water. Another problem, my hands are very chapped and dry, from the constant wind and sea on them. I'll use some "Neutrogen", a concentrated cream "as used by Norwegian Fishermen", it says on the tube, really? I must look after the hands though, I read in Commander Bill King's book, "Adventure in Depth", that he had to make an unplanned stop at Freemantle during his circumnavigation because the skin on his hands just peeled off in the cold and wet of the Southern Ocean.

Wednesday the 4th February. The Yanks trounce the Aussies 4-0 in the America's Cup. Sounds like a commercial fiddle to me, it breaks my heart to think of the money spent on those 12 metre yachts.

We work our way across the vast Pacific, the weather the usual pattern of storms and calms, rough seas and not so rough, but the sea is never calm, and if the wind should drop, life is very painful, being thrown about in the post-storm swells. Mind you, this leg is easy compared to the last. I've hardly had a really severe storm, and none of them more than two days duration. I'm being lucky with the winds too, no disastrous High Pressure head winds as I had in the Indian Ocean, they are what knocks the averages down.

Thursday the 5th. Am feeling much better since changing to the bottled water supply, the tingling sensations have gone and I feel more energetic. It was definitely that hull tank, which has some rust spots in it. I can now see that it was a mistake to use the hull steel as a water tank, or at least I should have either fibre-glassed it, or given it a cement-wash treatment. But I believed the advice I was given that 'Water Tank Black" paint would do the trick. That'll be another big job for me.

One of the many successes on board though, has been the "Fastnet" paraffin lamps, I have one amidships, and one in the aft cabin. They cast a cosy glow which doesn't ruin night vision, and give out a surprising amount of heat.

Maybe we haven't had the terrific storms of the Indian Ocean, but it's still quite rough enough down here. The weariness of the motion came upon me again this morning when we were bouncing to the South. A trip from the cooker to the foremast where I stow the drinking water bottle, all of 25 ft, there and back, left me groaning inwardly as I bounced left and right, off doorways and workbench, grabbing for handholds every inch of the way, putting feet in corners where they wouldn't slip.

Back at the galley, carefully pour water into the cup which is rocking wildly on the gimballed cooker. Fine judgement is required for this. Water into saucepan and onto the burner. Second bruising trip all the way to the foremast and back. This crawling around the ship goes on all day, every minute, when we have rough conditions, which is 75% of the time. Many's the time I slide and hand-hold my way to the sea-berth seat, groan with weariness, slump in the corner and rest, and think, then up to the dome for a look, or do a job, or... every day, every hour, it's a long trip.

Looking ahead, I check the chart of "South Eastern Part of Tierra Del Fuego", to start feeding basic information into my head regarding Diego Ramirez, Cape Horn, lights, distances, and bearings etc. The Admiralty List of Radio Signals says there is a weather report from Diego Ramirez twice a day, in English, for the Drake Passage. That will be useful, I hope.

We bustle and roll our way East, on the 8th of February, we have less than 1,500 miles to go to the Horn! Clocks are now advanced to G.M.T. - 6, and only 2 hours to go to Cape Horn Time. There's plenty to do aboard, as well as running maintenance jobs, plenty of writing too. There's this book of course, which I not only write as I go along, but type too, there are the Sea Letters to the Fan Club.

And I've started on the letters I shall have to send off at Stanley. Can't leave them all till I get there or be writing all the time I'm in port.

Sunday the 8th of Feb. Having been up into the 40°S, partly forced up by wind and current, and partly voluntarily, to keep 60 miles North of the Ice Line, which moves up to 50° hereabouts, it's now time to start heading S.E. for the Horn!

Journal. "I get the feeling we are moving into less - friendly climes. The dozing Southern Ocean giant, having allowed us a fairly easy run from Hobart, is stirring in his deep grey waters. The swells are bigger and longer, the sea is greyer and darker, the wind sounds "heavier".

Oh well, there are really only two ways home from here, and I don't have the fare for the Panama Canal, so S.E. we go, and take what comes.

I have a viewing of Mr. Moon this evening, having not seen much of him lately. He is low down on the Northern horizon, his declination being

28°N., I see from the Almanac. We being at 50°S., he would be low to the North. It's a "Big" world down here, big seas, high pale-blue sky, massively high-piled cumulus squall clouds, a region of extremes. Storms and lulls, sun and squalls, "exciting, ain't it?".

I still hear nothing of the B.O.C. fleet on the radio, but tuning through the wave-bands, I pick up many interesting conversations on the "Ham" network. There's a lot of chat between North and South America, the Antarctic Scientific stations staff and their wives and girl-friends. Also, I've a "Fun" African station on 15,477 Mhz, which jabbers away in French, English, and African. It turns out to be Radio Gabon! What are they doing down here?

By the 10th of February we have 5,000 miles logged and are in a position about, 1,000 miles West of the Magellan Strait. Wow! We really are getting near to Mr. Horn."

There's plenty of wind down here, a Force 9 Sou'westerly gives us a rough ride but good miles. At 52°S., 99'W., we are a little over 1,000 miles from The Cape.

Big news is that at last I have picked up the B.O.C. Fleet network, mainly by luck and tuning through the bands. They weren't on the frequencies or at the times given to me by Robin K-J. I didn't get many positions before I lost them again, but will be better prepared next time.

Thursday the 12th February. Listening in on the B.O.C. radio sked, on 14.240 Mhz, I pick up, "Pedro", in Santiago, Chile who is the Ham operator covering the Race for this area and I get plenty of information and positions, plus weather forecasts, very useful. He tells us there is a deep Low at 53°S., 77°W, giving Easterly gales in the Cape Horn area for the Race leaders. A Canadian, John, aboard, "Joseph Young", has lost his mast and has a damaged coach-roof. He plans to erect a Jury Rig and make for Talcahuano, Chile, for repairs. Poor chap, he has a long haul ahead of him. Pedro gives out plenty of other information and positions, but most of them are well to the South of me.

Sunday the 15th of Feb. We are at 90°W. and three-quarters of the way Round The World. Only about 10,000 miles to Home!

B.O.C. News: A boat called American Flag is way North of the majority of the Fleet, at 52° - 18'S., 103°- 09W., only about 700 miles astern of me. Maybe I can waylay him and get a message to home. For the first time, I regret not having a transmitter, I'd love to be able to talk to these guys, even if only to let them know I'm here!

Tuesday the 17th of Feb. Position, 54° 35'S., 83° - 25'W., Day's run, 165. 165?? No, I haven't started flying a spinnaker, it's just that I haven't had good sun sights recently, and when I did get a good fix today, it put me 45 miles East of my D.R. position. This confirms the fairly strong current indicated on the chart, good, all extra miles are welcome. Only 565 miles from the Horn now and getting excited. Am still trying to intercept American Flag, I believe he is about 150 miles astern making 7.7. knots.

Wednesday the 18th

This evening I reckon that American Flag is very close to me, visibility is poor and I have my all-round white light and the Xenon flasher on. I call him on V.H.F. but hear nothing. I keep watch for most of the night, for a 60 to 70 ft Ocean Racer to come looming out of the murk at 8 knots, but he doesn't.

Thursday the 19th. Listening in on the B.O.C. Chat Show, I hear Hal, of American Flag, telling one of his buddies, "Last night? Oh, I had a bath, changed all my clothes and bedding, turned in and slept like a baby for 8 solid hours!!!" Well, I'm glad he had a good sleep, "I was up watching Hal, even though you couldn't know it I was there".

Getting close now, Noir Island is only 130 miles to the East, "The worse lee shore in the world" is close enough, and I run S.E. as best I can, tacking downwind, with a N.W. gale on my tail. 6,000 miles on the clock today, and only 350 to The Horn.

"CLOSING THE HORN"

Friday the 20th Feb. At 56°S., 76W., the weather is very stormy. I have adopted a "working rig" of just two panels of each sail, which is good for winds of from F.6 to F.10, which is just what we're getting right now.

Log 1330. Something caught my eye astern. Bloody Hell!! An enormous shape in the wake. A swell lifts, and a great big beautiful whale surfs down its face. "Mind my log line", I shout to him! He cruises up the Starboard side, about the same length as Roamer, grey and mottled. He has a magnificent tail. As he moves ahead I rush to the pulpit. He swerves to Port, turns his light green underbelly upwards, and lies there, directly in our path! "Get out of the way!" If we hit him he may lash out with that great tail, but as we close on him he slowly glides to Starboard, gives a flick of his flukes, and is gone. What a wonderful experience, the most beautiful creature I ever saw.

Saturday the 21st. Most of the B.O.C. yachts are past the Horn now, just "Lone Star", and "Colt Byratic" are South and West of me. It's very windy, and I'm hoping that the storm may blow over and give us some "peaceful" weather for a Cape Horn rounding on Monday. I've been tuning in to the Diego Ramirez frequency for weather information, but have heard nothing.

Sunday the 22nd. 56° - 26'S., 69°- 45'W. Cape Horn 87 miles. The stormy winds continue, and the seas very big, but we're well used to them both by now. I've more worries than the size of the waves!

We close the land, and this afternoon I'm confident of seeing the inhospitable islands of Southern Tierra Del Fuego, about which I've been reading and dreaming all these years, will the dream become a nightmare?

At Noon sight time the weather is foul, S.W.F.7 to 8, very rough seas, flying cloud. I get a dubious fix, my eyes watering in the icy wind, which somewhat confirms my D.R. position, but I'm rather nervous. The funny thing is, I could solve all my worries by doing, as "Mark" on "Lone Star", says he will do, a passage far enough South to clear Diego Ramirez, the island group about 30 miles South of the main islands, and of Cape Horn. But - I want to see it, having planned and dreamed all these years, to sail by out of sight, or during the night, is something I can't do. So, reckoning I am 30 miles S.S.W. of the Ildefonso Islands, and encouraged by a barometer reading of 1000 mb, quite high for this region, I head N.E. towards "The Land of Fire". 1655. "Land Ho!!" Low and black, on the Port bow, are the Ildefonsos, a few miles off-shore, and like Pedre Branca at Tasmania, very helpful as position-fixers. It would be difficult to say where I am otherwise, with just a line of grim grey-black mountainous islands across the Northern horizon. My, what an inhospitable place it looks, and is. Get shipwrecked here and no-one will ever find me! Near the Ildefonsos the sea colour changes from the grey of the deep Pacific, to the light bottle-green of the shallow waters of The Horn. The huge swell reduces some, but it remains very rough, and the wind, ignoring the 100 mb barometer, increases to a full S.W. storm Force 10!

Damn! I'm not in a good position, close to the land, night coming on, and a storm a - blowin'. I run North as far as I think is safe, and till almost dark, up to within a few miles of those jagged grim outposts of South America, before reefing right down to the storm triangles. Then I gybe her, and plan to plod slowly S.E. through the stormy night for a rendezvous with Cape Horn, in the morning!

What a night! The terrible icy wind shrieks and howls over us, a near-hurricane, huge, violent seas buffet us, steep and tumbling in the shallow water. In this fearful situation, and I am afraid, I freely admit it, I dare not sleep and keep a lookout as best I can, through the dome mostly, but out in the wild, black night sometimes. Fearing that "Colt Byratic" may come this way, not knowing I even exist, I put on all my lights, and hope that the Finn aboard will be looking out too.

Monday the 23rd of February "CAPE HORN DAY".

Dawn was never so welcome, at 0230, and an easing of the wild storm with it. I see the black rocks of Diego Ramirez, too close for comfort on the Starboard bow, and relieved to know where they are, I alter away from them to the East. The storm has ripped open a foot of stitching on the Mainsail which I must fix soon before it gets worse. But, with full daylight and a further easing of the wind almost a mere gale, I go below and make hot strong coffee, with a good slug of Rum. After the coffee, a big pot of baked beans and corned beef, then more coffee.

Sailmending time, and I spend a very cold hour stitching the seam, a "fun" task in the icy wind and rough seas, but it has to be done, and is. After thawing out my fingers, I gybe and head N.N.E. to close the land again, to find Mr. Horn. The wind is S.W. F.7 - 8, sea rough, but not wildly so.

1155, Land appears and at first I think I have Cape Horn dead ahead, but, seeing more land to the East, realise that it can't be. Checking the chart shows the land ahead to be the Hermite Island group, starkly rugged and beautiful. Ah!, but there, to the East, I know that shape, having gazed at it many times, with dreamy eyes in photographs and paintings, that high triangular rock: THAT IS THE HORN!

I turn East and run down wind, which is very strong again. Having hoisted a panel of sail earlier, I now have to reef right back down to the triangles. I'm very excited. Steering Roamer in these conditions is like handling a dinghy, and taking photos at the same time makes life very "hairy", but today everything is possible!! 5 or 6 miles from the Horn, and I'm speechless with fascination at the sheer size of it, much higher than I ever expected, it's ABSOLUTELY MAGNIFICENT!!!

We continue to run downwind. I'm hungry and have a picnic lunch of Corned Beef, Biscuits and a Beer in the cockpit. All is action, huge seas, roaring wind, photographing, eating and drinking. I'm delirious with happiness, singing and laughing in the storm. Even being thrown into the cockpit from one of my photography positions, and hurting my left hip painfully, can't damp my exuberance.

The wind blows stronger yet and I get the feeling that the seas are steeper and more dangerous as we get closer to Horn Island. A bit of sense comes to me and I gybe away. We are only 3 or 4 miles offshore and maybe the strong East-going current is disturbing the seas. I force myself to calm down, the seas are very big and it won't do to broach here.

Wow! Look, a yacht. Between me and the Horn, so insignificant I hadn't seen him before. It must be the Finn, Petta, in "Colt Byratic". I add to my "things going on", fetch the V.H.F. radio and call him up, but get no reply. He's probably got his hands full, for he is much closer to the Horn than I am, and he disappears entirely in some of the deep troughs.

THIS IS A WONDERFUL EXPERIENCE, AND I SENSE THAT IT IS POSSIBLY THE HIGH POINT OF MY ENTIRE LIFE AND THAT, I SHALL ALL ALMOST CERTAINLY NEVER COME HERE AGAIN.

I gybe again, back towards that fantastic, wonderful rock face, a magnet drawing me towards it, for closer photographs, until the seas become too dangerous again, and gybe away.

A thought comes to me. "Whatever would Sir Francis (Chichester) have thought. A whole race fleet of singlehanders have just passed the Horn, followed by this working-class chappie, Bob Burns, gybing in front of the Rock in a Force 10 Sou'wester, taking photographs, eating a picnic lunch as though he's a-sailing off Brighton Marina!

I know I'm not though, and at 1600, having spent a wonderful afternoon "At The Horn", I officially declare myself past it, and turn away S.E., away from the fabulous rock, Cabo de Hormos, Sentinel of the meeting place of the Pacific and Atlantic Oceans. An impressive, and suitably grim sentinel.

I have a short chat on the V.H.F. to the Chilean Navy post behin Horn Island, a very friendly chappie with quite good English. He is full of amazement and praise for "A Brave Marinero" when I tell him I'm alone in an 11 metre boat. Suddenly I don't feel very brave. I feel deflated, bone-weary , and am glad to roll slowly S.E., away from the Horn and out into the safety of the open sea.

I need sleep, and though my next course should N.N.N., there are dangers that way, so enough for today, I take a last look, maybe forever, at Cape Horn as it fades into the evening haze, go below, and sleep the sleep of satisfied. I HAVE ROUNDED THE HORN – ALONE!!! Tuesday the 24th. I'm up at 0430 after a short but welcome sleep, and gybe to the Port tack and course of N.N.E. for Staten Island, or more correctly, Isla de los Estados, and roll heavily in the still - strong wind and big seas. The wind gradually eases, though the seas don't get much smaller, and at 2030, with my estimates of 40 miles to Staten Island, I make a "safety gybe" to the S.E. for the night. Shortly after, I take a sight of Sirius, the plotting of which puts us only 27 miles South of the Island. How to get into trouble! The Cape Horn Current must still run strongly here. The wind now being fairly light, we roll severely in the swells rolling up from the S.W. (Will the rolling ever stop?)

The end of the last bottle of Bundaberg Rum, is close, so, drinking toasts to all the folks back home, especially Jack & Betty at the Roundhill Tavern, who presented me with a bottle of "Pusser's" before I left I finish it off. Another good reason for getting to Stanley soon.

I sleep for a few hours during a quiet night and at 0230 hoist sail to 3 panels each and gybe her again to a Northerly course. I'm surprised to see a small vessel's lights which cross my bows to the West. In the early light, is that land in the haze to the North? Another hour confirms that it is, and the jagged peaks of Staten Island gradually appear.

After the appalling weather of the past weeks, today is calm and quiet, and as the sun rises, (it's warm!), I open up the ship, all hatches wide open, all wet gear up top and hanging from the rigging and guardrails. It's ages since I was able to have a good dry-out like this. Everything dries, as we are becalmed 15 miles South of Staten all day. I can see the Le Moire Straits, the channel between Staten and Tierra del Fuego, and am tempted to motor to them, and get North of the island, but all I've heard and read about Le Moire, makes me decide not to. Its swiftly changing weather and equally swift tidal currents have wrecked many a ship over the centuries.

A current seizes us here, and in a sea-state which reminds me of a tide-race off St. Alban's Head, we are carried to the East, past the spectacular peaks of Staten Island.

During the afternoon I grab an hour's snooze, and awake to find fog banks drifting down on us from the N.E. and in a few minutes we are in dense, cold, wet and very undesirable fog. I just have time to stow all the "laundry" away before the ship drips with a heavy dew.

The fog only lasts two hours, then clears as quickly as it came down on us. Staten is now to the N.W., the current still carrying us to the East at about 2 knots. A wind pipes up, but from the N.E.! Just where I want to go. What a life! Storms, calms, fog, now a head wind, shades of Tasmania.

But that's how it is, for the next 5 days I have the old familiar struggle into light head winds over the bumpy Burdwood Bank, where the "Pilots" tell grim warning of icebergs grounding, and lying in the fog banks, but I see none. We work our way painfully North and East. I worry about Beauchens Island. A rock outcrop 25 miles South of the Falklands. In more fog, we seem to be drawn to it, like a magnet, but, on Sunday the 1st of March, the elements decide they have played with us enough, the visibility clears, there is no Beauchens, and on a Westerly F.7, we bound North. There is a last night at sea to be survived, surrounded by fishing vessels and other ships, then, come the dawn, the Falkland Islands lie low and grey to Port.

With the Lo-Kata R.D.F. I pick up the radio beacon at the new Mount Pleasant Airport, which helps me to identify the coast and lead me to Cape Pembroke lighthouse, tall and conspicuous on a low spit of land, easy to see with its black and white bands.

The winds, which eased during the night, now pick up strongly from the West, and we have a long, cold, wet battle up the South to Port William. The small waves sheet back down the deck from the bows like icy bullets, but we must struggle on till the last. On and on up the long Sound, but at last, at last we motor through The Narrows" and into Port Stanley, to tie up at the Town's Public Jetty, thankfully!

Chapter Fourteen

Port Stanley – Triumph and Disaster
During which 'Roamer' is dismasted

Customs and Immigration Officers come aboard and "enter" me into the Islands. Steven, the Customs man, is also the Harbourmaster's Assistant, and presents me with a Bill for £30 for Harbour Dues.

"Hell", I protest, "That's dearer than Brighton Marina!"

"Ah", he replies, "But not so exciting though, eh?"

Well, that true, but still a painful blow. "Immigration" is a plump, bearded, cheerful policeman. As he climbs onto the jetty, his large peaked hat blows into the sea and I have to do a quick rescue job with the boat hook. "I don't like boats", he says, pulling his dripping hat down firmly.

So, here we are, at Port Stanley in the Falkland Islands, another of the "Romantic Places" I've long wanted to visit. The "Deep South" has for a long time been a fascination to me. The stories of Scott's and Shackleton's heroism in the early days of Antarctic exploration thrilled me when a boy, (and still do), and now, although not exactly "down the ice", I'm fairly close.

When I was in the Navy, I tried hard to get onto the "South America and South Atlantic Station", whose ships included H.M.S. Protector, and later H.M.S. Endurance, the Ice Patrol ships, based at Stanley. I never did get any of the ships or station I volunteered for though. Rumour had it there was an office in "Naval Drafting" which sifted these "Requests for particular Stations", and sent the volunteers to the opposite ends of the Earth. Sailors keen to see the Far East would find themselves on Fishery Patrol off Iceland, those choosing "Home Waters" would roast up the Persian Gulf! Certainly my stream of requests for the cold seas of the South Atlantic had me sweating in Singapore or Malta! That's Naval Drafting for you. My friend George Bunkin made it though, on Protector <u>and</u> Endurance. George sent me a set of photographs of "The Ice" which I still treasure.

But here I am at last, in the harbour at Stanley, with Roamer lying quietly at the end of the Public Jetty, while I sit in the cockpit, viewing the scene, much relieved to be in the harbour, and triumphant at having Rounded the Horn. The brisk West wind blows down the sound of the Inner Harbour and moans in the rigging but we are safe in Port.

Stanley is a small but attractive town, very much on the lines of Norwegian or Icelandic communities, with multi-coloured wooden houses grouped fairly closely on a hillside. They face to the North, to the warmth of the Sun, their backs turned to the Antarctic winds. The impressive Cathedral sits squarely at the foot of the hill, and other notable buildings front the town along Ross Road. The well-known three-gabled green front of the Falkland Islands Company's Offices, the F.I.C.'s West Store, the Globe Hotel, and Aha!, there it is, the Upland Goose Hotel, another of my ambitions is at hand.

I'm a happy chappy, and having secured Roamer, and stowed all sea gear, I set out to explore for the basic necessities of life, like Money, Bread and Beer. The first I find at the Chartered Bank where I can draw £50 a day on my cheque book, no problem there. Bread is a problem though. Shopping in the West Store, I can't find any. "Where do you hide the bread?" I ask a young assistant. "No bread" she tells me rather sharply. The Bakery closed on Friday." Help! The Bakery closed, is there only one, and it's closed just as I get here? It appears so. Bloody marvellous, why me? I do love to get a crusty cheese sandwich down me on arrival in port.

Beer is no problem of course, it seldom is, given that you have money. Not a lot of decisions to be made as to where to have a drink either. There's the "Globe", just 200 yards from Roamer, straight in from the jetty, or the "Victory", 100 yards further up the hill, and that's it. There is a third pub, I'm told, the "Rose", but it's closed at present for renovation. The Upland Goose, it appears, is strictly hotel patrons only, we'll see about <u>that</u>.

There's a healthy packet of mail for me at the Post Office, and I send off arrival telegrams. To Brother Terry and The Family, "Cape Horn Sailor Arrived Stanley. All Well." In the mail are plenty of Good Wishes and Congratulations, plus a book from my old skipper John Ridgway, its envelope covered in red 26p stamps! J.R. also warns me of weather conditions between here and Rio. "Beware of ambush", he says.

The strong winds of Monday ease, and during the week I enjoy myself nosing about, making friends, soaking up the atmosphere of this fascinating place. It's like a small English town dropped off into the South Atlantic, with a steeped-in history of seafaring and the sailing ship era. The English town might be Whitby, for Stanley reminds me of that fairly remote, cold and windy town on the North East coast. I used to go there quite often in my rigging days to service the radio equipment at the Coastguard Station.

Reminders of the old sailing ships are all around, wrecks and hulks abound, some of them still in use as store-rooms for the Falklands Island Company, others just wrecks, lying forlornly on the beaches or, like the iron three-master "Lady Elizabeth" still standing proudly upright on the shoals of Whalebone Cove. "Condemned at Stanley" an informative little booklet by John Smith of Stanley, records 16 wrecks in the Inner Harbour alone.

Then there's the more recent history of General Galtieri's Argentine troops invading the islands only five years ago. Few signs of that invasion remain, except for the still-heavy Army presence. I was very impressed though, by the 1982 War Memorial, which stands to the West of the town, near to where a large new hospital is under construction. The Memorial is a fine one, and lists the names of all who lost their lives, and the ships which were sunk, as it says in bold words, "To Liberate Us." The Memorial was raised by Public Subscription and built by local labour, without pay, in their spare time.

Terry phones with further congratulations, and is all agog with questions about Cape Horn and Stanley. So do B.B.C. Radio Brighton and I do rather a garrulous interview for them.

Stanley is definitely "my kind of town", very basic and unsophisticated, just like me! Just like the inhabitants too, who have no airs and graces about them, they call a spade a spade, and I get on just fine with them.

The "Globe" is a natural "watering place" for me, mostly in the evenings, and I soon make many friends. Ron Buckland, the Licensee, is ex-Portsmouth, and ex-policeman. His pub is full of characters, like Les, his potman-cum-barman, who comes complete with a "West Ham" woolly hat, even though he's a Liverpudlian. Les is the good chap who lights the blazing peat fire on the cooler evenings, which are most of them now, as the Southern Winter approaches early, for we are still at 51 South, only 300 miles North of Cape Horn's latitude.

Sailor's Falkland homage

LONE sailor Bob Burns is to make a special pilgrimage to Goose Green.

Bob, who served with the Royal Navy, has arrived in the Falkland Islands after rounding Cape Horn on the toughest leg of his solo voyage round the world.

In a 20-minute telephone call to his brother Terry, Bob said he would visit Goose Green and San Carlos Bay to pay his respects to British troops killed in the Falklands war in 1982.

Terry said Bob, who left Brighton Marina in July 1985, was tired but elated at reaching the islands after narrowly escaping death in a severe storm two days before tackling Cape Horn.

He said: "Bob was very lucky to survive.

"He was almost dashed onto the rocks of the Diego Ramires Islands near Tristan da Cunha but managed to escape disaster.

"He had a fantastic reception when he reached the Falklands — and his first pint of British bitter in 18 months!

"He bumped into a group of tourists from Redhill and they made a tremendous fuss of him.

"He's planning to leave Port Stanley next week after visiting the battle sites.

"It's quite an unusual thing for Bob to do, but that is how he feels at the moment.

"He tells me the boat is in good shape and dozens of Falkland islanders have offered him help with repairs.

"He should arrive back at Falmouth in about ten weeks."

Bob, 47, who sold his Ditchling Road flat to fund the trip, has already started a book on his adventures and plans to continue writing on his return.

Evening Argus
7th March 1987

205

Apart from the fire, the pub is pretty much bereft of comforts, a good old "spit and sawdust" pub, the like of which I haven't seen for many a year. The toilet is really awful, painted black, rather grotty, but covered with "interesting" graffiti! I love it.

Just up the hill is the "Victory" bar, and bar it is, for it can hardly be called a pub, as it comprises of one small room. Bill and his customers make me very welcome, it may be small, but when crammed full of soldiers, sailors and locals, it's very warm and very friendly.

Around the corner from the Victory, is the "Woodbine Café," wherein I was able to buy the best Fish and Chips I came across on the voyage, really good, and plenty of them. I just had to buy one of their sweatshirts. "Woodbine Cafe – The Southernmost Fish & Chip Shop In The World"!! (And you can have a glass of wine with your F & C, Red or White!)

In these three cosy social centres I meet a large proportion of the population of Stanley, and hear plenty of stories, have lots of laughs. One thing I want to know.

"How come the lighthouses are out of action. Is there a security reason?"

"Nar", says one of the crew of the "Monsunen" the F.I.C.'s coaster, "The Argies vandalised them while they were here, and then, after the war a bunch of R.A.F. guys were sent down to the lights, to clean them up, but got their orders all wrong, maybe, and cleaned them out, threw all the gear away entirely. Now the Islands Government and Trinity House are arguing about who pays to re-light them. Meanwhile, no lights at Cape Pembroke or Mengeary Point."

I also hear that M.P.A., or the new Mount Pleasant Airport, is having a new harbour, Mare Harbour, developed close by, and the day may not be far away when Stanley finds itself out in the cold. The locals seem unworried. I suspect that new airports and wide-bodied jets do not impress them.

Another topic of interest to me is the foreign fishing fleet, some of which I saw when approaching the islands. It appears that literally hundreds of fishing boats work inside the 200 mile "Exclusion Zone" around the islands. These fishermen pay the Government a royalty which now makes the islands self-financing. In Berkeley Sound, a huge natural harbour to the North of Stanley, the Fishing Fleet's "Mother Ships" are at anchor, receiving the catches from the trawlers, lying there for months on end. They are mostly Japanese, Taiwanese, Korean, Polish and Spanish boats. Prior to the 1982 war, these foreigners used to trawl the ocean around the islands for free, paying only minor amounts for facilities in Stanley, such as fuel or water. Another case of an ill wind blowing somebody some good.

I work too, of course, but there's not much to do aboard the Good Ship Roamer, and I'm in no great rush to get away. Billy and Dennis, two pals from the Victory, introduce me to Mike Robson, who runs a farmstead down at Goose Green. "Would you like to come for a visit, Bob?" Wow would I? Goose Green is probably the most famous name of all from the '82 war, except maybe for San Carlos Water and the Mountain peaks. But I have a better idea. Why don't we take Roamer up Choiseul Sound and stay the weekend? It sounds like a great idea and we plan for it by buying a couple of charts and "Falkland Island Shores", a Pilot Book by Ewen Southby-Tailyour, the notes for which gave much detailed information to our Forces in the war and enabled the amphibious landings to take place. It is a fascinating book, full of information and hints from a man who obviously loves these Islands.

So we plan to go on Friday, all is well, I'm in harbour, having a good time, achieving ambitions. Another one is to have my "Pint at the Upland Goose." Des King, the hotelier treats me to this pint, gives me a very pleasant evening, and has his daughter take a photograph of the happy event. Thanks Des.

Ah! but such are the way plans are made by men and unmade by the elements. Dennis and Billy can't leave till Saturday, O.K. no problem, we'll go then, but on the Friday, it all goes wrong.

Having a drink with Ron in the Globe at Friday lunchtime, I get talking to some "squaddies", young soldiers. They are a bit glum, not much fun for them down here, nothing to do, nowhere to go. We get friendly and the outcome is I invite them back aboard in the afternoon. We take a carry-out" and have a fun time with beer and cheese sandwiches, (I found some bread!) and bagpipe music, some of the lads being Scotties. At 1700 they have to be making their way back to Base, "It's a long walk." Walk? why don't I run them down there, to the East end of the harbour, in Roamer, no problem? It's a little windy, but then it has been since I arrived.

So, all aboard, let go the ropes, run down the wind and tie up again alongside a huge "Coastel", an accommodation barge which is anchored just off the shore. It's not the one they live on, theirs is in a restricted corner, and the wind is a little more blowy now. "Why don't you come up to the N.A.A.F.I. for a couple of wets, Bob?" Why don't I? the wind is breezy, but alongside the Coastel it's calm and protected. We put out four headropes, plus the usual stern lines, springs and fenders. She should be O.K. here for a few hours, and I'll take her back to the Public Jetty later.

Up at the "Shed",as the N.A.A.F.I. is known, all is fun and warmth. I take the Port Owen Songbook, the beer flows and the hours pass. At Closing Time it seems not a good idea to return to Roamer and move her, I have had quite a lot of beer, and a few rums. It's quite windy, but surely Roamer will be O.K. in the lee of that enormous barge, and with plenty of ropes out, won't she? I sleep aboard the Army's Coastel.

DISASTER

Saturday morning, 0600. I awake with a cold sweat of apprehension sweeping through me. Where am I? Hell, where's Roamer? Even in the depths of the huge accommodation barge I can <u>feel</u> the wind, vibrating the structure. I <u>know</u> it's all gone wrong. Up, a quick coffee, and out into the wind – The Wind!! It's a monster! I can hardly stand in it, and have the greatest difficulty in making into it for the half-mile to the other Coastel, where I left Roamer in the only-breezy conditions of last evening. I hurry as best I can, for I just <u>know</u> she's in trouble, but I'm almost blown off my feet by the blast. Staggering across the long foot-bridge to the barge, I am pressed to the lee guardrails, the wind a shrieking, tearing beast. White water flies under the bridge, spray fills the air. I'm terrified, thinking of what I will find when I get to her. Off the bridge, along the deck, across the stern, and ... Oh NO!!!

My worst fears are realised. I look over the side. Poor Roamer rears and wallows beneath me, already a wreck. The wind has veered from the S.W. of yesterday, to N.W. and now howls straight down the Sound of the Inner Harbour, a fetch of about three miles, funnelling down between the hills. In this N.W. fury of wind, the waves, <u>in the Inner Harbour</u> are 6 to 8 feet high, short and steep, and during the night chafe and strain have broken all the ropes I put out, and which "ought to be O.K."

Well, they're not O.K. now, they're all parted, and Roamer has been driven down the Coasters side into a huge and deadly massive anchor chain, which angles down from the barge's deck. Pinned against the side by the wind, and thrown about by the waves, her Mainmast has already been sawn through by the chain, and lies in the sea, ropes and splinters are strewn over the aft deck and doghouse. After the Main had broken off, she drifted back again, and now that deadly chain is sawing through the Fore, is already halfway through it.

Though horrified and sickened by the sight, I can also see that if the Foremast goes, she will drift aft again, and the next anchor chain is much lower. This will tear the stern gear off her, completely wreck the deck gear, and then what's left of my once-beautiful ship will blow clear to be destroyed on the rocks and shoals to leeward.

Imagine how sick I feel, having brought this faithful ship three-quarters of the way round the world, past the stormy Cape Horn, and now I've all but lost her, in harbour, due to my negligence in leaving her uncared-for last night, just one night, but the Gods of the weather allow no mistakes.

Sick at heart I may be, but the situation calls for action. No help is around, no-one appears to live on this Coastel. If she is to be saved, it is I who must save her. Over the side I clamber, and drop onto Roamer's rearing deck. Ropes, sails and wood splinters lie in utter shambles. Down below there is an equal shambles, the viewdome has been smashed, shards of Perspex cover the floors, books and cassettes are strewn around, water is everywhere. Priorities first though, more ropes to prevent her drifting further aft. The two 18 mm Nylon Anchor ropes, they are in the furthest aft stowage, under quite a lot of other gear, but I dig them out, quick.

Up on the foredeck, I have to sit down, as the only way I can steady myself to uncoil the ropes. I sort out the first, and double it. My eyes are full of water, is it the wind, spray, or am I crying for my ship? Whichever, I wipe the eyes clear, and, carefully choosing my moment, dodge under the deadly chain as Roamer plunges down into a trough. The Starboard foredeck guardrail stanchions have already been wiped out, I must be very careful here. Or must I? This is life or death for Roamer, why not for me too, who has put her in this situation. But the will to live and to save my ship is strong, up in the bows I clear away the broken ropes ends, secure the doubled-up Nylon and heave the rope onto the Coastel's deck. Another dodgy run under the anchor chain, climb up the Coastel's side. Rain and spray drench me. Hurry though, hurry, the cruel chain bites into that beautiful mast. Even in this tragic situation I marvel at the strength of it, how even now, half-sawn through, it stands tall and proud, resisting that terrible chain-saw. Richard Mason can be proud of his craftsmanship. I take the Nylon rope as far forward as possible, avoiding chafe as much as I can, and secure it to a strong cleat.

Back aboard, a second death-defying venture on the wild foredeck, under the chain, secure the second rope, up on the Coastel, and secure it. I try to pull her forward , but the wind and sea are too much for me.

Already I'm half exhausted from climbing about in the screaming wind, flying spray, pouring rain.

What now? At least she is secure for a while. I expect the mast to go at any moment, but there is nothing I can do for it. Help is what I need, to pull her forward from under that merciless chain, which is battering the decks as she plunges and rears. The Port side is getting cruel treatment as she pounds onto the Coastel's side. Oh how it hurts me to see it all. Better try for some help though. I hasten back to the Army's Coastel, but get little joy.

"Sorry Chum, but everyone's just getting up."

"Don't you have an Emergency Party, as we used to in my Navy days?"

"Well yes, that's the Inniskilling Fusiliers in that cluster of Portakabins over there. There should be a Duty Officer."

Indeed there is, but he also has only just risen, and is half asleep. Fortunately his Sergeant arrives and is much more use, he promises me two men, shortly.

I stagger back to Roamer through the roaring wind. While I've been gone the Foremast has broken off and only the Nylon lines hold her from certain destruction.

The two soldiers arrive. Bloody Hell!! <u>These guys</u> fought off the Argies? Surely not. Two half-grown skinny denizens of the back streets of Belfast are here to help me, and are no help at all. They have less strength in <u>them</u> than I have in me and we are unable to move Roamer forward at all. Damnation!! I send them off to beg for more men, but from their looks I know they won't try very hard.

After a while I go back to the Sergeant again, begging "Please Sarge, my whole life is being battered to pieces out there." He sounds like a good man and promises more help, six men this time. Again I totter and stagger back into the gale, which has relented not a bit, force myself through the torrent of wind, back to my poor ship, but unable to help her, painfully watching her torment. The harbour is a maelstrom of white water, I can't think of taking her off the Coastel by engine, we'd just be blown away.

"Looks like you got trouble, Pal." A North-country voice speaks the truth.

"Yeah, I do have a problem."

"Can we help? There are four of us on board." It's the Engineers of the Coastel, and they, good chaps, and me, almost at the end of my strength, do manage to pull my poor battered ship forward 50 yds and from under that deadly chain. We secure the ropes, and put out fenders, rubber tyres, lengths of rope, anything, to try to save her from further damage till the wind should ease.

A Corporal and six beefy Northern Ireland soldiers arrive, too late, but I thank them for coming, and their Sergeant. The Engineers take me inside from the tearing wind and feed me strong black coffee which I drink from a cup held by shaking hands.

What now? Well, she's safe for the moment, but is still being thrown against the Coasters side and is still in some peril. At the moment I still have a hull, engine, steering gear etc, and, apart from masts and sails, am still a going concern, but how long will it blow for?

I go aboard and start clearing some of the debris, on deck and below. She rears and plunges, bounces off the Coastel, sounds of anguish squeal from the ropes and the hull. I can't leave her here for another night, she'll never survive it!

Short of ideas, I decide to go into town and ask Les Halliday the Harbourmaster if he has any. An army lorry gives me a lift which is just as well for I would never have been able to walk the two miles into the wind, I'm whacked. More problems, it's Saturday and Les isn't there, his office locked. Damn.

I go into the Globe for a rest and a drink. "Hell, Bob, you look rough, what's happened, where's Roamer?" Friendly Ron gives me a beer and a rum, I need both, and tell him the sad tale.

"What are you going to do then?"

"Wait till the wind goes down, I suppose."

A short, stocky chap detaches himself from a group of young local guys in the corner. "That won't happen for 48 hours, maybe more," he says.

"Mike Mckie" says Ron.

"Hi Mike." I tell him the situation, talking about it seems to ease the tension in me. He listens quietly, eyes me steadily, he looks like a useful fella to have around in a crisis.

"Is your engine O.K.? What do you have?"

"A 42 H.P. Perkins Tractor engine, 20-inch, 3-bladed prop."

"Hmmm", he says, "that ought to get you off the Coastel and back up here, wanna try? Me and the boys will give you a hand."

"I'm game Mike, but I don't want anyone hurt, suppose we have a look-see first?"

"O.K. lets go."

He gathers three of his mates, we pile into a Landrover and back to Roamer. It's still very windy, but just a little less so. Mike and I weigh up the situation, decide to give it a try, and lay our plans. He plus one aboard me at the controls, the other two on the Coastel to let go the ropes. Bow lines first, then I will "spring her back" on a doubled-up back-spring to force the bows out against the wind. We lay the plans carefully, there will only be one chance.

First I have to clear all the ropes and debris from the hull. I cut and hack without thought of saving anything, no time for that. The masts and trailing rigging blow away in the fierce wind, but we manage to keep the sails aboard, and lash them down.

Time to go. I started the engine earlier, and it warmed up whilst I cleared away the masts and rigging. I bring her forward a few yards, Mike and the lads ready the ropes.

"O.K. Mike? Let go forward, and hold on tight." The bow lines come flying on board, half astern on the engine, and the Port quarter crunches against the Coastel as we strain against the back springs to force the bows out. Slowly, rearing and plunging, she comes away, the quarter is taking a bashing, but out we come.

"O.K., let go the springs," I shout, "Quick as you can." I stop the engine, the last ropes fly onto the deck. A quick check that none are in the water, then it's Full Ahead and Hard a Starboard to get her away. Hell, that forward Coastel anchor chain is close, but it's "Go" time, no turning back. The bows blow off to Starboard, rearing wildly, Midships the helm to stop the stern swinging, the chain passes very close down the Port side, and we're away. There is no time for feelings of relief at getting away though, the full force of wind and sea hit us, solid sheets of water fly across the boat.

"Get below Mike, there's a bottle of rum down aft."

Mike and his mates clamber down the hatchway, and I begin an hour-long battle against the wind and sea... Beating, yard by yard, into short steep waves and howling wind, with constant sheets of icy water blasting aft, making it almost impossible to see. But, yard by yard, we make it, working our way not only West, but a little to the South too, to close the shore where the waves are smaller. As time goes on, less and less water sweeps over us until at last I can see the Public Jetty and Mike's other mates waiting to take our lines.

Phew! what a battle, but we make it. At the jetty it's not all that calm, but the wind has backed to the S.W. again, and we are able to "hang off" just one of the bollards, with <u>eight</u> bow lines out.

My saviour Mike, and his courageous mates, depart. The pub is shut now, but I promise to meet them this evening for "drinks all round", the least I can do for their marvellous help, but they are unassuming. "Ah, it was nothing at all" they say.

With the wind blowing us off the jetty, 6ft waves still rolling down the harbour, and no masts to steady her, Roamer rolls abominably. But, I feel more than lucky to still have her, and to be alive and all in one piece myself.

Down below, I wander around, gradually, mechanically, cleaning up the mess, stowing all the gear, cleaning the floors, pumping the bilges, checking for damage all round. My mind starts nibbling at the edges of the problem. "How do I get her home now?"

I have often said, and believe it to be true, that I can and do, lose my temper quickly and throw short sharp tantrums at small irritating problems, or irritating people come to that, but, faced with a major problem or danger, I become very cool and clear-thinking. I certainly do have a major problem here, and instead of sinking into despair, or tearing my hair, my mind starts this "nibbling at the problem", circling it at a distance, not getting into it too deeply yet, whilst mechanically cleaning up the ship.

I also have two hours sleep, for I am very weary, cold, wet and hungry. Sleep first though, then up for a small hot meal, and to the Globe. I need company this evening.

Offers of help, and helpful suggestions, come from these friendly folk, and rough humour. I said they were a very basic people here, and so they are, I have to put up with a lot of jibes, like from Les, who removes the photo of Roamer from the cabinet on the bar, covers the masts with a piece of cardboard. "There's your ship now Bob." But I can take it, it's only what I was used to in Navy days, or on the rigs, and none of it is cruelly meant. The wry smile on my face is only strained by a woman in the Victory who finds the wrecking of Roamer absolutely hilarious. I return to the Globe and treat Mike and the lads to whatever drinks they want.

Sunday the 8th of March 1987. After a poor night aboard, cold, uncomfortable with too much to think about, I move into action early. The gale still blows strongly but has moved further into the South, and the waves in the harbour are much smaller. I get Roamer back alongside the jetty and make a start on clearing the decks so that I can assess the damage.

Struggling in the wind, I get both sail bundles up onto the jetty, the wind won't allow me to unroll them for a good look, in fact I have to lash them down, rolled up, or they'd blow away, it really is still windy. It appears, though, that the foresail is a complete write-off, the sail torn to shreds, all the battens broken. But the Main, probably due to there being less pitching while the Mainmast was being demolished, looks more hopeful.

Clearing all debris from the decks and cockpit, I then wash down with many buckets of water, and just to have clean decks boosts my morale surprisingly. I saw off the jagged remnants of those lovely masts, and wrap the stumps in several layers of black plastic bags, to keep the rain out.

Now that I can see the decks, I can assess the damage more easily. Well, what's the situation? The viewdome has a large hole smashed in it, and is covered by the ex-boat cover, loss of the viewdome will be inconvenient, but no big problem. The Levanter self-steering gear is smashed, and looks unrepairable. Although this is a blow, it's not disastrous, I've long had my doubts as to its efficiency, and have often wondered how much Roamer steered herself, and how much the Levanter did. So I reckon we can live without it. The L.V.M. Aerogen generator has gone, and this is a blow, for that was one of the pieces of the ship's equipment I really did value, but again, not a disaster, Roamer was always designed to be able to operate without electricity, and so we will.

Right forward, the 60lb C.Q.R. anchor's plough has been squashed flat, and the stemhead fitting bent out to Starboard. The pulpit frame is also bent over, though not a lot. The Port ship's side, for 10ft aft from the bow, took the worst of the pounding against the Coastel, and is badly knocked about. The toe-rail is bent inboard, and the deck plating bent and buckled in places. Looking over the side I can see that the plating has been battered and pushed in between the frames, but appears to be unholed. At first inspection I reckon this fairly minimal damage to the side to be due to the fact that Roamer is very strongly constructed, and has frames every half-metre, rather than the more usual one metre spacing.

The four Starboard foredeck guardrail stanchions have gone, the aft five bent flat to the deck. The Port side stanchions are O.K. The odd grabrail is bent, some paintwork has been damaged, but that seems to be the total of the damage, plus of course, the loss of the masts, and damage to the sails.

Bad enough of course, but when I recall the battering she was taking under that terrible chain, I can only think myself lucky that it's not worse.

Storm hits a world dream

ROUND-THE-WORLD yachtsman Bob Burns has had the dream of a lifetime shattered by the worst Falklands storm for 40 years.

But the Brighton sailor still hopes to limp home under jury rig following the disaster 7,000 miles from journey's end.

Bob's 36ft cruiser Roamer was moored in Port Stanley harbour when the storm ripped the boat from its moorings.

Both masts and most of the yacht's steering equipment were washed overboard.

Bob was in Port Stanley waiting to set off on the last leg of his single-handed 27,000 mile lone trip, which he started in July 1985 after selling his Ditchling Road, Brighton flat.

The catastrophe has left the 47-year-old sailor "heartbroken" but his brother Terry, of Upland Road, Hollingdean, says he is determined to make it home under sail.

He said: "Even though both masts have been destroyed Bob is going to put up some emergency rigging to see if he can make it.

"He is a determined man and he couldn't just watch his life's dream collapse like that.

"Bob is so single-minded that I'm confident he can make it even though a journey of this length with emergency sails must have the odds stacked against it."

The loss of self-steering equipment, sails, the generator and stores brought Bob close to giving up and in a phone call to Terry he described his "bitter dismay" at watching the storm smashing his steel-hulled cruiser against the harbour walls.

Luckily the construction of the boat left the hull without serious damage and Bob now intends to wait for the best weather possible before heading north to Rio de Janeiro.

Return

If he makes it there he will set sail for the Azores for the last leg back to Falmouth.

He will have to steer the boat manually, staying awake for long periods.

Terry added: "He was due back in June but this will now take three or four months.

"Roamer is his life and he couldn't give up without trying to make it home."

Family and friends had planned a huge civic reception and welcome home party in Falmouth for his return in the summer.

Terry said: "We will still have the big welcome but it is going to be a lot later than planned."

Evening Argus
13th March 1987

215

I'm quite sure that she only survived the battering because she was very strongly constructed, and above all, constructed of <u>Steel</u>. A wood, or fibreglass hull would have been smashed to pieces.

So, what's the situation? My thoughts are that I have a watertight hull, hence a home, I have an engine and steering equipment in good order, and if I can get a Sailing System organised, we're back in business.

More Positive Thinking shows that not only is Roamer in say, 75% working order, but that I am in good condition, and no-one else was hurt in the operation to save her. As an ex-Oil-Rig Manager, I can really appreciate this fact. Equipment is costly but can be replaced, not so people.

I spend the remainder of the Forenoon clearing up, the sun even shows himself through ragged clouds now and then. My tall, young friend Tim, with Veronica, Ronnie to her friends, who is the shop assistant I first spoke to about the bread, come down to commiserate, and then I join them for the "Glory Hour", in the Globe, from 12 to 1, the only hour's opening on a Sunday.

RECOVERY

"It's no good crying over split masts" says one of my "friends" in the pub. "Who's crying?" I growl. And who is? I've had a disasters before, and no doubt will again, an adventurous life cannot be a safe one, the art of living is to survive, and survive I will.

At 0600 on the Monday morning I set off in full waterproofs, walking boots, and rucksack on my back, to search the East end of the harbour for the masts, so as to recover whatever rigging and fittings I can. The wind still blows, but is at last easing. I walk a lot of miles along the rocky, kelp-strewn beaches, past the Coastels, right round the Whalebone Cove to the North East corner of the harbour, but not a thing do I find. I can hardly believe it, but Les Halliday tells me later that he's not surprised, "There are strong currents here, Bob, they've probably run out sea." He warns all the boats' crews to watch out for them.

That's the start of the recovery, the walk did me good, allowing me more thinking time, and the thinking is, that although the good people of Stanley are kind and helpful, as they always are to visiting "yotties", with their offers of telegraph poles for masts, and help in fitting them, I'm only going to stick with my designed-in Jury Rig. With only one Junk sail, two masts would be no good to me anyway, there would be problems in installing poles, plus the time factor. Winter approaches fast now, I must get away as soon as possible, or the Southern Ocean storms may wipe me out before I can get North to more moderate weather.

So, the Jury Rig it is to be, for which I have rigging already made-up, and two Jib sails, especially bought for it.

During the week I gradually get into gear, having made the decision. Bill Morrison, the F.I.C.'s East Jetty Foreman, gives me some space in the hulk of the wreck of the "Egeria", "Condemned at Stanley" 115 years ago, and used as storage space, her enormous timbers still in good condition in the cold dry air of the Falklands. The "Sail Loft" is cold and gloomy, but is out of the wind, which continues to blow, and blow, and blow. I think the wind never stops here.

It has eased some more though, and Maritime life begins again.

I am in the cockpit, sorting out ropes and rigging, when the "Bransfield", the British Antarctic Surveys supply ship enters harbour. She has come from Punta Arenas, Chile, and is leaving soon for South Georgia on a last visit before Winter. The F.I.C.'s smart green coaster "Monsunen" leaves for another tour of the Islands, and down at the East end of the harbour, the lean grey shape of the frigate H.M.S. Dover enters harbour and picks up a buoy.

I look at these powerful, well run, well crewed ships, think of my perilous future voyage, and, for a while at least, wish I was on any of those ships, instead of being about to set out alone on a long and slow passage up the entire length of the Atlantic.

Such gloomy thoughts are cast away though, and I keep myself busy. I have the mast raised by Wednesday, it looks a trifle spindly for a 9,000 mile voyage, but it's all I have. I plan to lower it again later for improvements, if and when I get a quiet day weatherwise. That's how it has to be, when the weather is half-decent, I work on Roamer, or gather stores, when it blows and pours or hails, I'm to be found in the "Sail Loft."

Repair of the Mainsail is my major task. Where the chain beat down onto the sail bundle while it was sawing through the mast, has cut and chafed the sail cloth quite badly, but only in one vertical plane position, so that 75% of the sail is in good condition. The other 25% gives me plenty of work though, I have to cut out and patch all the tears and chafed areas, a lot of hand sewing. I cannibalize the Foresail material, but soon run out of sailmaking twine. All I can buy in Stanley is a rough roping twine, which, while good and strong, is rather thick, and I have to pull every stitch through the material with a pair of pliers. A long job, but I have it done in a week.

I send Terry a telegram, "Tez, Disaster, Roamer Dismasted Me O.K. More info later. This brings a worried phone call from him, and I put him in the picture. B.B.C. Radio Brighton also call for an interview, so I have to spread the sad news far and wide. "About the best thing I can say," I tell them, "is that I was a victim of circumstance. Having got into harbour after a long and arduous voyage, I let my guard down for just one night, and the worst Summer storm for 40 years came and got me." But it sounds rather lame, lone sailors should never let their guard down. I think of John Ridgway's warning. "Looks like I got ambushed John."

But, we press on. By Monday the 16th I feel fully recovered from my traumatic experience. The "Improved" Jury Mast is up, the 28ft high Bipod now has a wire fore- and back-stay, with two 12mm Nylon rope extra backstays. The wire backstay has a 12V fluorescent lamp wired up to near its top. There is a Jib halyard, lazy jacks, topping lifts etc, all necessary rigging in fact. I've straightened up what bent guardrail stanchions I could, hacksawed off those I couldn't, rigged makeshift guardrail ropes.

Ron the Blacksmith has spread the sides of the anchor, Bill Roberts of the Radio Station has made me a radio aerial. Ah! The Good People of Stanley, I shall long remember them.

Between Monday and Saturday I top up with 100 gallons of Diesel, 140 gallons of water, 10kg of potatoes, 10kg of onions, 30 grapefruit , and lots of oats, baked beans, biscuits and other basic food stuffs. It's going to be a long trip.

The yacht "Northanger" from Essex, comes into Stanley. Her Mizzen mast lies along the deck. She was knocked down to the South of the Islands in the same storm which dismasted me. Soon after, the Schooner "Anne", a beautiful Steel 70-footer, also arrives, both these vessels have come up from the Antarctic Peninsula, and have interesting tales to tell. "Anne" came through 90 knot winds between the Antarctic and the Falklands, according to her Skipper Reid Stowe, a young American. Roamer is about as ready to sail as I can make her, and I have time to chat to the other crews, and relax a little.

Bob and Rose Peart invite me to their home for delicious Roast Lamb suppers, and I am very greedy with their cabbage! Also, just as delicious, is a soak in a hot bath, ah! Ecstasy. We watch videos of sailing ships, of the building of the War Memorial, and of their son Daren on an Agricultural farm down at Fox Bay. Their other son Anton, was the only policeman on the islands during the Argentinean Occupation, behaved very gallantly during those difficult days, and has a Citation from the Queen in recognition of his conduct. Bob gives me a bag of vegetables from his own garden, Tim gives me 5 gallons of paraffin, his girl-friend Ronnie brings me some bread, Ron at the Globe treats me to free lunches out in the kitchen with his two young sons. Island people are wonderful people.

On Thursday I speak to Terry on the phone. "Is this Jury Rig voyage wise?" he asks.

"No way", I say, "But I don't have lots of choices. I started this voyage, and all the time I have a ship, I shall keep trying to get her home.

B.B.C. Radio Brighton calls again, and the interviewer gets his ears burnt when he suggests that Rounding the Horn is "enough", and now I ought to take no more chances.

"What do you suggest," I growl, "I should throw Roamer into a corner and fly home?"

Patrick from the local Falkland Islands Broadcasting Service also voices "Opinions of some locals that it's unwise for me to attempt such a long voyage under Jury Rig."

"Sure it's unwise," I agree, "But so is sailing around the world, and even more unwise to do it alone, wisdom has nothing to do with it!"

"Fools rush in where wise men never go," but wise men also stay ashore, live in big houses, and never get their feet wet!

By Saturday I ready and rarin' to go. But the wind never has really dropped since the "Disaster", and now we have a S.W. 9 forecast. I haven't been able to hoist the sails, let alone do sail trials, so no way am I going out into a F.9 with an untried rig. I'm not that unwise! So I sit out this latest blow, resting and relaxing, trying to build up a bit of strength. It has been a taxing time, hanging on the end of the jetty, wide open to the weather, never able to relax, shifting Roamer from one corner of the jetty to another as the wind changes, half terrified that another storm would come in.

This gale isn't too bad though, it certainly blows hard at times, but is mainly S.W. and no large waves build up in the harbour.

The delay allows me some last-minute thinking about it all. Obviously I was a damned fool not to listen to the weather forecast at the time, but I had only just got into port, and my defences were down. It's possible to consider that with a storm of such long-lasting ferocity, some damage was inevitable, and maybe I got off lightly. Supposing, for instance, I had left her on the Jetty, and she'd broken away from there? She would have been blown onto a rocky shore somewhere for sure, or maybe even blown out to sea, and lost or completely wrecked. Or, suppose I had been approaching the Islands as the storm had come in? I'd have been blown clear past, and out into the vastness of the South Atlantic, short of food and water.

At 0640 on Monday the 23rd of March, on a cold, but sunny morning, 21 days after arriving, I let go our ropes from the Public Jetty of Port Stanley, and, while no-one was looking, we leave. We motor slowly down the Inner Harbour, out through The Narrows, into Port Williams Sound, with many a backward look at Stanley Town. As at Cape Horn, I have the feeling I shall not be here again.

Good People of Stanley, I shall miss you.

Chapter Fifteen

Port Stanley to Recife – The Painful Voyage

> Now this Port we are leavin',
> For old England give a cheer,
> Fare - ye - well, ye dark-eyed damsels,
> Think of me and shed a tear.
>
> Goodbye friends, we're bound to leave you,
> Haul the tow-rope, all in-board,
> We will leave the Falklands sternwards,
> Clap on all sail we can afford.
>
> (Sea Shanty, "Rolling Home".)

Monday the 23rd March, 0700. Motoring out through the Narrows, we are pursued by a smart green cargo ship, the "West Moor", and her attendant tug. I circle off to Port, out of the Fairway, and let them pass, then follow them down Port William Sound, the fresh Westerly wind comfortably astern. Schools of porpoises and penguins, gambol alongside, giving me a cheerful goodbye. As we near the open sea, the two ships ahead clear the reefs off Cape Pembroke and turn to the South, probably heading for Mare Harbour. What concerns me, however, is how they are pitching in the swell, it's still pretty rough out there, have I come out too soon?

There are usually a few butterflies fluttering around in my stomach when I go to sea, but today there are whole squadrons of them. Here we are, heading out into what is still the Southern Ocean, in late Autumn, with a half-wreck of a ship, an untried Jury Rig, Jibs I've never flown before, a hurriedly-patched up Mainsail, and maybe as much as 9,000 miles to go! No wonder I'm nervous.

Oh Well there's no turning back, so we press on, out into the ever-increasing sea and swell, with the further difficultly of avoiding large "rafts" of kelp, torn away from the rocky coast in the recent storm. It's a real danger to the propeller.

Clear of Cape Pembroke I hoist the Main, just one panel and the top triangle, and the White Jib. The wind veers to the N.W. as we clear the land and we make off to the N.E. at about 2 knots. I shut down the engine and secure it for rough weather by closing the seacocks. It is quite rough, but sea and swell abaft the beam, there appears to be a strong Northerly current, and we make good progress.

By 1600 the Falklands' low grey hills have disappeared into the haze, and we are out on the boundless ocean again. It's not very comfortable, with the N.W. F.6 wind blowing across the left-over Southerly sea and swell, but we're not looking for comfort, what we want is to get as far as possible from the Islands and the Fishing Fleet before dark.

I've had to rig all manner of ropes on the Main to stop it flying about, but all appears well with the rig and we continue to make 2½ to 3 knots.

At 2000 I test the Radio aerial and the backstay fluorescent light, both are O.K.

During the long and almost sleepless night, I see the amazing sight of the glow of the Fishing Fleet's lights, 15 miles or so off to the West, illuminating the whole horizon. Far astern I believe I can also see the glow of the Mother Ships at anchor in the peace of Berkeley Sound. No ships come near me though, and we survive the first night, which is always the worst.

On Tuesday the wind pipes up to N.W. F. 6 - 7 during the forenoon and I have to change out the White Jib, and hoist the "Wee Brown 'Un". I'm taking no risks with the rig in these early days. The White Jib has a long luff which just about fills the forestay, a 10ft foot, and an area of about 120sq ft., so we aren't exactly flying a lot of sail!

This sail change is the first of many, and the operation soon makes me realise how much easier it was with "the old rig", where I reefed from the cockpit. With these jib changes I have to crawl around the foredeck, for she really roles and plunges without the steadying influence of the masts. Clawing down one jib and lashing it down, changing sheets and halyard, hoisting the other. Already I can see how many times I'm going to repent the "Stanley Disaster".

However, the Noon Sun Sight shows we have made 80 miles to the N.E., of which probably 25% has been current, but still a useful start.

We settle down for the "Long Haul North".

"It's not much fun", becomes the catch-phrase, and it certainly isn't. Roamer's motion is painfully wild and makes all on-deck operations hard work and dangerous. I trail the 50ft Orange Floating Line as a Safety Line for the chances of being thrown over the side are much greater now. It's damn cold too!

It's definitely "Not much fun". Wednesday brings no wind and a cold clammy fog, the rolling is terrible. Thursday, a Northerly head wind, drizzle, more fog. "dark, cold, wet and nasty", says the Log.

Friday the 27th March. "Happy Birthday To Me - 47 Today". And what a day! Apart from the pleasure of opening cards, it's a day of unrelenting nastiness. The Northerly wind increases to Gale 8, then backs to N.W., throwing the sea into a more confused state, but when, in the early hours of Saturday, it backs further, and quickly, to S.W., we have to suffer one of the most horribly confused seas we've ever had to suffer, and suffer is the word, for, with hardly any sail up in the Gale, Roamer is just a hulk, thrown about and rolled unmercifully by the short steep pyramidal waves which attack us from all directions. Not much of a Birthday!

After a week out, on Monday the 30th, we are 400 miles N.E. of Stanley, and the Falkland Islands Broadcasting Service is becoming too weak to pick up. This is a sad blow. The F.I.B.S. was just like a "Village Radio" to me, with news and views and local announcements, and I feel a wrench at being unable to hear them any more. I just loved their "Jingle", too. "F.I.B.S., Number One in the South Atlantic!!"

So, having run 400 miles, we are at 47°S., 50°W. The Journal says "Very mild tonight, long johns off soon?"

Tuesday the 31st of March, 0800. Journal: "No Falklands weather forecast this morning, decided to let them go, and store them in 'My Happy Memory Box'. Gave myself a vicious haircut, being fed up with trying to drag a comb through the tangled locks. Just grabbed handfuls, and snipped away with scissors, looks not so bad though, and certainly feels a lot better. No one is likely to criticise, and I'm not planning to go out anywhere for a while!

Thursday the 2nd of April brought the Southern Ocean back up to us. Dark clouds gathering in the afternoon, black clouds at dusk, and then really black clouds very low overhead. Down comes the rain, in comes the wind to give us a horribly stormy night. Next forenoon I hoist and lower the "Wee Brown 'Un" several times as vicious squalls sweep over us. I try to make progress, but without endangering the rig. We certainly are back to Cape Horn weather, with full waterproofs, three layers of clothing, gloves, Safety Harness etc. Some of the seas are big and breaking, and we take a bit of water in through the viewdome, even though I have it covered by the old boat cover, and lashed down tight, but not very much.

Friday night is spent virtually hove-to, flying only the Main Storm Triangle. "Not much fun!"

We have time for Ornithology though. "There are a pair of enormous and anciently beautiful albatross with us. Two of the biggest I've seen, with wing spans of 10ft or more, cruel long beaks, and great big eyes looking dispassionately at me as they glide by."

The wind continues to blow F. 8 - 9 from the West and we make poor progress under next to no sail. I curb my impatience to raise more sail though, by quoting yet another maxim. "We're not in the Storm Business", it says. Survival is everything, put up a jib now, break the mast, and I'm just about a dead boyo. I must remember that, all the time and be patient.

So I sit below, reading what is probably my No. 1 favourite book, "Seven Pillars of Wisdom", by T.E. Lawrence, "Lawrence of Arabia". Favourite book, favourite film.

Although we are many miles from land, I have a worrying time as we pass close to a "14 metre shoal" marked on the chart as "Unconfirmed". In the big seas which are running , a 14 metre shoal could be the end of us, but I have little control over the course, no control over the weather, and couldn't pin-point our position within 10 miles anyway, so I just have to worry. We pass the position without seeing anything.

Sunday the 5th. I make a repair to the Main after the storm passes. The sail cloth is tearing at the luff above the second batten. I make up a short length of seat belt material and, reeving it through a lacing eye, sew it up tight on both sides above the tear. That sounds easier than it actually was, trying to stand on the rolling, rearing deck. It looks very efficient, I think.

My thoughts are casting ahead to passing over the 40°S. line, and officially leaving this wild and windy Southern Ocean that I've seen so much of these past months. It shouldn't be long now. Also thinking that the rig seems to be standing up O.K. so long as I nurse it in the rough stuff. So I can probably forget the first of my Emergency Plans, which was, if the rig didn't work at all, to make East on the prevailing wind, and current, to Port Owen, and refit there, where I have friends and could get a job. But Emergency Plan Two, to make a half-way stop at Recife, if progress was poor, looks rather likely at present, for we aren't going very fast. 14 days out, we have only 715 miles logged, at an average of 55 m.p.d. 'Twill take a long time to get to Falmouth at that rate!

Wednesday the 8th. Journal: "Am a bit down in the dumps at present, can't get into anything. Just lying around, loafing, reading, sleeping, living from meal to meal. Maybe if we can get North of 40 I'd buck up. Oh 'ell, the mood will pass. The weather is no help, Force 5 - 6 Northerly, cloudy, grey, showery, choppy seas. At least it's not cold, very mild in fact."

Friday the 10th. We log 1,000 miles, in 18 days, at 55 m.p.d. Not so wonderful, but a thousand miles is a thousand miles whichever way you look at it.

Journal: "Shades of the Indian Ocean! The Lone Sailor skulks below while mountainous seas roar by, and we soar and plunge over them. No serious waves have hit us since I hove-to with the wind just abaft the beam. She rides nicely like this, even makes a knot or so, North, on this occasion. Down below I doodle with the rig for "Roamer Mk II" She looks interesting in these early days, a Schooner Junk Rig, (of course), but this time with a smaller Fore than Mainsail, and provision of a bowsprit for a jib, and various stays, one of which will carry a staysail between Main and Foremasts. She had a pretty good rig before, but I need to be able to fly more sail in the lighter winds."

Lunch is a very tasty hotchpotch of last night's Veg stew with an Oxo and other "things in it". Heating it, and transferring it to a bowl are acts of acrobatic skill in the wind motion, and to eat it I wedge myself in the sea berth with one foot in the lower Wendy House window to prevent being thrown out. A wild day, she blows strong." I'm in the best place here, 'tis no place for a young sailor up top today, or an old one like me!"

1800: "Have been below since 1100, still she blows strongly and there are plenty of black squally clouds to windward. I pass the time thinking, mostly, which is why I'm maybe not so wildly happy at the moment. I have plenty to think about, like how long am I'm going to be at sea, trudging along at 2 knots or so, or, what happens if the mast falls down? And the worst thoughts of all, which I try to prevent myself from dwelling upon, how it would be "If I had my masts". Real killer thinking that is, for it reminds me that I brought all this agony upon myself. But for one foolish evening and night, Roamer and I would be a long way North in the sunshine, with all our equipment, having sailed swiftly through this rough area of beam N.W. winds. Instead, I'm slouched in the sea berth, wedged in the safest place , with Roamer just lying stopped in the water, rolling, pitching, lurching and heaving over the mountainous swells. Ah, sad thoughts. It could be worse of course. I still do have my bonny ship, she is still dry and cosy below, and I am warm and well fed and watered. So, we must slouch on, waiting for the wind to go down, hoping to be able to set a little sail before dark, or we might be laid here all damn night – we'll see!"

Sunday the 12th. We pass a line of four fishing floats, buoys and poles. "They must have broken away from the shore." I think. Then I pass another set. Damn! Alarm bells ring in the head, but I'm lucky enough to sight and pass the 200ft Fishing Vessel which has laid them, before dark, and he disappears into the murk and rain astern. Are there any more though? It's a very worrying business, but I see no-one else.

We reach 40°S. Latitude on Tuesday the 14th, but the Southern Ocean pursues us across the line with a series of gales and storms, rain, hail and big seas. All these give me a hard time on deck, reefing and gibing, holding on tight in the revolting sea conditions as the wind backs, and backs, and backs. Round and round in circles it goes, sometimes 360 in 24 hours!

As the wind backs, I have to follow it round, until the course gets to South of West, then I have to gybe. Gybing Roamer nowadays is a terrible business in these awful sea conditions. Because the Jury Rig has a backstay, the Mainsail has to be reefed right down to the Triangle, to allow the sail to pass under the stay. Once reefed down, I then have to lash the boom amidships, then untie the mainsheet blocks from the pulpit guardrails, pass them under the backstay, and secure them on the other side. Of course, they get into a terrible tangle during this operation, and, with little sail up, she rolls wildly, making it all a very painful game. Having crossed the sheets, were then ready to gybe, but, because of the restricted way I had to rig the Jib halyard, the jib either has to be dropped before the gybe, or during it, depending on the strength of the wind, and the sea state. But we put the helm over and get her round one way or the other, and then have to re-rig the jib, and re-hoist the Main, and I've had to do all this sometimes several times a day. An exhausting business.

The weather conditions are not good for progress. Progress!! April the 13th, 25 miles, 14th, 40, 15th, 60, 16th, 20! Hopeless. But life goes on. The 16th turns out to be a pleasant day, sea down, sun shining. We are at 38 S., 38 W.

In the improved weather I start on my Job List. I always have a Job List at hand, maybe it's a hangover from my Oil Rig days, when I always had a list ready for the drilling crews for their spare moments.

On a bright sunny morning, I start on the list. It's quite hot on deck, and I wear a long-peaked "welder's" hat, in red and white stripes, a very cheery hat. I'm very much aware of the dangers of sunstroke as we move North. We haven't seen much hot sun in the last 6 months.

I have a busy day, and later can write, "Jobs done. Trimmed off and sandpapered the broken teak coaming on the cockpit, Stbd side. Broke open steering shaft brake, removed cladding in Wendy House, freed stiff steering. Whilst at that, rigged down compass repeater box. Sawed off bolts and chocks, Port side of foredeck, of the aft jury mast holder, plugged holes with corks till I do the scrape and paint job. Restowed a lot of the canned veg in the aft cabin. Restowed and sorted, log books, journals, paperwork." Who's a busy boy then?

The "pleasant day" lasts for only 24 hours before conditions are nasty again. Wind N.N.W. 7- 8 and atrocious seas. At Noon I have to write, "No position worked, no progress made. None!!"

I am not in a happy mood. A big old albatross flying slowly past gets no friendly words. "Shove off South." I tell him, it's flying fish I want, not albatrosses.

I keep myself busy and modify the surviving Stern light into a more important Bow light, by painting its lens inside with Red and Green ink in the appropriate sectors. Rigged and wired up on the pulpit, it's yet another improvement to our situation. Of course, with the loss of the masts, all the Navigation lights went, and the Bow light too. Much as I am an optimistic chappy, there are times when I do get depressed, and Monday the 20th is one of those times.

"The Rocky Horror Show of this part of the ocean goes on, and on, and on. We have terrible weather, different, but still terrible. Yesterday's dawn brought series of hot, torrential rain showers, the sea state is really awful, a real horror of holes and pyramids. How can I make any progress through this?

In the past week, our tortuous rollings have taken us, on the chart, 210 miles N.N.E. Wonderful! But we must struggle on, it's the only way.

We are 1,200 miles due West of Tristan Da Cunha, and Inaccessible Island of the black memory. I have no temptations to go for another look, but another day? Another year? In the Summer?

A "fresh" cup of coffee after lunch made from rain water caught an hour earlier tastes amazingly different, and <u>very</u> nice.

Thursday the 23rd of April. St. George's bay. 30 days out, 1,575 miles logged. Thoughts fly to this time last year, at Port Owen and the rescue of "Zanj". What a year since, and Port Owen is only 2,500 miles to the East.

Progress is still hopeless, the chart line is ridiculous zig-zag up Longitude 38W., as the wind constantly changes and I gybe, and gybe, and gybe again, ever trying to get North, or East.

Life goes on though, slowly, slowly, maybe things are improving. Ever the easily-cheered optimist, I write at 1900 on the 25th. "Lots of lovely things are mine these days, gloves and long-johns are just memories. The hatch is open and the washboards out all day long, decks are dry, the ship is warm. I like it, after long months in the cold and wet. No doubt I shall be complaining of the heat soon!

Thursday the 30th. At 32°S., we at last appear to have escaped the Southern Winter. Journal: "0930, changed into shorts, sports shirt, bare feet. 1030, Bath and dhobeying in the cockpit. Sun! Heat! Calm!!"

May Day. Day 40. Position, 31° - 30S., 32° - 50 W. 1,955 m. A busy day which starts at 0130. Having gone to bed early with Roamer stopped and becalmed, I rise early to find a wee breeze from the S.S.E. and I hoist sail to it, but it barely moves us along. Later I try a plan of flying the Main Ghoster sail in place of the Main Junk sail. I have to tie two figure-of-eight knots near the peak to shorten its height, but even so, the experiment is a failure. Even in the fairly calm sea, she rolls so much that the sail just keeps collapsing, and soon I tire of the game and stow the Ghoster away.

We pass a fishing float with mysterious air bubbles and swirling water around it. I keep well away, "Curiosity Kills Cats". In the afternoon I start Polly Perkins the faithful diesel, to try for some progress. In fact, I've motored 25 hours since Stanley, whenever the wind has fallen off, and the sea conditions allow. Some "Purists" might regard this as cheating, maybe, but I can't afford to be pure. I'm in the survival business, and must use whatever facilities I have, to make to the North.

Later in the day, the chart tells me we are passing over the "Rio Grande Plateau", a submarine table-land rising to 650 metres from the average depths of 4,000 metres. The charts are full of interesting information like that, showing undersea valleys and cliffs, and the occasional mountains rising from the depths. Two of these are not far to the N.N.E. of us now, the Islands of Trindade and Martin Vaz. I'm hoping we might see them, partly to check my navigation, but mostly just because I like to see land now and then.

In the evening I make out a "40day, 2000 miles Review", and look at all aspects of our situation, food and water stocks, progress, goose barnacles, and how things are going generally. The result is none too pleasing, with the daily average down to 50, I doubt that I'll have enough stores to make it to Falmouth in one leg. I'll have to see how things go, and when we reach the longed-for S.E. Trades.

More bad times come upon us in the early days of May. Northerly winds predominate, and if I try to go East, the wind goes to N.E., if I try for West, it's a Nor'Wester I get. I have a bad time, very depressed, throwing tantrums wholesale at the unfairness of it all. We spend four whole days trapped in Latitude 29 5., four days!! Bad times indeed. Life aboard is very painful with the incessant heavy rolling, murder up top to work the ship, murder below just to exist. Look at this! 0400, Wind North Gale 8. 1400, Wind South 7.Force. 2400, Wind South Force 3. What chance have I got?

Friday the 8th. No position worked, no sights, too rough, and we haven't gone anywhere anyway.

Sunday the 10th. Noon sight very depressing, 45 miles to the E.N.E., in two days!

Tuesday the 12th. Mr. Weather relents, and gives us a F.4 Easterly and calmer seas. How I need a break.

Three beautiful whales keep us company for several days, swimming slowly round and round us, basking in the sun, blowing gently. Fascinating creatures, they even pose for photographs close to the stern.

As a makeshift Radar Reflector, I rig the two black metal "Anchor Ball" shapes on a boat hook lashed to the stern guardrails. I'm beginning to worry about meeting shipping as we move North and back into busier waters. Well off the shipping lanes, I've seen no-one since the Falklands except that one fisherman.

Checking around while motoring, I find the stern gland very hot. The copper pipe which should supply the gland with cooling water from the engine has broken, but I have spare olives and fix it without too much trouble.

Poor weather returns soon though. Journal, 2100 Friday the 15th of May. "I have to record that after 54 days of struggling and trying hard, maybe for the first time in the whole circumnavigation, I am weary of it all, have reefed the Main, dropped the Jib, and am hove-to. I'm fed up with the whole business, trying to make North on either tack, whichever I choose, the wind seems to lean over and push me off to the West, or the South. So, will take 9 hours off till daylight and then see what's what. Not that it's going to be any great rest, we roll and pitch like a bucket, the water tanks gurgle and boom. Great life!"

Saturday the 16th. I can see that I needed a break last night. But I didn't take 9 hours, only 5½ in fact, was up at 0230, and the wind having fallen light, was motoring by 0315. Put in 3 hours motoring, then tried to sail again, but with light wind still in the North, I can't make better than East on one tack, or West on the other. I give up again for a little while and spend a couple of hours repairing stitching on the Main.

But we persevere, and gain a few miles North most days, if not all. I look for any hopeful signs that we are "winning". "I've just realised that the cluster of stars lying across the Northern horizon, which looked vaguely familiar, is Ursa Major, the Great Bear, or the name which I prefer, the Big Dipper. I can see the resemblance to a water dipper, but none at all to a bear. So, the Northern stars are beginning to show themselves. If I can see the Dipper, it shouldn't be long before I have Polaris in sight, and the two planets Venus and Mercury both very bright in the pre-dawn sky.

Sunday the 17th. After lunch, I pop up into the cockpit for a breath of fresh air, automatically cast my eyes all round the horizon, and ... what's that? On the Port bow, an Island!

It can't be! I only fixed our position an hour ago, and the nearest land is the twin islands of Trindade and Martin Vaz, almost 250 miles to the North of us. But it's there, low in its Western end, with a couple of offshore islets, rising to quite a height in its centre. White stratified clouds swirl around those heights. I can't believe it, from the bows I strain my eyes through the binoculars, I even get the spare sextant out and check the readings of both, but they agree.

What to do? Well, the island appears to be 15 miles or so away, and we move at only a couple of knots, so I go for a nap. Hopefully it will be gone when I awake!

Two hours later, it's still there! But is it somewhat a different shape now? Have those offshore islets faded? At dusk I still haven't been able to decide if it is a "Rock" Island, or a "Cloud" Island, and I spend quite a few hours in the pulpit, during a squally evening, before the horizon eventually clears, and I can assume that it was, only a "Cloudy Island."

On the 18th the Falklands potatoes are finished. Quite the strangest spuds I ever had, they were very dark, soft and I reckoned they wouldn't last long, but they did, and were very tasty too. Only 4 onions remain, and Recife is 1,000 miles to the N.N.W.

Wednesday the 20th of May. A "Red Letter" day. We have some Good News to record (A commodity which has been in very short supply of late.) At 0800 Roamer and I crossed our Outward Bound track, at 22° - 45'S., 28°- 46 W. In doing so we have "Tied the Knot" and are now, Da-Da... "Circumnavigators of the World". Hooray, at least we have achieved something in these terrible days of contrary winds, rough seas and hopeless progress. At times like this the only thing worth thinking is that "Surely it must improve soon." Mustn't it? Please?

Passing under, (or over?) the Tropic of Capricorn at 22½°S., we move into the Tropics. I am full of hope that the weather will improve and that the long-sought Trade winds will soon blow upon us. We have also reached the latitude of Rio de Janeiro. John Ridgway's letter at Stanley warned me that J.R. and Andy Briggs reckoned they had some of the worst weather of their non-stop Circumnavigation between the Falklands, and this latitude. I agree, whole-heartedly, with their assessment!

Saturday the 23rd. We have three more Wonderful Whales with us again, or the same three? I am able to call to them the Good News that the Russians have given up whaling, and their Antarctic Fleet is on its way home. They are unimpressed, "About time too", they boom, "there are hardly any of us left."

On Sunday morning I am in the pulpit at 0515. There hasn't been a breath of wind all night, and there's none now. The silence is wonderful, it's so quiet there is a roaring in my ears. Under a dome of a million stars, the restless black ocean undulates slightly. The brighter stars' reflections skip across the oily sheen of the water. In the East, Venus, Mercury, and a crescent Moon point to where the Sun will soon rise to roast us in this calm. Regretfully, I have to start the engine, and shatter the quiet, but I need the miles.

By mid-forenoon, motoring has become onerous in the hot sun, and though there is still no wind, I stop the engine, and Roamer soon glides to a stop in the calm blue sea. She stops rather sooner than she ought, and this is mainly due to the growth of those loathsome goose barnacles on the hull. They not only look horrible, great fat slugs hanging onto my ship's side, but really do put a drag on progress, and that's bad enough as it is. So,

I had been planning an attack on the beasts for some time, and the time has arrived.

I had also planned some "anti-shark" precautions, such as wearing dark clothes and socks, and hanging the aluminium ladder over the side amidships on the side I was working, but, I have a good look around, and I see nothing in the sea except my two attendant little pilot fish which have been with me for a while. I rig a rope along the ship's side to hold on to, grab a scraper, strip off, and leap into the clear warm sea.

It feels glorious, but we're not here for fun, and I get scraping. Hell, there a thousands of the bloody things on the hull, some as long as two inches. They come off easily though, and apart from the amusing nuisance of the pilot fish wriggling around my body, and at my hands as I scrape, I have no bother, and the job is done in two hours.

I'm much relieved when it is done, and I'm back aboard, for although I was for ever looking round the surface for dorsal fins, sharks don't always announce their arrival in that way, so I had read. I don't actually like going into the sea much at all, and getting killed off by a shark, after all I've been through, would be the last straw, literally!

During a quiet couple of days, we drift, sail, and motor past Ilha Martin Vaz, about 30 miles to the East, but though I saw several "Islands" in the clouds, I don't believe I sighted it.

There's an interesting programme on the "Beeb" in the evening called, "Australia Bound", about the Sailing Fleet leaving Portsmouth to re-enact the sailing of the "First Fleet", which took the first colonists, mainly convicts, to Aussie. The event is similar to that which Merv Palmer of Canberra was organizing until his sponsors fell through, and in which I had planned to become involved. After that programme, I treat myself to a peaceful hour in the cockpit, lounging on two cushions, like a Roman Emperor, enjoying the quiet, which is only disturbed by Handel's Water Music, floating up from the saloon.

But this idyll doesn't last. Journal, 26th. "Last night was one of the nastier kind. Wind backed to S.W. 6 - 7, with heavy rain squalls, the night as black as your hat, and, of course, a revolting sea. This morning we head N.W. at maybe one knot in the horrible chop. I feel washed out having been awake most of the night. Can only hope that the wind will now go South, we gybe and then get a S.E. or E. wind. Full of hope aren't I? I don't know where I get it all, would've thought all optimism would have been knocked out of me by now!"

A survey of the 30°S. to 20°S. section of the chart. 2nd May, 30°S., 33° W. 26th May, 20°S., 28°W. Direct distance, 680 miles, logged distance, 1040 miles. For 24 days, Direct average, 28.3 m.p.d., Logged average, 43.3 m.p.d. Wonderful progress eh? 24 days for 680 chart miles! These Northerlies are killing me!

By the 28th of May, at 18°S., and still no sign of the S.E. Trades, I finally decide that we'll have to go to Recife for stores, as it seems obvious that it's going to take more than 90 days to get to the Equator, and at least 70 more to Falmouth. There are too many risks involved in heading into the open wastes of the North Atlantic short of stores and water. Supposing the mast should collapse? I'd be in big trouble. Stores are short, already. Journal. "All fresh veg finished with the eating of the last onion last evening. They, and the Falkland potatoes, kept very well. Porridge oats are finished, too many items are finished or in short supply. The days pass, but not the miles."

A 2-day calm follows, which finally decides that we must go to Recife, and I have a "binge" on the food, with a slap-up breakfast of Meat Balls/Baked Beans/Tomatoes/Biscuits and coffee, which is enjoyed to the music of Tchaikovsky's 1812 Overture, complete with cannon and church bells!

In the afternoon, I'm busy typing up this book, when I decide to reef the Main right down to save chafe in the rolling of the "calm". "I'll do that and treat myself to a swim," I say. So, up top and, as I'm doing the job, who do I see in the clear calm water than the biggest and meanest shark I ever saw! (Checking in my Survival Book later, he was a Mako, one of the most dangerous.) About 10ft long, he swims around us, black and menacing, and I can appreciate his beauty, from the safety of the ship. He has three attendant pilot fish, two striped, one not, which follow his every move. "My" two pilot fish cower under the hull. I get some good photographs of him in the calm water, and abandon my swimming plans! Better that I "snap" him, than he "snaps" me, eh?!

I wonder where he was when I did the de-barnacling job the other day?

May the 31st. "In this continuing poor progress, my nerves are very jangly. Many things on the ship make me fly into a temper. The chain of the inside wheel tapping, the tool drawers rattling. I threw my track suit top over the side last night, exasperated by its habit of hooking the horns of the hatch-way. Then the floppy sleeves of my shirt do the same, the blue waterproof coat always manages to hook itself on the corner of the chart table. All the ropes on deck are anti-me, and knot and seize and tangle every chance they get, when they aren't actually wrapping themselves around my body or feet!

I think I need a break, but I'm not getting one. It's <u>excruciating</u> to know that the Trades can only be a few degrees North, but I can't get up to them.

Ah! The Trades, how I dream of and long for those steady and true East winds which I know are not far to the North. They've got to be, they are always there, but where?

Monday June the First. I start a new month, (and the 11th week!) with the treat of good hot fresh water wash and neck shave, clean the teeth, and enjoy breakfast of Baked Beans and Meat Balls, pretty much the most luxurious food I have on board, but I'm easily cheered, and ever optimistic.

Feeling energetic, I do a job which has been bubbling in my mind for some time. Gybing Roamer, as said before, is a very painful task in the prevailing conditions, so, I get brave and transfer the backstay and mast-raising tackle from the padeye on the aft end of the aft cabin roof, and rig them to an 18mm Nylon strop secured to the lower part of the pushpit guardrails. This has the effect of moving the backstay several feet aft and will allow me to gybe with one panel of the Main still up, but, even better, I won't now have to move the sheet blocks from Port to Stbd and vice versa. This should be a great labour saving move.

We are at 17°- 12'S., 26°-50'W., and have logged 3,285 miles in 71 days at an average of 47 m.p.d. Hopeless! At noon I logged a "run" of 35 miles, and that was for <u>two days</u>. We have been "stuck on a stick" again, with the Northerlies blocking our way, unable to go East, not wanting to go West. Hopeless!

Ah! But at last, at last, they had to come sometime, and, on Wednesday the 3rd, at 16° - 30'S., 27°- 00'W., we appear to have picked up the Trade Winds. They come in with a bang. 18 hours of severe squalls with plenty of wind and very heavy rainfall, but we have them. Steady winds from the East, and it's like changing gear in a car, all of a sudden we make good progress to the North. 60 miles a day, one degree up the chart, every day, not a lot in normal circumstances, but after what we've been used to. It's heavenly!

In these lovely winds, with bright sunshine too, after the squalls pass, we head North and a little West, towards Recife, which at Noon on the 7th of June, is only 430 miles N.N.W.

I now regret that we have to go there, as the wind is much more suitable for carrying on due North, but I've made the decision, and will stick with it. Even though we have the Trades, we're still at 12½°S., and at 77 days out, it would still take 90 days to "The Line", so the same rule applies, we must go to Recife for supplies (And a rest!).

The B.B.C. World Service churns out streams and torrents of words on the up-coming British General Election. Always heavy with News, the radio is overburdened with it now.

Friday the 12th June. Tories have won a comfortable victory in the Election, and Mrs. Thatcher is in for a third term. Well, that's a relief, I'm not madly keen on any politicians, but better her and the Tories than that other bunch, who remind me of a bunch of noisy, troublesome schoolboys.

On Sunday the 14th, amazingly, we have logged 4,000 miles from the Falklands, a long trip. We are about 130 miles from Recife, and I'm homing in on the R.D.F. beacon, though it's signal is O.L.D., not R.E.C., on 380Khz, as in the R.D.F. Signals Book. I assume this to be a change from Recife to Olinda, which is the name of a very bright lighthouse just to the North of Recife. I'm lucky, (is it luck?) that I have a chart of "Port Do Recife", one of a bundle of the South American coast picked up cheap from a pile of dusty old charts in Brighton Marina Boatyard three years ago. I'd be in an awkward position without it. It even has a pencilled notation telling me how to get to the Yacht Club. I check the lights and buoys of the out of date chart against the up to date "Lights List".

As we approach the coast, ships' lights start to show, and I rig one of the Tilley Lamps on the aft cabin roof if and when I take a sleep. We're getting close.

We do quite a lot of motoring on the Monday, our course being now West, and the East wind having fallen light. In the evening, as the sunset glow fades, another glow takes its place, a glow I assume to be the city lights of Recife. I'm wary of being set on-shore by a current all the books warn me of, but we must be way off, Olinda's light has a range of 34 miles, but I can't see it.

I take a sleep from 2200 to 0200, then, tempted by that glow, motor across a calm sea towards the coast. I motor on till 0630, when a very heavy squall catches us up, and I hide below from the torrential rain, stop the engine, and breakfast. Motoring again at 0800, plodding on, and on, where is Brazil? Not until 1110 is the cry heard, "Land Ho!", and the low shore of the South American Continent appears on the horizon.

Using the R.D.F., I head slightly North of its bearing, the beacon being shown as about 10 miles South of Recife, at the Airport. As we close though, I'm confused by the layout of the shore, I see skyscrapers to the S.W., surely that must be Recife, but the R.D.F. bearing is to the North of them. It takes me a while, and much peering through the binoculars, before I identify the tall Black and White Olinda lighthouse, and work out that the R.D.F. beacon has not only been changed in signal, but in location, and transmits OLD. from the lighthouse.

Having worked this out, I alter course to the S.W. and plod on through the increasing heat. Occasional squalls unhelpfully wander in from the sea and blot out the shore, but, at 1430, we pass the Green lighthouse of the Outer Breakwater, and enter Recife Harbour. Their lights system appears to be the opposite to that of Europe, where entering harbour, Red lights are left to Port, Green to Stbd.

Recife is a large city, and appears to be a busy port, about 20 ships lie alongside the wharves, and 3 more lie at anchor in the Roads.

Skyscrapers abound behind the port area, and there are many more to the South. Guided by the chart, and enjoying the bliss of flat water, we motor South past the ships, the sweat pouring off me in the humid heat, and worrying about the engine's temperature, it having been running continuously for the last 7 hours.

We reach a point where my anonymous yachting friend has written on the chart, "From this point, keep 10 to 25 metres from the wall." Hmmm, looks dodgy all the same. A mud bank is shown on the chart, and I can see it clearly ahead, the tide must be fairly low, but the chart gives no depths after this point". There's a lot of debris in the water, palm tree fronds, and bunches of what looks like the great clumps of hyacinth that used to float down the Great Berg River and clog up Port Owen Marina in the Autumn. While I'm circling slowly, eyeing the presumed channel to the Yacht Club, a boat with 4 Brazilians approaches, 2 young men, and two boys.

"Yacht Club, Yacht Club?" they shout.

"Si, Yacht Club." I reply. They swarm aboard, one has a little English.

"Me Piloto, steer to Yacht Club." Dubious, but tired and trusting, I let this guy on the helm, and we chug slowly South. One of the boys is looking down the hatch, sees my biscuits store, in the Wendy House lockers, from which I have removed the doors some time ago. "Senor, Senor," he calls, pointing his finger to his mouth. I catch on and nod, "Dois," I tell him, my 8-Language Dictionary at hand.

He dives down and returns with 2 packets of Digestives, and he wolfs the biscuits hungrily.

The "Piloto" runs us on the mud, we back off, "Over, over", I tell him, we need to be closer to the wall. I go forward for a look-see, he runs me on the mud again. Back in the cockpit, I then notice that my watch has gone from the piece of rope on the stump of the Mainmast, where it was hanging.

"Hey!" I say to these boyos, "Where's my watch?" I get blank looks from them all. I stop the engine and indicate in sign language that I want my watch back, but the blank looks are expressionless. I enter a foreign port, all friendliness, let them aboard, give them my friendship, give them my biscuits. They run me aground, and steal my watch. "O.K. Vamoose, Out, Git". They get that message and pile into their boat. Bloody pests, but I'm not going to raise too much of a rumpus for a £20 Casio. Maybe I'm lucky, for my camera, R.D.F. and binoculars lie in the rope boxes. "Piraticos Bandidos", I shout after them. Bloody pests.

I wipe them from my mind, let's get in, time is pressing, it's now 1530. We appear to be afloat, so I steer slowly for the wall till I am 10 to 25 metres from it, and head South. We bump a few times, but I know what's on the bottom of Roamer's keel, and worry not. The Depth Indicator doesn't seem to want to work, maybe there's a goose barnacle sat on it. We slide slowly along the mud towards where I can see some yachts' masts, and then the entrance, looking very narrow, and very shallow. A 36ft Motor Boat sits up on the mud to Port, this must be Low Water, Oh well, better to run aground now, than at High Water! We creep in through the entrance, a blue-overalled figure on the wall waves to me to turn to Port, where about 8 yachts lie stern-to, to the wall.

A dead-looking dredger lies on my Port side, and some of the yachts have Bow lines across the Marina tied to it. Stopped, but drifting in the slight breeze, I indicate these ropes, from the foredeck. People appear on the yachts' foredecks and slack off the lines.

It's rather restricted in the small Marina, I'm obviously going to have to anchor off, and moor stern-to with long ropes. Damned awkward on my own. I motor slowly across the slack bow lines, get to windward of all the yachts, for a bit of breathing space, a French chappie, Marc, comes alongside, and offers to help, and is, a great help.

A German chappie, immediately christened German Jim, is no help at all, shouting from the shore, "I Zink you are dropping your anchor on mine."

Hot and tired, I call back, "How do you know, you have underwater vision?"

But, with Marc's help, we get anchored, drift back on the breeze, Marc takes a line ashore for me, and I can stop the hot engine. Phew! I'm bushed, the anchor winch played up and seized up, and I had to do a lot of chain heaving. Sweat pours off me.

But, we've arrived, and seem to be O.K., it's 1630, 'Tuesday the 16th of June. 4,150 miles and 85 days from Port Stanley.

Quite a trip, the "Painful Voyage".

Chapter Sixteen

Rest at Recife – Hot and Steamy

Paying out chain forward, and then warping in on the rope aft, I work Roamer's stern in close to the beach, drop the 10ft aluminium ladder over the stern, climb down, and step ashore in Brazil. More ropes are needed, a long one from the Starboard bow to as far along the wall as it will reach, and another, shorter, from the Starboard quarter. Now, at Low Water, the stern is almost beached. Where the rest of the yachts are, the water goes right up, but I'm happy to be where I am, rather than hemmed in by other boats. I like a bit of room, and wouldn't like my stern gear close to the wall anyway. While laying my lines, an English voice greets me.

"Hello, I'm Terry Hawkins. It's nice to see another Red Ensign; I'm surrounded by French and Germans." Terry is ex-English but has been in South Africa for 18 years, he has a 44ft Swan, "Thunderbird of St. Helier". We chat a little, but I want to get Roamer settled. He invites me to "Thunderbird" later for a beer and a braai. Wow! Is <u>that</u> a welcome invitation for a for a lone sailor just in from 85 painful days at sea, in a hot tropic port, with no local money, hungry and thirsty?

"Thanks a bundle, Terry, I'll be along shortly."

And so I am, as soon as I have Roamer secured to my satisfaction, and all sea gear stowed. I wash and change into a decent pair of shorts and shirt, down the ladder, up the beach, along the wall, and on to "Thunderbird".

It's a lucky break for me to find Terry, his beautiful wife Glynis, and their peaches-and-cream-complexioned teenage daughters, Samantha and Michelle. Two hours after entering a strange port, hot, sweaty and thirsty, here I am – in the cool cockpit of a real "yacht", drinking cold beer and chatting to three lovely females!

239

Terry and his Brazilian friend Flavio, from "Taiyo", next alongside, are on the wall attending to the braai. In the cockpit, we are joined by Flavio's beautiful sun-tanned wife, Regina. This is nice! Naturally, after my long voyage, I'm extremely garrulous, but although I keep apologizing for it, the ladies encourage me to talk. We have mutual friends in Cape Town, they have my Practical Boat Owners articles about Roamer lying on the cockpit table, and obviously think I'm someone famous. They are all ears for my salty Stories! Words just pour out of me!

The braai food is ready, and is passed aboard. At first we eat the very delicious chicken, steaks, wonderful (to me) fresh vegetables, and freshly baked bread rolls, in the cockpit, then a windy squall blasts in from the sea, rain blows under the awnings, we retreat below. What a beautiful ship, spotlessly clean and amazingly spacious, the seven of us, plus the two young boys from "Taiyo" fit into the saloon no problem.

I have a terrific evening, but my tiredness and the beers have a heavy effect on my eyelids, so I have to tear myself away, must have some sleep. The tide has risen and Roamer sits 10 feet off-shore! No problem here in the tropics, straight into the water I walk, pull myself out on the stern line, up the ladder and inboard. It's been quite a day, but aren't they all?

Wednesday the 17th of June 1987. The Journal starts the day. "How wonderful it is to be calm, still and quiet." So it is but all is not absolutely perfect. Though I slept from 2200 to 0430, a long time for me, it was very hot below, and the mosquitoes soon took a liking to my body lying on top of the sleeping bag. Even at 0600 I'm sweating, just sitting, writing. On deck it is slightly cooler, and I survey the surroundings. We are in the Cabanga Iate Clube de Pernambuco. The Marina lies at the South end of the river, and only 200 yards from us, are two wide bridges, which, night and day, carry heavy traffic. Brazilian drivers must be among the noisiest in the world, "driving on their horns", rather than their brakes. This makes the Marina rather noisy, and, at night, well lit by the highway lighting.

The Marina is only partly built, and all further development seems to have halted. One small dredger lies just inside the entrance, another, larger, lies outside, off the channel. Huge pipes, used by the dredgers, lie around the Marina in disarray, on the beach, on the wall, a bit of a mess.

To business. First day in, and I must gather the well known basic necessities of life, Money, Beer, and Bread. Plus, in this foreign port, the Authorities must be visited. In South Africa, Australia, and the Falklands, Customs and Immigration come aboard, but not here.

I unlash the folding dinghy from the Workshop bulkhead where it has lain since we were 500 miles West of Cape Town in November '85, rig, and launch it as transport to the beach. I rig a pulley system to get the boat from ship or shore.

"Ship's Papers" wallet in hand, with all the paperwork I hope need. I'm ashore by 0900, and, with helpful directions and suggestions from Terry H., head for town.

It's always a pleasure to me to take a long walk on getting into port, so I don't mind at all the two-mile hike. I walk along the wall which on entering I kept "10 to 25 metres off", the tide is high now and there is no sign of the mud banks. A cooling breeze blows in from the sea.

Along the waterfront road, over a bridge, the noisy traffic rushes past. Into the town and I'm all eyes at what is my first really "foreign" port for years. The sights and smells remind me immediately of Singapore, the contrasts of main roads and back alleys, expensive stores and street traders, "million dollar" banks and obvious poverty.

Money is my first objective, can't manage anything without that. So I wander around till I come across the "Banks area", looking for the "Banco Credito Nationale", which my Barclaycard information pack tells me is Barclay's agent in Brazil. But I can't find it, and can't ask anyone because of the language barrier. Ah! But what is this? a familiar green sign, "Lloyd's Bank", surely someone must speaka da English here?

By brandishing my Passport and cheque book at the security guards, and saying loudly, "Inglez, Inglez, Por Favor?" I manage to get them to bring an English-speaker to the door. This helpful chappie gives me the gen on bank opening hours, 1130 to 1600, and draws me a map with directions to the B.C.N. Bank, only a few hundred yards away.

I'm in the B.C.N. almost an hour while they phone B.C.N. in Sao Paulo, which appears to be Brazil's Commercial capital. B.C.N. Sao Paulo phone Barclays Sao Paulo and eventually the message comes through that the "Banco Mercantile de Sao Paulo" will accept my Barclaycard. B.C.N. have been very friendly and helpful, and now direct me to B.M.S.P. Keep Smiling Bob!

Unfortunately B.M.S.P. are not impressed by my Barclaycard, (or my smile) and send me round the corner to "Banco Noroeste", where, at last, I do get them to accept the card. Not a soul speaks English here, but after more phone calls, I leave 30 minutes later with 10,375 Cruzados, which equals 150 U.S. Dollars. Dollars is the only currency they work in, not being interested in Pounds. I reckon 150 Dollars equals about £220. Phew! Quite a battle, but the smiles won through.

It's now 1300, and outside the air-conditioned Bancos, I'm melting in the heat, starving, and desperate for a cold beer. These problems are solved in a near-by Cafe where, to keep the language simple, I choose a Hamburger from the Menu, and order a "Cerveza Antarctica." Both are very welcome, and though I have difficulty in understanding the money, I keep smiling and give the waitress as many notes as she wants. Well I don't know what they're worth! Next, Officialdom. Armed with information from Terry H., and from Nick Skeates' P.B.O. article, "Ports of Call, Salvador". I work out that I must visit, in this order, (A) Policia Federal, (B) Receita Federal, (Customs), and (C) Capitaine de Porto. Fortunately, these offices are fairly close to each other in the port area, and with only one hiccup involving a return visit to the Customs for a Form they should have given me, I have it all done by 1600. Great Stuff! So, it's 1600, we have money in the pocket, paperwork done, it's relaxing time, and though the Policia Federal gave me a strong warning about wandering around alone, and the dangers of mugging, and worse, I ignore it, and have the odd beer in the odd sleazy bar. I also find the "Correios", and send off arrival telegrams.

(Later, when I work out the Currency, I find that the telegrams cost £11 each!!!!).

After the telegrams, a few more beers, and a steak, and I buy a large straw hat. No one I meet speaks English of course, but with sign language, common sense interpretation of the Menu, and plenty of smiles, isa no problema!

But as darkness falls, and downtown Recife comes to life, I judge it politic to jump into a taxi, and back to the safety of the Marina. By 2000 I'm sitting on the Terrace, sipping a last "Antarctica". A busy day but a successful one.

The Thursday I spend on board and in the Marina, planning the jobs which must be done. I don't want to be here more than 10 days, so must get started. Terry and Glynis are planning to go to the "Shopping Center", where it appears there is a Supermarket and many other shops, much more civilised and organised than the shambles of Recife itself, and they invite me along. The jaunt is planned for tomorrow, which is just fine.

During the day I work on my Jobs List, in particular on the steering wire sheaves, some of which are stiff. I find though, that by 1100 it's far too hot to work, and slope off for a shower, followed by a couple of beers and a "Sandouiche Americane". In the afternoon, a snooze, but it's very hot and sweaty.

I manage to work out the currency, to a degree anyway, I'd heard on the radio that Brazil had a bad inflation problem, and it's true! What I didn't know was that only recently, to try to solve the problem, they had brought in new currency, the Cruzado, which replaced the old Cruizero. But, notes of both currencies still circulate, the Cruizeros being worth only 1000th of what's printed on them. This explains how I appeared to be giving away 1,000's of Cruizeros/Cruzados yesterday. As an example, a "Cerveza Antarctica", the local beer, costs, say 27 Cruzados, about 45p for 600 ml, but, if paying with the old Cruizero notes, it's 27,000, which sounds a lot of money for a beer!

In the evening I am on my way for a walk to see what lay over the bridges, at "Boa Viagem", but Terry and Family waylaid me at the Club, so, I'm happy to spend the evening in their pleasant company, plus more beer, and a delicious steak. I like it here! What I don't like though, is the number and variety of "beasties" on the beach and on the shore wall. These areas are just alive with inch-long Sandlice, Ants, Lizards, Crabs, and in the quiet of the late evening, large Rats prowl along the wall. I'm very worried at the prospect of Roamer being invaded by these denizens of the shore, and keep her well held off.

The night air is filled with the whine of midges and mosquitoes, and after only a few days here my body is covered with bites and lumps.

Sleeping is a problem, it being very hot below, but it's seldom possible to sleep on the deck, for this is the rainy season, and heavy showers are frequent. Then, of course, there is the noise and light from the bridge highways.

Another disturbing nocturnal activity comes from the fishermen, either in boats, trawling, or on the wall or beach, with throwing nets. The Marina has a Security Guard at the front gate, at the road end, but at the river end is completely open to all comers. At night the fishermen, during the day all and sundry, walk about the Marina, fish, get water from the jetty taps, do their washing, and bath themselves and their children!

Already I'm keen to get back to sea.

On the Friday (19th June '87) we make our visit to the "Shopping Center", going by bus, a very crowded bus! The fare is 5 Cruzados, about 8p, for a 5-mile ride! The Shopping Center is impressive, with escalators, fountains, children's play areas etc. I'm mainly interested in the "Bompreco" (Good Price) Supermart, and soon fill a trolley with basics of my shopping list. Biscuits, Canned Meat, Coffee, Oats, Beer, Fresh Fruit and Veg, Bread and Cheese. The prices are very reasonable and this first trip gives me a good idea what is available and how much it's going to cost me. The trolley-load costs me about £50, but I really filled it.

The return trip is by Taxi, and is my introduction to the local traffic, and the local Taxi drivers in particular. A large proportion of the Taxis are VW Beetles, painted bright orange, unsuitable for stowing bags of Supermart stores in, but very suitable for dodging through the traffic at high speed, one hand on the wheel, the other constantly on the horn, with loud and lively Rhumba music to help us along!

Red traffic lights call only for a slight slowing down, a quick look, and through them. In all my time in Recife I never saw a Police car on the road, the traffic is completely wild, except in the City where some crossroads are controlled by slim young ladies in smart green uniforms and shrill whistles.

The return route from the Shopping Center takes us along the "Bahia Boulevard", the Beach Road. A 6-lane highway, this 3-mile, perfectly straight Boulevard is pure heaven to the Taxi drivers, who fly along it at 120 km/hr, swerving from lane to lane, hooting happily. I take my mind off the driving by looking at, on one side, the blue South Atlantic breaking gently on the golden sands, where sun-bronzed beauties and macho Brazilian boys play ball games, and on the other, high-rise apartment buildings and hotels. This is Boa Viagem, Recife's "over-spill".

We survive the ride, arrive at the Marina, and, with a struggle, on my part, transfer the six large paper shopping bags along the wall, down the beach, into the dinghy, and back aboard, all the time vigilant that I don't import any of the local "beasties".

It's hard work, particularly in the steamy heat, which isn't my favourite climate by a long chalk, but, by Friday evening, I've made a good start on the Jobs List, and the Shopping List, and best of all, I now know my way around.

Having a quiet beer on the Terrace in the cool of the evening, I am joined by Monsieur Paul Evin, a sprightly 80 year old French/Portuguese History Professor. He arrives carrying a large coconut, which the waiter takes from him, returning shortly with the coconut in a jug with ice, and two large whiskies. Whisky isn't my tipple, but it's "interesting" with the milk! I enjoy sharing the drink with this very pleasant gentleman. Whisky and coconut on a warm evening in Brazil, Aha, this is the travelling life!

M. Evin tells me he has a boat in Falmouth Marina, Sea Laughter II, and knows Alan and Rosie Cummins in the Club, very well. We hope to meet when I get there in September.

Over the weekend (20th & 21st June) I work on Roamer from early in the cool of the morning until the heat becomes too much, and by Monday have laid the mast down, renewed the forestay, rigged Lazy-jacks from the Masthead, checked all round, and rigged it back up again. I've also been all round the hull checking for barnacles, but have found none. There's a strange crackling noise under the hull which I assume, (and hope), is the action of small marine creatures known as "crackers", similar to those at Port Owen, which I believe are nibbling at the barnacles lower down, where I can't reach, and will clean the hull of them.

Though the Marina moorings aren't very good, the "Iate Clube" itself has very fine facilities. Bar and Restaurant, Swimming Pool, Tennis Courts, and an open-air theatre-cum-social centre. The Saturday I was there was the Festival of "San Joao", and the "theatre" was full of children acting plays, singing, and having a lovely time. The evening was only spoilt for me by another aspect of the Festival. It appears the done thing for the male Brazilians to let off loud fire crackers, endlessly, all evening.

My evenings are spent either at the Club, or on "Thunderbird". Both are very good social venues. At the Club, mixed crews of Brits, South Africans, Brazilians, French and Argentineans, (the German detachment never visit the Club), have equally mixed conversations, interpreted as necessary by Flavio, who speaks very good English. The Argentinean, Jorge, and I, banter each other over the "Falklands/Los Malvinas" question. I tell him, "Mrs Thatcher will throw me into the Tower of London if she hears me calling the Falklands, Los Malvinas!" But we are sailors, not politicians, and have no problems.

The "local" club members don't appear to be very interested in sailing. There are about four small yachts in the Marina, but they seem to go in more for great, horrible, noisy, smoking fast motor boats, ostentatious in the extreme, and seemingly inappropriate for a poverty-stricken country like Brazil, in debt up to its neck. On another evening I take the Port Owen song book and paddle down to "Thunderbird" in the rope and canvas dinghy, a Tilley lamp shining brightly in the sternsheets, and we have a fun evening sing-song.

On Monday I decide to "raid the Bank" again. Terry is going to town, so he and I, plus 14-year-old Michelle, are in the hubbub of the Metropolis by 1000. There's safety in numbers, and we keep young Michelle between us, also for safety. Her blonde hair and fair complexion stands out among the swarthy Brazilians, and I see young "Macho Caballeros" licking their lips. "I bet we could get a good price for her on the Black Market!" I call back to Terry. Michelle is not amused.

We spend a few hot hours in town, Terry is trying to get "Charter Price" airline tickets to Europe. He has a medical problem which won't allow him to sail his yacht on long voyages, and is arranging for a delivery Skipper to come from Cape Town to take her for him. He has asked me to, and I was certainly tempted, but decided my first priority is to get Roamer home as soon as possible.

In the "Correios Y Telegraphos". I buy stamps for my postcards, and have a sticky time with them. The stamps themselves won't stick and have to be glued on, a rather messy business.

In the "Banco Noroeste", I have a heart- stopping time when the Bank Official shakes his head over the Barclaycard, having rung Sao Paulo. Damn these world-wide computers!! But I'm saved by my Barclays Premier Card, a sort of "Gold Card", the first time it's ever been any use to me, and only 8 days before it's due to expire. The Banco gives me 15,000 Cruzados on it, more than I need, or want, but the language problem is difficult, it's better to have too much than too little, and anyway, it's for sure that anything I buy here will be cheaper than at home.

Back at the Club, drenched by a heavy rain shower, running with sweat, we find the Club Bar closed, and Terry has to save us with a cold "Brahma" from his cooler on "Thunderbird".

I need to complete my Job List and during the week, pump out and clean the Starboard water tank, having done the Port one at sea. I plan to use only the Starboard tank for this last lap. I sew a patch on the peak of the Mainsail, where some of the Herring-bone stitching is pulling apart, check out the sail, and repair a few feet of seam stitching. The whole ship's side gets a coat of paint, which won't do it a lot of good, but improves her appearance.

From a garage just outside the Marina I buy a can of Engine Oil, run the engine till it's hot, and do an engine and filter change, the sweat absolutely pouring off me as I work alongside the hot engine. Another hot task is to load 48 gallons of Diesel fuel, carried in 6 trips of two 4-gallon

Jerricans, from the same garage. This job really makes me sweat, and the shoulders ache, but is preferable to taking Roamer to the nearest fuel pump, at another Yacht Club across the Bay.

For the "Diesel Operation" I turn Roamer round, running the anchor chain from the stern so that I can sit the bows on the beach and use the ladder rather than the dinghy.

While I have her turned round, I warp her close to the water tap to top up the tank and containers. "German Jim" suddenly becomes very friendly and loans me his water hose, which is much appreciated, even though I had already arranged to borrow Flavio's.

I make several more trips to "Bompreco", complete my shopping list, clear the Job List, and by Friday am "ready to go" again.

I pay the Marina charges, which are about £3.50 per day, a little expensive for what the Marina is, but acceptable for the facilities of the Club.

Its good to know my 'grams got through. I'm rather surprised not to hear from Terry or B.B.C. Radio Brighton though.

Friday afternoon (26 June) is devoted to "clearing" with Officialdom, and, knowing my way around the system now, I whistle through the Policia Federal and the Customs Offices. At the Main Gate of the Capitaine de Porto, however there's trouble. The young sentry at the Gate, stops me, shakes his head, points at my legs. I pretend not to understand the problem, but I know what it is. Terry Hawkins had told me that at Salvador he had been refused entry in the same way because he had been wearing shorts, as I am now. Damn, this is a nuisance, it will be a right drag to have to go all the way to the boat, put trousers on, and then all the way back, just for this laddie.

I protest, in a loud voice, "Mia Capitano Inglez, Have Documento Mucho Importanto, Capitano Inglez," I tell this young lad who, faced with a noisy, red-faced English Captain, looks for help toward the Reception desk in the building.

Taking advantage of his confusion, I make off towards the entrance. Reaching Reception, I put on the Big Smile, say to the Petty Officer there, "Por Favor Senor, Yacht Documento?"

"Si. O.K.", he nods, and I'm in. Phew, that was close. Ten minutes later I'm clear, leave the building, tip the sentry a wink and a mock salute, and make off to a taxi, fast.

24 hours to go, a last quiet evening and spent at the Club, a last quick visit to Bompreco on Saturday morning for fresh bread, cheese, fruit and

veg, and, my last buy, two typewriter ribbons, so that I can press on with this book during my last lap, and I'm back aboard by 1000.

The "Thunderbirds" get me to make an entry in their very interesting Visitors Book, a very last beer and a "Salado Mixta", up on the Terrace, give the last Cruzados and Cruizeros to Manuel, my favourite waiter, and I'm finished with the shore.

Back aboard, scrub the dinghy's bottom, hoist it aboard, dissemble and stow it. Turn Roamer the right way round, and prepare to go on the rising tide at 1430.

Terry H. will let my shore lines go, but of course, Murphy's Law prevails, and at 1400, wind and squalls with heavy rain sweep in from the sea, to spoil my departure. I had the extension speaker rigged, and bagpipe music ready to play me out of harbour, but have to stow it all away.

Terry lets my lines go just before the rain arrives and I lie to my anchor awaiting a lull in the squalls. I heave in as much chain as I dare so that I can scrub it in. It's thick with black mud and I can see the last bit of heaving in will be a messy business.

1500, O.K., time to go. I give 4 toots on my fog horn to let Terry and the other yachts know I'm coming and they can slack their bow lines off. In with the anchor chain, I give a burst ahead on the engine, run forward, pull in the chain, burst on the engine, run forward, pull in the chain, several times, the chain piles up on the foredeck, a black sticky mess.

Wash my hands in a bucket of water, back to the controls, another burst on the engine, up forward again, and this time I get the anchor, and leave it awash to clean. Wash hands, back to cockpit, sweat pours off me, it starts to rain again. Oh for a crew at times like this.

I motor slowly out of the Marina, "Auf Wiedersehn" to "German Jim", "Au Revoir" to the French boats, and "Bye Now, Thanks for Everything", to the "Thunderbirds". Lots of toots to the Club and my friends the waiters, and I'm out of the entrance and motoring down the channel to the Commercial Port. Here I stop, drop the anchor and chain again, then winch it slowly in, giving it a good scrub, don't want any drying, stinking mud in the bonny ship, do we now? It's hot, hard work though, for here, by the ships, there's hardly a breath of wind.

Secure the anchor, secure the ship for sea, out through the breakwaters, and we're heading for home, on the Last Lap!

Chapter Seventeen

Recife to Falmouth

We motor out between the huge stone breakwaters, and back into the rolling swell of the Atlantic. The wind is very light, and a Northerly current almost gets me into trouble, pushing us towards the shoals of Punta Olinda. Searching in the lumpy sea for the small Port Hand buoy, I at last find it, way out on the Starboard bow. Much relieved, I alter course, pass it safe to Port, and all is well.

A breeze comes in from the South, to which I hoist some sail, and we make slowly East. The current is strong and helps us away from the shore, Recife's lights are soon dipping below the horizon in the swell.

Olinda's very bright lighthouse flashes fine on the Port quarter as we roll off to the N.E. There are several ships about and I have the backstay fluorescent light on. I feel very tired, but doubt there will be much chance of sleep. Tonight's Motto is, "Take it easy, keep out of trouble."

Sunday the 28th of June '87. We did keep out of trouble, but it was a long night of squalls and calms, rolly seas, ships, fishing boats and fishing floats. We wriggle our way through all of them, motoring at times for progress. I managed one hour's sleep. Now, at 1030, we must be about 10 miles offshore, since I can see no land. From 0830 to 1000 the engine pushed us through a small fleet of fishing boats and out to seaward of them, into deeper water. I'm hoping we are now clear of the fishermen and their gear, floats and staves and rope lying in the sea, a danger to my propeller. Certainly the sea is more regular out here.

In a heavy rain squall I strip and take a delicious "Sunday Shower", singing loudly as I wash away the sweat and mosquito bites of Recife. "I'm gonna wash Recife right out of my hair, and sail along my way."

Not quite "South Pacific", but it feels good.

Sailing conditions are poor but at Noon I reckon we have made 40 miles on our way, a useful start. We are clear of the coast, which is the main thing.

Monday morning sees us making N.N.E. at about 2 knots on a light E.S.E. breeze. I'm feeling pretty well, and eating my way through the Recife fresh foods before they go off in the sultry heat. Breakfast is coffee, toast, cheese and tomatoes.

I have another bright idea, wire up the backstay light to the old Stern light deck socket, and can then turn it on from the switchboard instead of having to connect wires and crocodile clips to the battery terminals. The two black anchor balls are re-rigged as a radar reflector again. The Noon position is cheering, 76 lovely miles North, to 6° - 14'S., very nice too, we are 40 miles offshore.

In the evening I'm not feeling so good. Have a bad headache, feverish cold, aching limbs. Maybe my Sunday Shower wasn't such a good idea after all.

During the night I'm rather ill. I try to sleep below, but can hardly breathe in the stuffy cabin. Up in the cockpit, with shirt and shorts, tracksuit top, anorak and a bath towel wrapped around my legs, I alternately sweat and shiver. I feel terrible, weak and wobbly, my jaws ache and feel as though they may lock! What bugs have I brought from Recife? All night I twist and turn, in the cockpit, or in the cosy chair. When I doze I have vivid hallucinations, ships all around me, swinging deck cargoes over Roamer, some of which fall on the deck. (It's me, falling into the cockpit well from the seat.) Ship's crews are fighting and swearing all over Roamer. (That's me too, I awake sweating, shouting and trembling.) What a night! Come the welcome dawn I'm surprised to find only Roamer and me, all alone on the quiet sea, no ships, no crews. I feel very weak and am worse after a session on the toilet bucket which empties me completely.

On with the cooker, for strong coffee, with which I force myself to eat some biscuits, must flush the system out. Phew! What a night. I come to somewhat during the forenoon, but what was all that about? I put it down to (1) A cold fever from Sunday's shower. (2) Hallucinations maybe from Sunstroke, I hadn't worn a hat and shirt all of the time on Monday and got a bit burnt. (3) I'm suspicious of a can of "Fanny" Grated Bonito I'd partly eaten for supper. First time I had tried it and I'm always suspicious of fish for dreams and sleeplessness. I throw the rest of it over the side.

(4) Recife's Revenge, the well known stomach bugs we Northerners are susceptible to in the Tropics.

My Bonny ship looked after herself during the night, just as well, for I was incapable.

At Noon I find we have made 82 miles North! Wonderful, there must be quite a strong current.

During the day I take things easy and keep out of the sun, and in the evening feel much better.

By Wednesday (30th June) I'm almost over the "Bug" though I still daren't go very far from the toilet bucket, which I keep on deck, and use in the cockpit.

The Recife cheese gets a "float test." It's a very soft cheese, and though it tastes and smells O.K., it has been out in the heat for 4 days, so, anything I'm suspicious of, over the side with it. The bread is lasting surprisingly well, I finish a very juicy pineapple, the red apples are sweet and crisp, and a hand of green bananas is ripening nicely. I have a few potatoes, lots of onions and several nets of "Inhame" a very rough looking root crop I was recommended to try, as keeping better than potatoes.

We make good progress North and a little East in beautiful weather, real sparkling-blue Trade-wind conditions. I'm trying to keep some Easting in the course to counteract the Guiana North West towards the West Indies.

At Noon we are at 3°- 45S., 34°- 52'W., and have 270 miles logged. Not bad at all. We pass 60 miles to the West of Atol das Rocas, and now have no land or Islands to worry about. We head off into the wide open spaces of the vast ocean, soon to be the North Atlantic when we "Cross the Line" in a few days time.

Friday the 3rd of July. Journal, 0800: "Finished the bread for brekky, no more till Falmouth, then it'll be a good English Wholemeal bread, hard Cheddar cheese, and Cornish Pasties. All that is a long way away yet though. I've been practically living on coffee, bread and biscuits lately, trying to get this bug out of my system, which has my bowels feeling like water all the time, making me weak and sickly. Collected 5 litres of rain from a passing shower – it's very sweet-tasting in coffee or orange juice."

We "bound" North but the wind being East to E.N.E I can't make any Easting as I would like. At times I have the urge to set "Full Sail" that is, two panels of Main, but the wind is a brisk Force 5, sometimes a little less, sometimes a little more, and maybe the "little more" would be too much for the mast legs. So – Safety First is still the rule, must continue to nurse the rig on this, the "Last Lap."

On leaving Recife, I navigated on a Coastal chart, "Sac Luis to Recife" an out of date, black and white fathoms chart. Now, we run off it and transfer to the Metric Chart, "North Atlantic - Eastern Part," at 1: 10,000,000. The lower half of this chart takes us up to 35°N., and I don't allow myself to peep over the fold yet.

Saturday the 4th of July. 2200. I declare that we have "Crossed the Line" and are back in the Northern Hemisphere for the first time for two years. I celebrate with a couple of beers. One of them is a bottle of McEwan's "Strong" given to me by "Taffy" in Port Stanley. My, that seems a long way and a long time ago. I promised to drink it at the Equator and send him back the cap, which I shall do. It really is strong, more like treacle than beer, I shouldn't like to drink many of those!

Journal: "Supper was soup, with spuds and onions and half of one of my "Mystery" Brazilian cans. This one was "Lentilha con Palo e Carne." It was Lentils with meat as suspected, but what was the Palo?

At Noon on Sunday the 5th July we are at 0°- 30' North 35° - 40'W., and have run 537 miles in 8 days, very good, in our condition.

Toddling North, the water supply is replenished from passing squalls, the rain makes exquisite coffee!

I didn't entirely escape from Recife without some of its insect life. There are small flies aboard, hovering around the 'vegetables store" rising in a small cloud whenever I take something. I have sprayed them with 'Poison Gas', but they seem to like it!

Monday the 6th, 0830. I have to dismantle the Compass gimbal system which has ceased to "gimbal." The grease has dried in the ball races, I clean it out, re-grease and oil it and then the compass rocks splendidly.

I hear on the radio that the England cricket team have been beaten by an innings and 18 runs! By Pakistan!! Huh, I think that a Test Team that gets beat by an innings, ought not to be paid for that game. It might encourage them to try harder.

The weather continues to be very pleasant, a steady F. 5-6 Easterly, with not too much "sea." We plod on North at 2½ knots, slow but sure. During the night though, Mr. Weather reminds me that it's not all sunshine and blue seas. I awake at 0230, does E.S.P. warn me? I hear a squall approaching, the wind gradually rising, the sails taking the strain, rigging creaking and groaning. Better get up there quick. I struggle, only half awake, into the red waterproof jacket, up the ladder, through the hatch, into the cockpit - into a waterfall!! The rain teems down, but the wind is the danger, it's strong, too strong for the spindly legs of the mast. Must get the jib down. Roamer is lurching wildly in the suddenly-rough sea, the night as black as pitch. No time to turn a light on though, must get that jib down. I crawl along the deck to the anchor winch and untie the halyard, (now's the time to <u>know</u> the ropes, the knots, the <u>system</u>) and claw down the flogging sail. Secure the halyard, bowse down the sail, rain teeming down, waves leaping up. But with the jib down we are out of danger. There is only one panel of Main up, and that doesn't put much strain on the mast Back in the cockpit I adjust the helm and wait for the squall to pass. It's a long one, half an hour or more, but eventually it drifts off, the stars re-appear, and I watch them while waiting for the wind to come back. In another half-hour it doesn't, so I leave her and go back to bed, after drying off the lower half of me, which has had a welcome cold bath.

In the morning there is still no wind, so I motor for a few hours, until, at 1000, surprise, surprise, the wind does come back, F. 5-6, from the East again.

The Noon position is fantastic. There must be a wayward North-flowing current under us for we have made 95 miles to the North on the chart! Easily the best run since before Stanley, it whooshes us up to - 22'N., and our daily average becomes 70.7, since Recife – Terrific!!

Journal, 1830: "Had a tasty veggie soup for supper. Body and bowels in good shape at last, it's good to be well again."

By Wednesday the 8th, we are at 4° - 31'N., and "In The Doldrums." Hot, sultry weather, squalls, thunderstorms, all the usual fun. In the afternoon I have another tussle with Mr. Weather. The Easterly breeze is light, I try for my afternoon snooze, but it's too hot. So, on with the engine at 1400 and make some miles to the North. By 1430 though, the wind has freshened and I shut the engine down. Amazingly quickly the windward horizon is black, with white horses of the freshening wind standing cut brightly against it. I have full sail up, and start reefing. Looking to windward I mutter, "Better hurry Bobby-boy." I do, and have the sail down but not secured when the wind arrives, lots of it, all at once! I have to leave the Main, and get the jib down, quick-quick!

Motoring at 1430, with no wind, hove-to in a Gale 8 at 1500! I'm glad this one didn't arrive during the night. It blows hard for 90 minutes, and I even set the Storm Jib for progress, but it soon eases, the clouds disperse,

Mr. Sun re-appears. Down with the Brown Jib, up with the White one, and proceed. Tropical Weather!!

Supper is canned Tuna and sweetcorn over Inhame and onions. The Inhame is a great success, very tasty, like a firm turnip.

For five days we plug N.N.E. through the Doldrums, using the engine unashamedly, any time there is no usable wind, which is quite often. Must keep the miles up. The sail I can fly will never get us anywhere in these light puffs which only last an hour, or two, or four. The heat is oppressive in the middle of the day, from 1100 to 1500, and I hide below. The motoring is done in the early morning, and late afternoon or evening, averaging about 8 to 10 hours a day.

I eat later these days, "in the cool-cool-cool of the evening." Another Brazilian food success is the packet Macaroni, "Macarronada Instantanea – Preparo Rapido em 3 Minutos." It's good stuff, and I can prepare it "Rapido" with the aid of 5 little drawings on the packet. Yet another success – "Colombo Marmalada." Its recommendations are printed in 4 languages. "Packaged in rectangular cans making it easier to store and cut. Recommended by Doctors since 1892 for its high nutritive value. Respected product – Export quality." Most of all though, I like, "We use Grandmother's recipe, especially selected Guava Pulp, blended with sugar, and Love!" How nice? And it's not bad marmalade either.

Saturday the 11th, we are at 7°- 46'N., 34° - 45'W. 14 days out, 992 miles on the clock. P.D.G. Pretty Damn Good. I need the N.E. Trades though, and it's about time I got them. The Doldrums are much wider than expected, this far West.

Monday the 13th July. Up bright and early. Journal, 0300: "Dozed and kept lookout last evening, then we had a squall at 2330. Now the sky is almost clear and there's a whisper of a breeze from the N.E. I'm sure we're almost at the Trades, and plan a "Last Push" to get there, starting now. And I do. On with Polly Perkins and push on North, towards a bank of cloud with a very distinct dark base. As dawn breaks I can see pink clouds beyond, under the base. On and on, but I can't reach what I'm sure is some sort of front. Ah, we'll have a rest.

At 0600 I stop for breakfast. At 0745, the sound of wind – a squall coming? No, just wind, and it blows and blows, not strong, but steady, and as it holds. Yes, it appears that we have the N.E. Trades. They arrive at 9° - 30'N., and will blow us up to almost 30° N., during the next 20 days or so.

Thursday the 16th of July. Plodding N.W. wind and current are pushing us West, but this is to be expected. How far West is the big question. In calculating the distance to Falmouth, I reckoned we would go out to 45W., a long way, but it can't be helped. I had hoped to be able to make some degrees of Easting soon after leaving Recife, on the "South East" Trades, but they proved to be very much Easterly, with even a touch of E.N.E. in them, so that wasn't possible.

A fishing float passes close to Starboard, and a current flowing past indicates it is secured to the sea-bed. This seems rather doubtful, since we are in almost 5,000 metres of water, so, it probably supports a net, which means the proximity of fishing boats. Damn! However, I see the owner of the float at 1200, out to Port, and he moves astern, towards it. He looks like a typical Japanese or Korean, white hull streaked with rust. What a life these guys lead, dozens of them in that stinking boat, spending months at sea, years away from home, to earn a living.

In the evening the Northern horizon is clear for the first time for a while, and I get a clear sight of Polaris, the Pole Star, who will guide me to the North. He is out on the Starboard bow, of course, and be glad to see him on the other side in a couple of week's time, when, hopefully, we will be heading N.E., for home.

Plodding on through the Trades, I keep myself busy, mostly writing, catching up on this book, keeping lookout, listening to the radio. On the B.B.C. World Service the "Henry Wood Promenade Concerts" start, and the announcer tells me that the famous "Last Night at the Proms" will be on the 12th of September. Will I listen to it at sea or in Falmouth?

Wednesday the 22nd. At 16° - 05'N., 39° - 50W. 1,667 miles. 25 days out today, one third of my projected 75 days voyage, and going very well so far.

There is a problem with the water tank. It looks as though I have pushed my luck once too often with it. Only 25 days out and its contents are practically undrinkable! I have to strain the rust out, and boil it and still it tastes foul. Unwilling to upset my stomach again, I start on my "Emergency Water," about 12 gallons kept in various bottles and containers. Intake is reduced to one coffee for breakfast, one cup of Orange at lunch, one coffee with supper. I shall be on the lookout for rain clouds, and fully expect more squalls at the Northern end of the Trades.

Friday the 24th. A ship's lights pass well off to Port. He is heading S.E., probably from the States, or maybe the St. Lawrence Seaway, Canada, to the South Atlantic. He reminds me of the lights problem. I'm still not showing any, and am increasingly worried about being run down as we approach the busier Northern waters.

We sail on, to the N.W. crossing this great river of wind the N.E. Trades. Across 20 degrees of Latitude it blows, a 1,200 mile wide stream, creating its own current, blowing forever round the North Atlantic "High." The wind blows to the Caribbean, and peters out, the current continues circulating, back across the Atlantic, now as the Gulf Stream, then South, and West again, for ever and ever.

The weather is quite hot, although the wind keeps it cool on deck. Down below is stuffy and humid, and I try to keep the hatches open as much as possible. This, occasionally, as has just happened, allows the odd wave which might jump onto the foredeck, to cascade into the washroom. This is alarming at the time, but is relatively harmless, as the water just runs through the "shower" holes in the floor, thence into the bilge sump, and I pump it out later.

Saturday the 25th of July. Four weeks out today. This evening we are at 19 North, Recife lies at 8° South, so we have made 27 degrees North in 28 days, which is very satisfactory. That's 1,900 miles, averaging 67 m.p.d. 2.8 knots! We have been on the Starboard tack every day and 90% of that with only the white jib and one panel and the triangle of the Main. That's about 220 sq ft. of sail, not a lot to push Roamer along. Sunday the 26th. I have a bit of fun with the sextant today. We are due to pass under Mr. Sun, as we move North, and he moves South. At 1145 I go on deck to take a Meridian Altitude Sight, not really expecting to get a usable one, more for the experience. But, to my surprise, I do get one, out over the Port quarter, at 1155. The Angle, after two corrections, for Dip, and for Semi-Diameter, is 89° - 27.1, which gives a Zenith Distance of 0°- 32'.9, which added to the Sun's Declination, gives a Latitude of 20° - 01'N. So, we are "North of the Sun" for the first time for 2 years, and I must get into the habit of looking for it to the South!

The sea is rather rough today, the Trades a boisterous Force 6. I lost my last plastic bucket earlier. Dropping it over the side for washing-up water, I got a "full load" and the handle pulled out. Damn! That leaves me with only my old faithful black bucket, which I've had since prior to "Aries." In fact, I mixed the fibre-glass resin for her fitting out in that bucket.

Tuesday the 28th. Two years out from Old England today! Shades of Richard Henry Dana's "Two Years Before The Mast!"

During tonight we should officially pass out of the Tropics, crossing 22½ North, the Tropic of Cancer.

I'm trying hard to keep the course as Northerly as possible, not only on principle , since that is where we want to go, but to keep us "on the chart." Having been pushed out to 44° - 10'W., my plotting is now very near the left-hand edge of the chart, and I have nothing for further West.

In fact, on Friday the 31st, the last day of July, I have taken our course line off the actual chart, and on to the border. Fearing falling over the edge, I transfer the chartwork 10 to the East. Damn!, we are out to 45½° W. That's a long way from Falmouth.

The Trade wind gives us good mileage to the North though, even if it is painful work. I have to steer a middle course between making as much Northing as possible, while keeping the daily run up to about 60 miles. It's a delicate battle at times, but any attempt to steer too much to the North just stops her in the water.

The constant rolling, and "falling off to loo'ard" are very wearying, but it's no good me asking "How much more of this can I put up with?" for, however much more there is, I will have to put up with it. There's no respite, no taking a day off out here. I must just "Grit the Teeth" and look ahead to the day soon when we will be out of the Trades. But then I doubt that I shall enjoy the calms of the "Variables" for very long!

I'm still chancing my luck by sailing without lights. My night routine consists of taking a look every half-hour or so during the evening, except when I take a nap, about 2200 to 2300, then look out again till after midnight. Even during my "long sleep" period, of 0100 to 0500, I get up once or twice for a look-see.

It's dangerous though, and when the ships start appearing frequently, I really will have to show a light when I'm not looking. Trouble is, I don't have the battery power to keep an electric light on, nor sufficient Paraffin to have a Tilley Lamp going all night.

Mind you, I'm not at all sure that ships can be relied on to see my lights! It's my belief that, shipping economics being what they are, very tight, there is probably only one man on watch, away from Coastal waters. The Auto-Pilot steers her, day after day, night after night, and if that one man is slumped in a cosy chair, reading "Playboy", I've got no chance!

Monday the 3rd of August. It looks as though we have run out of the Trades, at 27° - 30'N., 46° - 50W. We have a light Easterly breeze, the sea is calm, and very blue. If this is the end, we have had a good run on the

Starboard tack. <u>For 37 days and 2,475 miles,</u> the sheets have been on the same side, and I've not needed to use my new gibing system.

Whilst waiting for the Sun to reach its Meridian Altitude, I see a ship approaching from the Southwest. He heads directly towards us, and at 1300, the "Donau" of Hamburg, passes half a mile astern. I call him on V.H.F., hoping to get a "Report me to Lloyd? message out but get no response. I see no-one on the bridge either, but I am suspicious of the radio. The "TX On" indicator doesn't light when I press the "Talk" button, so I have to assume that the radio is U/S. "Donau" goes steaming off to the Northeast, she'll be going "Up Channel" in not many days time, unlike me.

The wind has gone, and I settle into a motoring habit again, putting in 8 hours or so a day, heading N.N.E. to claw back some Easting.

There is a lot of rubbish in the otherwise sparklingly clean sea, a large piece of green netting, plastic drums, bottles, (with their tops on!) pieces of timber etc. All indications of shipping lanes. Of course I have to throw <u>my</u> rubbish over the side on these long voyages, but at least I make sure all my cans sink, and fill any bottles with water. The "Ocean Passages" chart of "Main Routes for Power Vessels" tell me we are on the shipping lanes between Ushant and the Caribbean. We'd better show lights from now on.

Journal, 1930: "Supposing Donau had been 9 hours earlier? 0400, sleepy bridge staff, me asleep, no lights on, right in their path. Could have been the end of Roamer and me. Must show lights."

The very next night, at 0300, lying becalmed. Another ship passes only half a mile ahead - it's getting crowded!

The silence on these calm nights is marvellous. Utter peace, stars' reflections twinkling on the undulating black ocean, the hum of my "personal computer" is the only sound. It really is amazing how much noise my head makes!

I finish, at last, the 500g tin of Co-op Coffee powder bought in Stanley. Now I can start on the Nescafe "Pete" granules from Recife. The difference in taste is remarkable. I bought 2½ kg, in 100g jars, "They've got an awful lot of coffee in Brazil!!"

These are quiet days, when I'm not motoring, and quieter nights. 0100, the 5ᵗʰ August, Journal: "Up top and looking. It's wondrously calm and quiet. An aircraft's lights pass ahead as we lie stopped, pointing East, and it's so quiet I can hear it faintly, a whisper of sound in the vast sky. It is probably 20 miles ahead and at 50,000ft."

0930. A freighter passes to Starboard, about 8 miles off. It's very hot, and calm. I dissect the V.H.F. radio, but on seeing its "innards" put it back together again. There's a miracle of miniaturisation in there, but I see no reason why it won't work. But, it won't, so no radio to get off ZD2 messages, (Report me to Lloyds), no radio to contact the Coastguards when I near England. Better brush up on my Morse and try flashing messages, and, as a further contingency plan, maybe I can call in at the Scillies and give the folks prior warning of my arrival?

Friday the 7th of August. Pumping up fuel to the header tank, I find the upper tank is now empty, which means there is only about 60 gallons remaining, maybe 300 miles motoring. I'll now have to start economising with the engine, using it only when we are absolutely stopped through lack of wind.

There is a shocking amount of rubbish in the sea, here at 36 N., 44N. Mostly plastic buckets, drums and bottles. I pick up two useful floats whilst motoring, and would have had a third, if I hadn't been so busy. I was sat on the toilet bucket, and steering for a rain cloud, which I wanted to catch up with before dark, and so couldn't stop. I caught the cloud, and got 10 litres of sweet water from it.

The hot weather has brought out the midges again, which I thought I'd exterminated. They must have been semi-hibernating during the cool winds of the Trades.

The sea around here is rather "dead." No birds, no fish, no anything. It gave me a gift though. I picked up a 15ft aluminium pole with two floats. It had a bullet-spattered radar reflector at its top, and a cement weight at the other end. I chopped off both extremities, and will modify it for a useful dan-buoy.

"Auntie Beeb" has been promising me a Prom all week, Rachmaninov's Piano Concerto No 2, one of my favourites, but this far West, reception is poor until about 1900. So, since I can't pick up the B.B.C.'s performance, I have my own, with supper, courtesy of the cassette player.

Sunday the 9th is a long and busy day. I sleep on deck these days, a wonderful experience, but at 0200 I'm up to make a gybe for a better course. At 0430 we get a heavy shower and again 10 litres of water. Another dan-buoy comes in sight at 0730, so I pick him up too. This time a 20ft pole, with floats and a weight. It carries passengers, half a dozen crabs, which I have to chase over the side, I don't want them aboard, thank you.

A large brown whale passes 200 yards to Port at 0820, but shows no interest in us.

The middle part of the day is very hot, and I hide below from the sun. Later in the afternoon though, a little breeze pops up from the S.S.E. and we sail slowly E.N.E.

Sailing when I can, motoring N.N.E. when I can't, the course starts to tend towards where we want to go and we are back on the chart, at 31° - 32'N., 43°- 25'W. We have run 2,780 miles and have approximately 2,100 to go.

Sunday 10th August. 2100. I sit in the hatchway, relaxing listening to the radio. There's a lot of electrical crackle, and I can see the cause, very bright flashes of lightning., to the East, rumbles of thunder roll across the sky. Soon though, the thunderstorm isn't a distant one, it's coming my way! A black-as-pitch cloud approaches from the East, even though the wind is Southerly. The lightning becomes severe, off radio and isolate the batteries, dress for a storm, it looks as though we are going to sail right through it.

Great forks stab across the sky, and become too bright to look at, thunderclaps boom and reverberate across the heavens. All this isn't too serious, being steel, Roamer will conduct electricity into the sea, and thunder I actually enjoy. What I don't like the look of though, is, right in the centre of the blackest part of the black cloud, is a persistent fork of thick lightning, it stabbing down directly into the sea. There must be millions of volts in that and suddenly I feel very vulnerable, the only object on the sea's surface, just begging to be a conductor for that thick rod of silver. It is only a few miles off now, and I can actually hear it crackle as it stabs down, seemingly from only a few hundred feet above the sea. I daren't let that hit us, it would, at the very least, melt thc mast, at the worst, burn me to a frizzle. Time for action!

Down with the jib real quick and lash it to the guardrails. Start the Perkins, and having got it going, turn off all electrics. I judge the storm is moving N.W., so I motor off to the South, to outflank it. South is, of course, pretty much the last direction I want to go in, but that doesn't matter to me right now. The lightning , almost non-stop, crackles and forks overhead, the thunderclaps are physically painful, and I cower over the wheel under them. The blackness of the cloud at the storm's centre is impenetrable, except by that rod of fire which continues to stab into the sea. We are moving away from it now though.

A new problem! Strong winds come out of the storm and the Main, with two panels up, is on the wrong side. The rigging creaks and groans alarmingly, I want to reef but can't as I have the rain-catcher rigged along the boom, and the lazy-jacks are inside it! Bad news, things happen quickly when it's all going wrong. I quickly rig the Port stand-by backstay as a lazy-jack, let the halyard go, and the sail comes down in a heap. Never mind, I lash it into a bundle and concentrate on steering away from the black nasties in that storm centre. The wind blows strongly, the rain lashes down, but I have my "Cape Horn" jacket on, up with the hood and I'm cosy. I only have it and a shirt on, the legs can get wet, and it's quite warm.

More revs on Polly Perkins to get round the side of the storm clouds. We are making it O.K. getting towards a lighter area of sea, the full moon shining down on it. We bustle through the choppy sea, rain, wind, thunder and lightning, what a life! We escape from the clutches of that inky black cloud, and arrive eventually in the moonlight, the wind falls off, the rain stops, and suddenly it's all over.

The thunder is now a murmur, the lightning flashes, but now distantly, we wallow in the choppy sea for a while, but it soon settles down. It's 2330, off engine, sort out the mess of the Main, hoist sail to a little Easterly breeze, down below to dry off, and bed. Another crisis survived.

Yes, Sunday was a long day, but not a long run, Monday's Noon position shows we moved only 22 miles in the 24 hours. Not so good.

Monday, 1800, Journal, "The Southerly wind has held all day and if it continues we should have 50 to 60 miles to the East tomorrow. Not exactly the course I want, but any wind, just about, is better than no wind! Life is rather uncomfy in the chop, but I ought to be used to it by now. I wonder what tonight holds for us?"

Later; "We plod on, sometimes I think we'll be plodding on for ever. Its a long, slow task, but only one way to see it through, and that is to keep trying, keep plodding."

Two ships pass today. They are a real menace. They appear so quickly, in 20 to 30 minutes from not being there, to being upon me. I show a light all the time now, when I'm sleeping. I do seem to be up to see them all though, is that E.S.P. working? That's if I do see them all, of course, if I miss any I'll never know!

By 1800 Wednesday 12th August I reckon that the Southerly wind that we've had for two days, is drawing to the West of South, and that it's time to gybe to the North. So, round we go, no bother these days, and, when round, we make 345° (T), which, with Easterly current flowing, will take us North. Present tactics are to work our way Northwards, keeping well to the West of the Azores, pass N.W. of the Islands, then N.E. for the Channel.

1400 on Thursday brought my closest ship yet. Journal, 2000: "I saw him coming in from the Port beam, when I popped up for a look-see after lunch. He was heading East, and looked as though he would pass across the bows, but I didn't like the way his relative bearing remained steady. I was right to feel uneasy; I was under sail, making about 2 knots North, and this huge tanker, I reckon about 200,000 tons, passed only 200 yards ahead of me. I had my binoculars on the bridge, and never saw a soul up there, or anywhere else on the shop. I didn't need binoculars to read his name, "Brazilian Vitoria", I could even read the "No Smoking" notice on the superstructure! She was steaming at about 15 knots, and pushing a pressure wave a good 30 feet in front of her great bluff bows. (I wonder if that pressure wave would push me out of the way?) As she steamed past, I was rocked by her passage, and then could see on the enormously wide transom, her Port of Registry, "Monrovia"! Say no more! Seeing that name convinces me that they never did make any alteration of course for me, and indeed, were probably all at lunch. Monrovia, Liberia, has probably the world's worst reputation for "Flag of Convenience" ships.

Of course I was ready to start the engine and save myself, but supposing this had happened at night? What chance have I got, if they don't see me in broad daylight?

Later; "Am feeling despondent this evening, it all seems such a long plod, and we haven't made much progress lately. For two days I went East and even a little South, now I head North and a little West! It seems impossible to get into the Northeast quadrant that I need to be in. Then there's the speed, or lack of it. Plodding on and on at walking pace across the vast oceans - it's very dispiriting at times.

Friday the 14th of August 1987

Position 33° 06' N 40° 20' W Total run 3,045 miles. Meridian Altitude a nice surprise, almost a degree North-and 20 East, nice one!

During the afternoon the light Westerly wind pipes up to F4 - 5 and we head NE / NNE, slow but steady.

There's Spam and pickles, baked beans, coffee with whisky AND Wings on the music box. All hatches are open, and its warm and sunny. At 2000

I advance the clocks 1 hour to GMT -2, which cheers me up more. I continue the 'party' with more of the same menu but this time washed down with two cans of 'Brahma Chopp' Brazilian beer. I've saved them and am chuffed to find yet another can underneath these two. A 'Happy Day' for me too.

As night falls it's good to see Ursa Major and Polaris on the Port bow, and they're getting higher in the sky all the time. All I have to do is to keep plodding!

Next day is not such a good one, we only make 35 miles in the 24 hours, and that just about due East! Disturbances in the sea indicate a current, which I suspect is setting S.E. Not so good. Sea conditions are poor, with a lumpy sea which is bad enough, but there's also a long groundswell which creates its own wind, throws the light Westerly breeze out of the sails and backwinds them. Each swell leaves us rocking wildly after its passing, sails slatting and banging, and ruining our efforts at progress.

Over the weekend we trudge slowly North on light breezes, using the engine now and then to keep us up to some sort of average, until 0830 on Monday the 17th August. We had been stopped all night, then motored from 0615 to 0815, when a squally wind got up. It didn't last long though and at 0830 I had to start the motor again. As I put it into gear I hear a loud crack. The forward gear has always 'cracked' but this time sounds somewhat louder than normal. I disengage gear and pop below for a look. All appears ok so, up top again, into gear with only a light 'snap'. Ah, that sounds better, revs on, but no progress, what now? Below again, prop shaft turning, and all looks well. Up top, I look over the stem but oh dear, prop not turning which can only mean one thing. Damn and blast, the prop shaft has snapped inside the stem gland I don't have much time to think about the implications though. The squally wind is rising again, and I hoist sail into it and we head N.E. But – problem upon problem – a look over the stem shows that the propeller is dragging the snapped shaft out of the stem gland and will jam the rudder if I don't do something about it.

DOUBLE DAMNATION! Down with all sail, strip off and into the choppy sea with ropes to lash the propeller forward away from the rudder. The sea is cold and rough, and the barnacles inflict many cuts on my naked body as I struggle to get a knot on to the prop. But I manage to get it done, climb aboard and tie the rope to a guardrail stanchion amidships on the Starboard side. Never satisfied though I go back into the sea leaving a trail of watery blood on the deck. My reward for going back in is to pass a second rope. As I struggle again, a series of larger waves come along, and Roamer's stem pitches high, and one of the rudder's wooden steps hits me on the left temple. I am knocked out for a few seconds and come to only a few yards from the ship, spitting out sea water and with my left eye red with blood. I manage to reach the stern steps and hang on for my life until I regain full consciousness which is helped by the chill of the water. I pull myself aboard, dripping blood and water, looking, and feeling, as though I've had a tussle with a shoal of piranha fish!

Journal 1100 So we are now a pure sailing vessel, or rather, half a pure sailing vessel. No engine and no radio to tell anyone about it. Certainly a problem, though not so much for now, since we are short of diesel anyway, rather more of a worry for later, when closing the coast, for I'll be unable to work my way into a port, disabled as I am. Oh well! I have plenty of time to work it all out don't I?

Later 1130 Had refreshing rain water bath in the cockpit

1140 Had large Scotch and water

1200 Had lunch

1215 Fell asleep and slept through Mer. Alt time.

1300 Awoke, kicked myself, and got a P.M. sighting.

Position somewhat dubious but it doesn't seem to matter a lot. We are becalmed anyway on a calm sea. Position approx. 550 miles S.W. of Horta, Faial, Azores.

In the evening we are still becalmed on an almost perfectly flat sea. I have cleaned myself up somewhat, and sponged some of the blood from the 1-inch cut on my left temple. The rest can fall off on its own, and it's rather painful.

I have a cheap rice/mixed veg/sardine supper and muse upon my situation. My musings are not entirely happy ones! Now engine-less, I shall feel very vulnerable at not being able to get out of the way of ships. I put on a life jacket and put some flares in the cock pit for ready-use. I'll have to further economise on the food stocks, but at least the water situation is good at present.

We cross the fold in the chart and I can now see our destination – 1800 miles to go. It looks a long way!

Thursday 20th August. 1987 2000 This evening we are on the latitude of the Straits of Gibraltar, but 1600 miles West of them. We have plenty of ships around us now. Yesterday afternoon, unable to sleep, I popped in to the cockpit only to find a huge ship passing 400 yards down my port side.

The 'Kapitan Sideris', with a tiny figure high up on the bridge looking at me through binoculars. We exchanged waves as the throbbing monster swept past. Then, today at 0730 I saw a ship in amongst the squalls to the N.E. He made a substantial course change to pass close to me. He was the 'Pascal', a French gas tanker. Several immaculately white-clad officers on the bridge waved to me. I wonder if they are looking for me ?

'Friday 21 August 1987 0730. Passed a quiet night, no ships and not much sleep. I just had an interesting experience! I was sitting below writing this book , when Roamer calls me up top by luffing the jib, which hasn't happened all night. Up there, I see we are about to run into four small whales sleeping on the surface. I up-helm to avoid them, then they sense me and gracefully flip their beautiful tails in the air and dive. Interesting, eh? Roamer calls me up to see = E.S.P.!

1300 Mer. Alt not so good only made 31 miles to the North. I believe we are being set S.E. by the Azores current. We are 325 miles S.W. of the 'Flores in the Azores'. That's one of the few poems I know two lines of. 'At Flores in the Azores, Sir Richard Grenville lay'.

Saturday 22nd August. Position 37 02 N 36 15 W. Weeks run 304 miles!

Wednesday 26th August 1987 Journal heading, Day 4l. No Position worked. No sun available. No progress anyway. Then 1800, where to start with today's tale of woe last night I suppose when I was continuously trying to coax her along, gybing, up jib and down jib. Left her at 0100, trickling N.W., up at 0300 to pump up the Tilley night light and she was on N. Up at 0530 to turn the lamp off, course E. and that's the story of the day really, a story of painfulness, puffs of wind from all directions, Roamer going in circles but making no progress. Has no sun for sights which doesn't matter since we've hardly gone anywhere. In the afternoon, rain woke me from my much-needed snooze, but wasn't really heavy enough to catch. The breezes aren't strong enough to be useful, and there's a nasty, choppy swell rolling us painfully.

Anything else? Oh yes, supper was a failure too, left-over meatballs, spinach and rice. Bound to be a failure I suppose!

So, here we are, having a really poor time of it, not going anywhere and suffering. Of course, everything goes wrong at times like these, radio reception is poor, everything rattles and clunks, my nervous system is jangly – tight and all is nasty. How long will we be stuck here?

Saturday 29th August 1987 sees us at last scraping across latitude 40 N., quite a landmark for me as I've looked forward to getting here for sometime. I have a feeling we are out of a hole and can soon expect fresher winds from the W. and N.W. 1210 position 40 17 N. 32 50 W. and I am <u>1325 miles from Falmouth</u>. Nothing now between us and the Lizard except for the curvature of the Earth.

I am re-reading Donald Ridler's 'Erik the Red'. He sailed from the Azores to Falmouth in 1971, in his engine-less, home-made, £200 Junk-rigged boat and had a hard time at this very time of the year. He had headwinds, calms and fog! It took <u>him</u> 35 days, so I am warned.

Tuesday 1ˢᵗ September 1987 0700. September started early with me up at 0100 to reef the main. The night was dark and gloomy, but I could see the loom of the lighthouses on Corvo and Flores to the South. Then, at dawn I could see the purply-grey lump of an island. LAND HO! but no spectacular sight and anyway of no use to me. We are sailing due E. on a southerly breeze. Then in the afternoon, heavy squalls and rain which gives me 9 litres of lovely fresh water, but better still, after the squalls, the wind stayed in the N.W. and we made off to the N.E. at a rampaging 2½ knots. WONDERFUL!

The ocean today is as different to yesterdays as chalk is from cheese. Yesterday, choppy, lumpy and full of 'races', whereas today a big ocean swell from the N.W. It's like being in a new world!

The nights are chilly now, and I'm back to wearing shoes and socks, trousers <u>and</u> a jersey, when its windy that is. My lovely N.W. wind soon gets round to the N. again though, and we can only make to the E. What a struggle I'm having making Northing being only one able to sail beam-on to the wind.

On Friday the 28ᵗʰ we were in Lat 39 48 N. on Saturday 40 17 Sunday 40 29 Monday 40 18 Tuesday 40 14 Wednesday 40 28 Thursday 40 29 Friday 40 56 and during that time we made Easting from 33 45 W. to 29 20 W. A hard struggle indeed. Not until the early hours of Friday 4ᵗʰ of September do we get a useful wind from the W. By 0630 its F 4-5 and by 1000 a lovely, lovely F 6 on which we make to the N.N.E. at our maximum now of 2½ knots.

I had a laugh earlier – a small, brown turtle was being harassed by a Dorado snapping at his rear flippers. The turtle promptly pulled in his aft flippers, paddled like mad with his front ones, and the Dorado eventually decided that the turtle was a tough lunch and gave up the job. There are still flying fish about and my resident pack of killer fish are busy hunting them.

The Mer Alt result at 1205 on Saturday shows progress to the N. of 57 miles! Great stuff, and nearly a degree to the E. – best news for some time. It does go to show that we can make some sort of decent progress if only I can get F 5 -6 winds from the W. or N.W. Ah, but the wind doesn't last long and my noon log report on Monday the 7th records a run of 15 miles

At 0630 this morning I went in to the sea again to tighten the ropes holding the propeller. I didn't want to, the water looked decidedly black and cold. However this time I wore a shirt, trousers and deck shoes. The job took half an hour but was well worth doing. Afterwards I treated myself to extra rations of coffee, biscuits and porridge as a reward.

At lunchtime we have some 'Good News', an item in distinctly short supply of late. Whilst up top for the Mer. Alt. sight, I see a ship coming from the N.E. He alters course to close me and though I don't believe my radio works, I try calling him and to my great joy he comes over clearly. I have a very useful conversation with the captain of the British ship 'Author' or should it be Ortha? during which he promises to report me to Lloyds of London and the coastguards and tells me there is a big High in Finisterre. I kick myself afterwards for not giving <u>him</u> the info that my engine is useless, but I was so excited I just forgot.

On Wednesday I force myself into the sea yet again to scrape off as many of the loathsome goose barnacles. Really revolting creatures they are too. I can see them festooning the lower part of the hull but cannot reach them. The water is cold and half an hour at this job is quite enough. I am afeared of sharks too, it would be terrible to get attacked now after all I've suffered. We are only about 1000 miles from home now, but its still a long way to go at a ridiculous rate of progress we're making.

I am in a gloomy mood. The journal says "Philosophical Thoughts" – Plodding is a very appropriate term for our disastrous progress of late, as, 1. A long-term prisoner plodding round the damp earth of his exercise yard. 2. The down-trodden peasant plodding homeward after a long weary day in the field, or 3. The defeated soldier plodding off the battle-field. This evening I certainly feel imprisoned, down trodden and defeated as we sometimes plod, sometimes not, rolling all the time, making desperately poor non-progress. Sometimes my reserve snaps, I can't stand any more of the flopping of the jib, the slatting of the Main. I rush to the jib halyard, tear down the sail furiously, tie it up tightly, sheet in the main hard to stop it's banging and creaking. I shout abuse at the sky, the wind gods, and anyone else who might be up there torturing me like this. Then I subside, first into despondent thoughts, then the fury will pass and I do something positive to take my mind off the agony

1930, Stopped again – wind gone – weather very ominous. Sky black-black, even though a full moon has risen in the S.E. The evening is full of silent menace – what happens now?

On Thursday 10th September. Noon we are through the 1,000 mile barrier and are only 985 miles from Falmouth. We are 76 days out from Recife and a note in the log says, "how now the 75-day chart which I started at our last port as the expected time to home". How now indeed!! During the afternoon the wind rises quickly and I'm soon reefed down to the top triangle and the storm jib, the barometer down to 1005, the lowest for months!

By 1930 I have been just in time to get all sail down in the face of a blast of wind from the South. Barom at 1930 is 998, wind S. F. 9 - 10. From becalmed to bestormed in less than 24 hours, what a life!! I gybe her at 2330 to the North as the wind goes West, and then I was up all night on lookout, hoping desperately that we won't meet a ship on such a wild night as we had. Great seas such as I haven't seen since about 35 South, sweep around and over us, and very unwelcome they are.

At 1130 on Friday 11th September, the storm degenerates into a series of violent squalls, which themselves terminate in a fantastic rainfall, a complete white-out of rain and mist, with 20 yard visibility. It still blows hard from the West, but the worst seems to be over. We make 2 knots to the North under storm sails, and sights grabbed between the clouds put us at 43 16N., which equals 34 miles of Northing and 48 miles made to the N.E.

After the storm gave us a bit of decent mileage, Mr. Wind did the dirty on me once again by going to N.W., then N., and then to where I most dreaded it would, the N.E., bang on the nose, a dead header, stopping us in our tracks!

On Saturday 12th September, I'm writing gloomy thoughts on starting our 12th week at sea. Progress is terrible, our total mileage for the 11th week is 230, an average of 32.8 per day, and worse, miles made good towards Falmouth, only 180!!

In the evening I tune into "The Last Night at the Proms", usually one of my favourites, but I'm in such a gloomy mood that I turn it off, unable to stand the sound of the happy young people at the Albert Hall.

I sit up top under the stars, becalmed yet again. Jib down, main sheeted in tight, in a mood of resigned sadness. "It's a hopeless business and I no longer have any hope," I write.

After a few days of uncomfortable gusty winds from S.W. and W., the wind goes again into the N.E. and blows a full gale from where I want to

Solo sailor Bob limps for home

ROUND-THE-WORLD yachtsman Bob Burns is heading for home — very slowly — after more than two years at sea.

The Brighton sailor has been spotted 100 miles north of the Azores and is expected to reach the British mainland in about a month.

The final leg of the journey has been anything but plain sailing and he is now limping along at a speed of only two knots, with makeshift sails.

In March, bachelor Bob feared his life-long dream had been shattered by the worst Falklands storm for 40 years.

His 36ft. cruiser Roamer was ripped from her moorings. Part of the steel hull was crumpled by the battering that followed and the mast and rigging damaged.

Now family and friends are preparing to welcome back the adventurer. Bob, who started the voyage in July 1985, is due to land at Falmouth before heading for Brighton Marina.

Evening Argus 10th September 1987

go. I heave-to on the Port tack, with no sail up. "Stuck on a stick" is how the log describes it – very aptly. On the evening of Wednesday the 16th I have to do an emergency gybe to avoid collision with a ship which appeared to steer away from my Port bow but then changed his mind and appears determined to run me into the sea. I hoist the storm jib quick-quick and gybe her round and he shoots by no more than 200 ft away! This is ridiculous. A bloody gale on the nose and trying to do me down! My language in his direction is not for printing.

The N.E. wind blows for four days and at the end of it, for all my struggles, for all my grovelling on the pitching, rolling foredeck with the jibs, for all my hours on lookout, we are 35 miles further from Falmouth than before that accursed wind started. I am somewhat unhappy!!

On the 19th I talk with a large bulk carrier, the "General Cruz", who promises to report me. Weather is hopeless, light airs and bumpy seas. The weather becomes more violent now, with squally gales from the W. and N.W. but at least we make some progress, and on Monday 21st September, the Autumn Equinox sees us at 44 50 N., 22 25 W, and only 800 miles from Falmouth. We get regular gales now, and cold winds with them. I live in my oilskins, never more than an hour below, fearful not only of the weather, but of the ever-increasing volume of traffic. I try to keep some sort of light on all night but don't have much in the way of lights or electricity, and am short of paraffin for the Tilley lamps. I want to save paraffin for the stove, not that we have a lot of food left either!

On Wednesday the wind goes into the N.E. again – and blows a gale. Next day I "chat up" a Blue Star refrigerator ship, the "Auckland Star", and a cheery English voice promises to report my position to Lloyds. That's the only good news, for this "killer" Nor'easter blows until Sunday and we lose more miles, blown back to the West 22 miles. For the gale I went onto the Starboard tack and headed N.W. instead of S.E. on Port tack. Already I'm worrying about being pushed into the Bay of Biscay.

During the gale I made a white bow light out of the remnants of the stern light as a base, a 10 watt bulb, and a jam jar. I've rigged it on the pulpit and it gives a good light, I think, but is rather bad for night vision. My plan is to keep it off when I'm up and about, and turn it on if a ship gets close.

I give myself a vicious haircut, hacking off large lumps of matted knots, and immediately regret it when the cold night winds blow on the back of my neck.

Another ship almost runs me down on Monday evening, even though I have the Tilley lamp on and flash "D" at him with the big flashlight. He comes up from astern and passes only 200 feet to Starboard! He's so close I hurl abuse at him across the waves – my nerves are strung up tight-tight.

I make an unhappy discovery! The oats I bought in Brazil are now rotten with weevils! Not that this makes them uneatable, but now I have to spend a lot of time picking out the little nasties. I wonder how many I ate before I noticed!

On 1st October we are 550 miles from Falmouth. Working hard to scrape a few miles each day in the right direction in ever-changing winds and choppy seas, but we are making it!

Then – a gale from the North, which blows us 75 miles to the S.E. before I realise what's happening, followed by another cruel Nor'easter, and on the 4th of October, revittys ottrefuiRecife, we are still 500 miles from home! What a struggle, but there is no way out, no getting off. We must plod on and we must make to the North. At 45 52N. and 15 40W, we are far too much to the East and in real danger of being embayed in the Bay of Biscay.

I treat myself to a "500mile supper" of Spam, Baked beans and macaroni – some treat, but it's better than some meals of late.

Journal: "Diary of the latest storm," Tuesday 6th October, 1930, wind West F.7. Drop big white jib for coffee break. 2030 set wee brown jib. To bed till 2330. Wednesday 7th, 0100 wind W.8, reef main to the triangle up till 0400. 0630, wind W.9, drop wee jib. 0930, wind W.10 - 11, drop and lash the triangle, hold tight. Terrific squalls, air filled with foam and spray. 1045, got a Mer. Alt sunsight, with difficultly!

Stayed below until 2300, awoke from snoozes to find she had gybed to Starboard tack and was heading South. Up top and gybe her back. I have to use my body as a "Storm Jib" in the pulpit to get her round. Fantastic seas in the moonlight. Wind N.W. F.10.

Thursday the 8th 0630. Up top to see if there's any chance of setting a little sail – no chance, wind still N.W. 8, and up to 10 in the squalls, which might blow my spindly jury rig clean away.

We make a lot of leeway in these storms, but there's little I can do with too much wind to show any sail to. We are at 47 N., and nearly 300 miles West of Brest, which I am very glad about.

At 0830 I start Polly Perkins, the faithful engine. I have a hell of a job to get her going. The batteries are way down and of no use except for the heater plug. I have to start her by hand – and foot. I tie a line through little blocks to my left ankle, start turning the heavy engine, and when I think I have enough revs, I shout "now", and kick my ankle away. Sometimes she starts first time, more often not, and I have to go through the procedure again. An exhausting business in the wind rolling, but I must keep the batteries up a bit for the radio and the 10 watt bow light.

By lunchtime I can fly some sail, and do, and get a dubious sunsight with the sun dodging in the clouds, a black horizon, Roamer rolling like a bucket, and the odd wave breaking over me and Sally Sextant. What a life!!

The wind goes down for 12 hours, but so does the barometer, and by midday on Friday we had another gale from the N.W. and are shut down again. Fearful of the leeway we are making, I made up a sea anchor out of my big 18mm anchor ropes, floats, and fenders to try to stop us drifting to the S.E.

I have yet another problem! My "Navigation" watch has chosen this moment to run out of batteries, and shows me a blank face. I have to use the other time-piece I have with a second hand, which is a bulkhead-mounted clock, and make adjustments to time signals.

The storm blows hard and waves drop on us from a great height. Quite a lot of water gets in through the tarpaulin over the smashed view-dome, I must try to improve it.

At 1700 I'm thinking gloomy thoughts again. Foul weather, too many ships about, and only 300 miles from Falmouth. Journal: "I feel like the crew of H.M.S. Saltash in "The Cruel Sea", thinking how silly it would be to get killed in the last few days of the war." Nothing I can do though except to put my little light on, it's too dangerous for me to be out there looking, and the nights are 11 hours long now.

But – up there I do have to go. I see the lights of four ships, and I just have to go out, with full Cape Horn oilskins and safety harness on, big flashlight hanging round the neck, pockets full of white flares; trying to work out which ship is the most danger to us, in poor visibility, Force 10 to 11 wind, and huge breaking seas!

We survive the night though, and next day she blows unceasingly, a screaming, roaring storm from the N.W., pushing us ever to the East, towards France, towards the Bay!

I can now pick up the B.B.C.'s Shipping Forecast, but to get it I have to rig up a copper wire aerial on one of the lazy jacks and hoist it as high as possible, making sure it doesn't touch any metal anywhere. The latest forecast tells me about N.W. gales in area Sole, which is just where I'm heading. Will these storms never let up? I've never known such a constant stream of them, every other day a F. 8 to 10 or more. I'm very tired, morale and strength are low.

I'm living on porridge, coffee, biscuits and marmalade for a few days as food stocks are low. I have "meals" for another 10 days, but even though I'm only 300 miles from home, I can't count on making 30 miles per day – ridiculous!!

During Wednesday forenoon, the 14th of October I meet a new menace, fishing boats... I was afeared I would, as I approached the edge of the Continental Shelf, but my heart falls when I see one in the mist and rolling seas. "Rain, cold, vile rolling storms, ships and now fishing boats – what a terrible life!"

But I soon recover. "I have 1. Collected rain to fill all bottles, 2. done the washing-up as last, in rainwater, 3. dumped the thunder-bucket. I scoffed a large pot of porridge and muesli mix, drank more coffee, with biscuits and syrup. I have Handel on the cassette player, the rain has stopped, clear weather lies to the West, and we WILL make Falmouth!!" Later, "Hundreds of seabirds wheel around us, or sit on the water in a chattering social gathering. A huge swell rolls in from the West. I have the deck hatches open - for the first time in two weeks."

During the night of the 14th/15th, the barometer, never very high of late, starts to drop alarmingly. 990 at midnight, 985 at 0300, 980 at 6! A very unwelcome and hard to understand wind come in from the Northeast. By 1200 on the 15th the barom has fallen to 974, at 1615 972, and blowing a gale from the N.N.E. with heavy and very cold rain. Something very nasty is a-brewing, and, after 111 days at sea, I can feel it in the groaning of the ocean swell.

At 1615 I advance the clocks 2 hours to G.M.T., then stream the sea anchor assembly of ropes, floats and fenders. We have a Northerly gale 8. I feel sick, probably more depressed than ever before. I have a new feeling too, one I don't recall except maybe for the brief periods of terror at Inaccessible Island, and the night before Cape Horn. I'm frightened, frightened of another storm, frightened of the night before me. I feel fear, and it's not a nice feeling.

At 2000 I pop up into the viewdome. Agh! There's a bright light to Port, white and red on its mast, a fishing boat! The fear floods through me. Into foul weather gear and up top quick-quick with the flashlight and flares into a Force 9 gale, with heavy rain. The weather is a small problem! All around me is the Sole Bank fishing fleet! I count 12 sets of lights! Bloody hell, what horrors are next? But action is required, got to get away from them, they'll never see my little 10 watt light bulb in this weather, in amongst all their working lights. So – in with the sea anchor, I feel weak and sick with fear, it's all going on too long, how much more can I take?

I stow the sea anchor gear and hoist the brown jib, though it's too windy really. But I must get away from these huge trawlers, who will sink me for sure on a night like this, without ever knowing. There is a black hole in the lights, to the S.W., down-wind, and I head for it, rain and waves pouring over us. We are making about 2 knots with the wind and sea behind us. 2 knots, to the S.W., the opposite direction to where I long to be heading, but – priorities – if I don't get out of here, I'll never see land again!

I make to the S.W. and get away from most of the fishermen, but one, about a ¼ of a mile to Port, seems to come with me and I have a difficult job to get clear of him. Damn! What's that? Flashing lights in the water ahead, it's a marker buoy, and we scrape past it, I can see floats and ropes swirling all round it.

We continue away and <u>do</u> escape from the trawlers. I drop the jib and manage half an hour below for coffee and to put on another pair of thermal trousers and socks, it's bitter cold up top. The barometer sits menacingly at 972, the lowest I can recall seeing it. After a while, the wind backs to the N.W., and, no matter how stormy, I don't want to go to the S.W. a minute longer than I have to. So, under bare poles, I gybe her and work my way round to the South of the fleet, keeping the nearest of them half a mile away, and on my beam. In this way I get South of them all and, the wind continuing to back, start to head N.E. She still blows a gale, but the rain has stopped and the sky is clearing. The sea-state is terrible though, and we are thrown around like a cork, laying hard over, then falling back on the windward bilge with a thump.

The wind continues to back, however, and we head North, back towards the trawler fleet! Damn!! I tire of the battle, it being 0100 by now, gybe her to Starboard tack, head South with the fleet on my stern, and creep away slowly from them. I go below, and manage 3 hours sleep till 0530. The Radio 3 weather forecast at 0555 tells of the Low which tracked across England during the night, with 100 mph winds, floods, roofs blown off. Trees uprooted. At 0610 I'm up top gibing to Port tack, and we head off to the N.E. under a panel of main.

During Friday the wind continues strong from West, then S.W., with severe squalls. We run variously North, or East, as the gybe takes us, the wind on our tail. In the evening the weather clears, but still the wind blows and blows. I open the last pot of jam, a Fig, and very sweet, but delicious. I promise myself a big pot of my favourite blackcurrant jam, with wholemeal bread, soon. Next week?? I hardly dare hope, it seems quite impossible that we'll ever make port, but we'd better, we're running out of <u>everything</u>!

Saturday the 17th of October. 1200 position 48 45 N., 8 35 W. Falmouth = 150 miles. Day 113. 1000. During the night we doodled slowly down the wind, under only the wee jib, sometimes on North, sometimes on East. No excitements I'm glad to say, the wind strong but steady, first from the S.W. then backing more to the South. I steered her from 0200 to 0430, towards, then past, a fishing boat, and left her for an hour's snooze. I set the alarm for the Radio 3 forecast, got up for it, and got – Cricket!!

Bloody cricket, on the only frequency I can pick up – Cricket!! I can't get Radio 4 without stringing the aerial around the rigging, (and then maybe not) and it's too rough to do that. What a life!! We plod on, the wind has gone South and back up to F. 7 - 8, sea rough. We roll abominably.

I have yet another worry. Something I've never had before, pain and inflammation in the navel!! Probably just general run-downedness and lack of a decent diet and washing. I give the offending area a good wash, and eat the last 3 Vitamin C pills.

1200, Big News!!! Visited by an R.A.F. Nimrod aircraft, their long-range reconnaissance plane. Sitting below, I hear a thunderous roar, rush up top to see the enormous aircraft zooming away. I grab the radio, and, as he banks round to make another pass, I make contact.

"Nimrod Aircraft, this is yacht Roamer over,"

"Hello Roamer, we've been looking for you, are you O.K. over?"

"Hello Nimrod yes I'm fine thank you, a little weary, but O.K. over." The conversation continues with these good chaps asking if I need any help, which I am glad to be able to say I don't need. I give them an E.T.A. for John Owen of the Western Morning News, of Tuesday or Wednesday, and they fly off to the N.E.

I hoist the triangle for progress, but soon after the wind gets up to F.9 again and I have to drop all sail. This weather is extreme.

Journal: 1745. "Yet again I cower below at the onset of night. The wind roars overhead, the ship lays over wildly, waves beat on and over us. How long can this go on? I am utterly weary of storms, storms, storms. Day after day, it all seems so unfair to get such weather at the end of my "Grand Voyage." It's so dangerous out here in a storm, with ships and fishing boats, and soon, land will be close."

Life seems so petty too. Here I am in the middle of yet another F. 10 storm, but I can't pick up Radio 4 to get forecasts. Radio 3 has cricket at the 5 minute forecast, there are hundreds of stations I can pick up, but the two I want I can't have! The cooker packed up on me this evening after cooking yet another fish/veg/rice stew, I'll leave it till tomorrow to fix. I'm out of muesli till I deweevil the last packet. I have two cans of "meals" left, a Feijado, and a veg curry, a can of spinach, one of runner beans, one of baked beans. It's lucky for me I bought extra oats, syrup and above all, lots of coffee, which keeps me going.

Life is so physically wearing too, my body is strained by the pressures of laying over, the normal bumps and bangs of hitting parts of the ship as she leaps about. My kidneys ache, my head aches, my legs feel weak, my hands and fingers sore. Rest is so close and yet so far.

Over the weekend we roll in a generally N.E. direction, and on Monday the 19th are through the 100 mile barrier! <u>Only 95 miles to Falmouth.</u> I chance my luck with Murphy's Law, and, during a fairly calm period, rig the anchor chain for instant use. I also rig the big Fisherman anchor onto the long anchor ropes. Being blown onto, or just drifting onto shore, is a real problem.

Tuesday 20th October. Day 116. No sun, no positioned worked. 1130. Journal: "Well, reference the last entry, I certainly did invoke the full force of Murphy's Law. I am reduced to writing a few words again, the painful facts, no emotions. Here I go.

Last evening was a hopeless case of light variable breezes, torrential rain, no progress. Collected 5 litres of water. We were becalmed all night and I lost count of the ships around us. We must have gone North close to the Bishop Rock shipping lane. Two ships came close enough to be very scary. I was up till 0200, and only felt able to turn in when I rigged the Tilley lamp on the jib halyard, (with all sail down) as well as showing the bow light. Since morning things have worsened a lot. Couldn't get any proper shipping forecasts but Radio Ulster weather says pressure is becoming high to the N. and E. of the U.K., which is bad news for me. We have a F.6 Easterly now with a cold wind and I am hove-to on it.

So - the situation is desperate, until this East wind goes away, we are stuck, with very little food left, and only about 80 miles from the Lizard, 30 miles from the Scillies. What can I say??"

On Thursday, only 52 miles from the Lizard, the Easterly having fairly quickly changed into a short sharp N.W. GALE, which gave us a nasty time, but a few more miles on the way. The Nimrod comes to see us again, with information on the weather, contact with the Lizard Coastguards.

It's all happening, all I've got to do is get there.

More good news in the afternoon. Lying becalmed, (this weather!!) I see a fishing boat working fairly close. I call him on the V.H.F. with a view to exchange cigarettes for food – no reply. He works closer, I wave my arms in a distress signal, and he comes over to me. He is the William

Sailor Bob limps home

THE family of round-the-world yachtsman Bob Burns have gathered in Cornwall to await his arrival.

His crippled yacht Romer has been sighted by an RAF plane 30 miles south-west of St Mary's in the Isles of Scilly.

Bob waved and radioed: "I am fit and well but it's lumpy down here".

He reported that his boat, which lost its mast in a storm, was heavily fouled by barnacles.

He is travelling at less than two knots but is expected to arrive in Falmouth tomorrow afternoon.

His brother, Terry, is in Falmouth with 16 other members of the family.

Weather

He said today: "Bob may have been thrown about a bit during the bad weather but we knew he would survive because it is a very strong boat. It would take a couple of torpedoes to sink it.

"Sometimes we haven't heard from him for weeks on end. It is a fantastic feeling to think that now, after all this time, he is almost in our back garden. We are all very proud of him."

The girl Bob hopes to marry drove into Falmouth from her Lymington, Hampshire, home hoping for a weekend reunion.

But Barbara Holder, a Devon farmer's daughter, says that the wedding plans might be delayed so that they can get to know each other again.

And the RAF Nimrod told Bob: "Your girl's waiting for you".

The Mayor of Falmouth, Major Bill Smith, will give Bob a civic welcome when he steps ashore.

Evening Argus 22nd October 1987

Sampson Stevenson, one of Stevenson's boats out of Newlyn, by Penzance. A big, burly man on the foredeck asks what the problem is, I tell him. He calls back to his Skipper in the wheelhouse, then returns to the foredeck.

"How long you been at sea?", comes the question in a Cornish drawl.

"118 days," is my reply. He blinks at this, calls back to the Skipper again, and after that, they are wonderful people, and give me two big sacks full of wet fish, bread, baked beans and all manner of wonderful things. I have difficultly in persuading them to take the cigarettes. I hate to think what their reply would have been if I'd said only a few days out, not 118! Very likely an ear-blistering. Fishermen don't usually like "yachties," and I don't blame them, but for anyone in real need, they will always help. Cheers to the Fishermen of England.

I have an initial stuff of beans, bread and butter, milk (real fresh milk!!), and apples and almost make myself sick! Later I give myself a good clean up, wash and shave, clean the ship and rig an ensign on a broom handle, for surely I'll be in soon now, won't I?

It's a busy day. Nimrod visits again later, with more news. I listen on V.H.F. Ch 16 and hear messages. Peter de Savary, the millionaire yachtsman, has bought Falmouth docks and has offered a tug to tow me in from the Lizard area! All the arrangements are going well, all I have to do is get there, I have a breeze – from the East! And it's cold, too.

After all the excitement of Thursday, I suffer the agonies of anti-climax all over the weekend as I am baulked by light Easterly winds and cannot make as much as an inch towards where I desperately long to be. Worse, everyone seems to have lost interest in me, no-one flies over me, I keep the V.H.F. on, but on-one calls me. I write, "No contact, no interest, how can they just leave me out here??"

By 1600 on Monday the 26th I am in a right old state. I think we have wriggled on wind and tide to within 35 miles of the Lizard. "I'm in agonies of suspense that something nasty is going to happen now that we are closer than ever! Light wind, heaving choppy sea, no speed. Man, I'm dying out here, and nobody ashore cares a damn. Why doesn't someone come and find me??"

Tuesday the 27th of October, 0830. "This ridiculous agony drags on yet!! Last evening the wind went to N.E. and though I actually had the Lizard light in view, we were pushed N.W. Visibility worsened, and a during a night in which I never got a wink of sleep, ten or more ships trundled past me. Two had to be driven away by the big flashlight. The

Lizard light finally faded in the rain at 0400. Now, we are stopped with a Northerly breeze, awaiting a promised N.W. F.5 I'm also awaiting the promised tow, but there's no sign of it. The Fishery Protection plane flew over at 1630 yesterday, but though I made a distress signal with my arms, nothing came of it. If anyone comes near me today I shall fire a red flare at them. I'm dying out here! I've eaten all the food the fishermen gave me, never believing that I could possibly be out here after the weekend, so now I have hardly any food again, little water, little diesel, no paraffin, the radio is U/S I think, and the weather determined to stop me getting in. Must I await a storm and get embayed in Mount's Bay or something before they'll come for me?

I've just had breakfast, two boiled potatoes and a few beans, delicious, I don't think! I reckon I'm between 5 and ten miles S.S.W. of the Lizard. So close again, yet so far.

A little later, a coaster appears out of the mist. I try the radio, and, wonders it works! The good Captain of it gives me a position of 8 miles 5.W. of the Lizard. The N.W. wind comes in and we head off N.E. The wind brings rain, which isn't so good. As we start moving in the rising wind, a warship appears on the Starboard bow. Right, flares, my big chance to contact the Coastguards and fix up the promised tow. But – damn and blast yet again!! No sooner does the warship appear than the wind whips up quickly to F.7 and I have my hands full handling Roamer. A big tanker is coming down on me from astern. Damn again, I have to let the frigate pass 1½ miles to Starboard, he's heading West. The wind is very fresh now, a good wind to blow me past the Lizard, even if not into Falmouth. We press on. Wow! The frigate has turned and is now running East, out on my Starboard beam. Has he been sent to keep an eye on me? I try the radio but can't make contact with him. I've had enough of this game – flares, first a white one to attract his attention. I hear him calling me, but he can't hear me. I force myself to let off a red flare, the first time I have ever done it.

The Royal Navy springs into action. I see his bow lift as he increases speed and turns Port towards me. "Tanker on my Port bow, keep clear of me and the small yacht," the tanker is told. The frigate, H.M.S. Manchester, I can now see, sits on my weather quarter, protecting me from the seas and the tanker. Hoorah for the Royal Navy! Now only 400 yards away, I am able to speak with him on the radio, and advise him of the situation. He quickly hooks up a communication system between me and Falmouth

Coastguards and we arrange the promised tow. A tug will be coming out right away. Phew! What a relief, are all my troubles over? It looks like it. The Manchester's seaboat brings over a "food parcel" filled with good things, hot scones, scotch eggs, a whole dish of cottage pie. Wow, it's good to be alive!!

We continue running on this lively N.W. wind towards the Lizard which is now clearly visible out on the Port bow. Lifeboat 47 - 012 is on passage between Penzance and Falmouth, he diverts and stands by me. I have too much sail up and Roamer moves faster than she has for many a month, but I don't care. With a frigate one side, and a lifeboat on the other, this is a great time to pull the rig down!! I feel great, I've made it, surely nothing can go wrong now?

I'm told the tug has left Falmouth and will be with me at 1600. The Manchester closes, and her good Captain sends over "survival rations" a bottle of whisky and a ship's plaque. Manchester then departs, taking warm thanks from me.

The tug appears to the North, and I stow the jib, and reef the main to the triangle. The lifeboat helps me to communicate with the tug St. Eval, and I prepare to take a 6" rope from him. The seas are quite rough now and the tug skipper handles his ship wonderfully to get his stern close to my bow. A heaving line is passed and then I pull over the 6" rope. Wow! I'd expected a 6" circumference rope, but this is 6" diameter!! A huge piece of towing line, but fortunately Roamer's towing bollard can handle it. We secure the line, I give the tug thumbs up, and dash back to the wheel. Powerful beasts are tugs, and the St. Eval is no exception.

We take off at a great speed probably only about 8 knots, but to me, it's like being in a speedboat, after a while I trust Roamer to steer herself in the calmer waters under the lee of the Lizard peninsula, and go below to the warmth of the cabin, and take a few tots out of the Manchester's very welcome gift. The whisky feels good in my stomach, and I soon feel warm all through.

North of the Manacles buoy, the N.W. wind strengthens, and lots of cold spray flies over my sturdy ship, but the waves get smaller and smaller as we approach the harbour in the cold darkness.

I'm not cold though. I'm feeling good, and wander round my good ship tidying up as best I can, and preparing ropes and fenders for the magic moment when we will be in harbour. Near the harbour entrance, St. Eval slows down, and out of the dark comes a big speedboat. It draws alongside and I am amazed to see, in the bright lights, a T.V. crew filming my magic moment. My eyes become accustomed to the glare of the lights.

The boats draw apart, for the St. Eval wants me alongside her. I go off to help with this operation, and the tug slowly manoeuvres into the docks.

Greeted by the Mayor of Falmouth, Cllr. Herbert Smith

With Roamer secured Port side to the tug, another, smaller boat appears on the Starboard side, it's "Schubert's Eighth" containing Tony Warren, the Falmouth artist, proffering large tots of whisky across the gap between us!

The St. Eval berths Port side to, and we're there. Have to clear Customs of course, but it's a joke. Then it's totter on shaky legs up the long gangway into flashing lights, and bright T.V. cameras. With several good tots of Scotch in me, I parry all the questions, happy as can be. The formalities are soon over though, the crowds drift away.

Terry and Mum had to go back to Brighton while I was stuck off the Lizard over the weekend, but they'll be back soon. We are off to John Owen's house for the night.

I'm a bit dubious about this – how can I leave Roamer?

I walk around her quietly, talking to her as I have done so much over the last two years. She won't mind me leaving her for the night. She will be resting too. I give her a last pat, and walk ashore.

Afterword

Random thoughts on Roamer, Rig, Route, and Routine.

As what she was designed to be, a sturdy small ship to sail round the world with one person aboard, Roamer was a complete success, and I have not one complaint about her.

This is not to say that I didn't learn a lot from the experience, and, since the dismasting at Stanley necessitates a new rig, I shall take the opportunity to improve the sailing rig. (See Appendix, Roamer Mk. II.) Our progress just North of the Equator, and then down to about 25 degrees South, was very poor due to Roamer's hopeless performance "on the wind" in choppy seas. Also, in any wind under Force 6, she was under canvassed. I hope to remedy both these faults.

After the "Magic Roundabout" I made the tactical mistake of sticking to "Ocean Passages" instructions to head S.W., even when the wind went to the West of South. I should have gone onto the tack which gave me most Southing.

The attempted visit to Tristan cost us a week, (and almost my life!), but I regret it not. After Tristan I should have gone further South, into the Forties in search of more wind, but was nervous of the Southern Ocean in early Spring.

On the Southern Ocean legs, she performed much better in the stronger winds, and but for the succession of Highs and East winds between Cape Town and Hobart, would have made better time. Going downwind was a problem, and I must admit I haven't solved it yet, unless it is to steer her. Tacking downwind was my solution on the voyage, but it certainly adds to the distance. I believe that the Self-steering wasn't strong enough, as it was installed, that is, with only the trim-tab steering her, with quartering or stern winds.

The Junk Rig lends itself very well to balancing the ship, and aiding the Self-steering, by reefing one or other of the sails. She was always at her best, and would make 6 knots plus, with a F. 5-6 beam wind, but we had precious few of those, until the last two legs when, unfortunately, we didn't have the masts and sails to take advantage of them.

The Junk Rig, reefing system, and the sails themselves, were excellent, apart from the following remarks. Peter Lucas and I had the sails strengthened at each clew above each batten, but we should have done the same at each "tack" as well. The battens, in most cases, chafed through their pockets at the leach, giving me a lot of bother. The battens themselves were too heavy and not strong enough. The usual reason for reefing was for fear of breaking a batten, never for fear about the masts. The masts were wonderful, as was the theory, in that, as I reef down, so the strain on the masts comes down to where they are thicker and stronger. The reefing system was nigh perfect, being able to control the sails from the cockpit was a real safety factor and work saver. True, I found it necessary to go to the sails and put lashings on, after reefing, but this could be done after the sail area had been reduced, and thus the main priority achieved, in two minutes or less. The "Top Triangle" Storm sails were wonderful, a 100% success.

The Ghosters were a waste of money. In light airs of F.2, which they were designed for, they wouldn't move Roamer. I think I'll make kites out of them now! And I don't mean Spinnakers!

The Jury Rig did marvellously, considering the small amount of sail I was able to fly, and was surprisingly well balanced. It was the 120 sq ft. White Jib which "got us home", the Junk Main doing not much more than balancing the Jib. (See Appendix, Jury Rig.)

Going back to the original rig, I found chafe much more of a problem than I had expected. This came from the Lazy Jack system, and the Mast Lift. Early in the voyage I had thought myself aware of the problem, and indeed check around for wear on the stitching, but it took me a surprisingly long time to realise that the lazy jacks were rubbing away as much as they were. Only much work with palm and needle made me pay more attention to the problem. The solution was to tie the "lee" lazy jacks out to the guardrails, clear of the sails altogether, which solved the chafe problem but gave me another when it came to doing any hurry-hurry reefing jobs!

If I forgot to re-rig the lazy jacks, I would find the sails falling to the deck as I lowered the halyard.

The centre cockpit, viewdome, and inside steering system, were all marvellous safety factors, especially in the stormy times in the Southern Ocean. Other good safety ideas were the 30" high guardrails stanchions, and ½" ropes as guardrails, the strong grabrails, especially the two high ones on the forward doghouse, and the array of guardrails around the transom, which were essential for working on the Self-steering, L.V.M., OR Main Sheets. The steel steps on the stern were very useful, not forgetting the two on the rudder, below water level.

I did very little anchoring, but found the 60lb. C.Q.R., 3/8" chain, and the system, quite satisfactory. I carried a 25lb. Danforth as a kedge, and a 120lb Fisherman for kelp or thick seaweed. (I've never used that big Fisherman, but it's nice to have it aboard.) The "antique" anchor winch worked splendidly, particularly as a "Jury Mast Lifting Winch", and as the Jib Halyard winch, on the last two legs.

Down below, starting forward, the Workshop and bench were very useful, the washplace fine, the "Bucket and Chucket" toilet system no problem.

My sea berth was very comfortable, except on the Starboard tack, when I sometimes had to chock myself in with a windvane. Many times I wished I had a Port sea berth! The Cosy Chair on the Port side was very welcome at those times, but I seldom slept in it. I used it mostly for resting and reading.

The Galley was good, and I was able to cook whatever the weather, albeit somewhat acrobatically at times! The cooker itself performed well, I changed burners but once in the 3 years that I lived aboard continuously. A disappointment though, was that the enamelled top lost its enamel, and rusted away to a surprising degree, and if I had wanted to use the interior as a heater, or warming oven, would have had my food covered in rust particles. The pump on the cooker's pressure tank gave me a lot of hassle, the washer just refusing to "pump". I'll carry a complete spare pump next time.

The Chart Table, Wendy House, lockers and saloon layout in general was just fine. A big problem in the saloon though, was the water tanks. I'm absolutely sure I asked Les Savage for baffles in the tanks, but I never got any, and suffered sadly from their booming and gurgling. As it was, they went rusty, and gave me some problems. Hull tanks are not a good idea, and I shall not use them as water tanks again. Maybe as Dry Storage though?

The Aft Cabin worked out just fine too, mainly as a Store Room, for I never slept in there. A cover or curtain on the "Wardrobe" would have saved my shirts and coats from a dousing when we were knocked over in the Indian Ocean. The pigeon hole lockers and ice-cream box system was very good.

The faithful Perkins D3.152 engine saved my life at least three times, and saved Roamer at Stanley. My original idea of having a "big strong engine to help me out" was certainly a good one. The Starter Motor played me up quite a lot, appearing to have a "blind spot" on it, but that's electrics for you. "Never trust electrics!" I started it by hand most times, partly for the exercise, partly to save the battery, but mostly so that I knew I could. The Fuel tanks, with baffles, were quiet, the Fuel System, where I pumped up fuel to a header tank, was a great success.

Miscellaneous Equipment Notes.
Yaesu FRG 7700. Radio Receiver. Very good, but its Memory, for storing frequencies, never operated satisfactorily.

Icom Hand Held Transceiver. Very Good. Except it failed after Stanley.

Lokata 5B R.D.F. Very Good.

Casio Watches Very Good.

Sestrel -Moore compass was very good in the main, but its card tended to go round in circles, bumping off its housing, in very rough conditions.

Concept compass. I maybe expected too much from this compass, it probably being only designed for Northern Hemisphere use. South of the Equator, it suffered from "dip", and was unusable by Cape Town. Its diaphragm leaked though, and that shouldn't have happened.

Clothing
I had two sets of Henri-Lloyd's Waterproofs. The "Ocean" suit was very good indeed, its insulation was excellent, and even when I was "submerged" during the pooping in the Indian Ocean, I never got any more wet than the cuffs of my shirt. The other suit, the "Coastal", was fine for more moderate conditions.

Damart's Thermolactyl thermal clothing cannot be praised too highly. I've used it for many years now, on my rigging job, and on the North Sea Rigs, and in the cold Southern Ocean, it was a blessing. The underwear, long johns and vests, were particularly warming, and I never took them off in the S.O. Their socks too, were very warming. I actually carried far too much thermal clothing, taking three sets of everything, but better too much than too little.

Various gloves were used, but I found Damart's and Mrs. Boons mittens more useful than gloves.

Seaboots. I started with four pairs. One "Paddy's" black heavy boots, which scuffed the paintwork and were soon stowed away. A green pair, which had such slippery soles I was sure they would kill me one day, so I stowed them too. That left me with two pairs of Damart "Derri-Boots", which had a warm lining and were excellent, at first. Then, after a little use, the inner lining pulled out, and was difficult to get back in properly, plus I found pieces of steel in the lining! In a bad mood one cold day, I tore out the complete lining, and found that a 100% improvement. I could wear seaboot stockings, and, if the boots got wet inside, a quick rub with a rag, and they were dry again. After this discovery, the boots made excellent seaboots!

Food

I stocked, ate, and restocked so many times that I can't recall all the food items I had aboard. Basically though, I liked to carry at least six months food, with a lot of it canned vegetables which brought their own water supply. On leaving a Port, I would have a week's supply of bread, butter, cheese, fruit etc, plus 10 kg each of potatoes and onions, an amount I found would last me about two months, if they kept that long. After the fresh food had gone, it was Fish stews, Meat stews and soups, biscuits, and jam, coffee. I ought to add that I am very easy to feed, being capable of eating just about anything at any time of day. So long as it's Hot, and there's a generous quantity.

As great a variety of food as possible should be aimed for. I like plenty of things to nibble at between meals as well, muesli, with nuts and raisins, toffees, barley sugars, Mars bars etc, are all very good for this.

Drink. I drink mostly coffee, hot, strong, and black, with honey or syrup as a sweetener, and brandy in it when appropriate. Tea doesn't do much for me at sea, but is nice ashore.

Alcohol. I liked to have a can of beer a day, and did, on the "short" Southern Ocean legs, and it was nice and cold, chilled in the bilges, close to the icy sea. As said, Brandy in the coffee was good in cold weather, and a Rum or Whisky "Hot Toddy" at lunchtime, otherwise I drank little spirits.

Medical

I am lucky in that I rarely get ill. I had that heavy cold and flu after Hobart, and the stomach trouble after Recife, but that was about all. I did get the occasional headache in very rough weather at times, but seldom. I carry few pills, my cure for all ills is Vitamin C and fresh air. I used two 200mg Vit C pills per day once the onions ran out, or if I got "Spotty", or felt run down. Six Brewers Yeast pills a day were also a booster if not feeling at my best. If teeth or gums became sore, a couple of Calcium pills, plus Halibut Liver Oil and/or Wheatgerm Oil pills as the mood took me. I carried three 2-week courses of wide spectrum Anti-biotics in case of food or blood poisoning, or bad cuts or gashes. I never used any of them. I had eye drops, eye wash, headache pills, indigestion pills, and Andrew Liver Salts.

I carried a general first-aid kit, a dental first-aid kit, and book to tell me all about it, "The Yachtsman's Doctor", by Richard Counter.

Lifesaving Equipment

Very little, Roamer was always my lifesaver, and a very few times would leaving her have done me any good? I carried a lifejacket, and two circular lifebuoys. No life raft was carried. I streamed two floating safety lines for most of the voyage.

Fuel, Paraffin, Meths

Diesel, capacity 150 Gallons, but I normally carried 50 to 60 gallons, which filled the lower keel tank only. On the last two Jury Rig legs I had 120 gallons aboard at the starts.

Paraffin, I usually carried about 10 gallons, and estimate consumption at about one gallon per month.

Meths. The cooker needs 10 c.c. per lighting, once or twice per day in the warmer climes, four or five times in the high latitudes.

Navigation Equipment and Systems

Many people seem fascinated as to how Singlehanders manage to do their Nav., practically, so I'll go into the matter in some detail here. As stated in the text of the book, I was ignorant of Celestial Navigation when I set out, and I'm no expert now, so this is no text-book, just how I did mine. I believe that Deep-sea navigation is a relativity simple affair, to the degree to which I did it anyway. I took one Sun sight in the forenoon, about two hours before local Noon, then got the Meridian Altitude, at "Noon", to cross the a.m. sight's Position Line. If all looked right, that was it, if unsure of anything, or if closing the land, I might take a second sight in the afternoon. I took a few Star Sights, and some of the Moon, more for the experience than the necessity, though the sight I took of Sirius, when close to Staten Island, may have saved me some hassle. All problems and queries were solved by Mary Blewitt's little green book".

I had several systems of actually taking the sights. In the early days, I was very conscientious, and, with a piece of paper secured to my left wrist with elastic bands, used to take five, or later, three sights, write them down, plus the time from a watch also on the left wrist, average them out, and plot the answer. Later though, and in the worst conditions, it was only one sight, but carefully taken, written in ball-point on the back of my hand.

In really wild conditions when it was impossible to write on anything, the time had to be chanted and remembered whilst making a hazardous trip, sextant in hand to the saloon, and written down there. I tried to avoid writing on my hand whenever possible though, for fear of dermatitis.

Originally I had two watches, both cheap, but very good Casio's, at £20 each. One was "Ship's Time", and was worn on the wrist, the other was G.M.T., and hung on the bulkhead over the chart table. I checked the watches against Radio Time Signals frequently and kept a record of their rate of change. After Recife, and the "Bandidos" stole one watch, I kept the remaining one on the Ship's Time, and just remembered how many hours behind Greenwich we were. I kept a chart of this item, also on the bulkhead, all the way round.

The Sextant was a plastic Davis Mk. 25, 'With Beam Converger", which means the full image of the Sun is available to sit on the horizon. This sextant was admirable, and did me a fine job. I had a spare, a cheap "Ebbco" , rather an inferior relation to the Davis, but it's nice to have a back up.

Nav.Books.
I used *A.P.* 3270, "Sight Reduction Tables for Air Navigation" Vols. 1, 2 & 3, in conjunction with "The Nautical Almanac", N.P. 314, and found the sights easy to work out, especially with a book of "Davis Worksheets for H.O. 249". (A.P. 3270), which takes the working of the sight through easy steps, with full instructions. The two books mentioned also make it easy to check the Azimuth of the Sun, to ascertain the Compass difference on True, a calculation I did every few days in the Southern Ocean when I

was "tearing" through lines of Longitude and Magnetic Variation difference. I actually never took much notice of Magnetic Variation as shown on the chart. I believe the Sestrel-Moore Compass Deviation changed quite a lot between Brighton and Cape Town, and I used the Sun's Azimuth, as described, to tell me the difference between (C) and (T).

Charts and Nav. Equipment
See separate Lists.

Faults and Failures.
Not many of these, I'm glad to say.
1. The G.R.P. Dinghy. A good idea in principle, but it became too cumbersome to be practical.
2. Compass Repeater. Devolved a high-pitched whistle which I couldn't stand, and eventually malfunctioned anyway.
3. Sestrel-Moore Compass Light. The thin flex snapped too often due to the rolling of the ship/gimballing of the compass. Luckily, I had ordered the compass "with Beta lighting" as well, which was quite sufficient. The 12V light was actually bad for night vision.
4. The Solar Cell "Solarvents" seized up whilst in South Africa because I had mounted them vertically and the high Sun never shone on the solar cells. I wasn't very impressed with them anyway, and they certainly aren't waterproof.
5. The Hull Water Tanks. As stated elsewhere, they rusted, and made much noise without baffles.

Appendix I – Chart List

All charts are Admiralty, except those marked Aus. or N.Z.

2675 English Channel.
536 Beachy Head to Dungeness.
1652 Selsey Bill to Beachy Head.
2050 Eastern Approaches to the Solent.
394 The Solent - Eastern part.
2219 Western Approaches to the Solent.
2040 The Solent - Western part.
2045 Outer Approaches to the Solent.
2611 Poole Harbour and Approaches.
2615 Bill of Portland to the Needles.
2255 Approaches to Portland and Weymouth.
2610 Bill of Portland to Anvil Point.
26 Torbay, Brixham, Torquay and Teignmouth Harbours.
3315 Berry Head to Bill of Portland.
1613 Eddystone Rocks to Berry Head.
1267 Falmouth to Plymouth.
32 Falmouth Harbour.
777 Land's End to Falmouth.
2565 St. Agnes Head to Dodman Point. Inc. The Isles of Scilly.
883 Isles of Scilly, St. Mary's and Principal Off-Islands.
2649 Western Approaches to the English Channel.
4103 English Channel to Gibraltar and The Azores.
4014 North Atlantic - Eastern Part.

4104 Lisbon to Freetown.

4020 South Atlantic - Western Portion.

4021 South Atlantic - Eastern Part.

1769 St. Helena. Tristan da Cunha, Bouvetoya & Gough Islands.

636 Table Bat to False Bay.

4070 Indian Ocean - Southern Part.

1033 Champion Bay to Cape Naturaliste. Inc. Swan River. (Perth) Aus,

114 Approaches to Rottnest Island. (Perth.)

4709 Australia - South Coast.

Aus. 794 S.E. Cape to Cape Pilar. (App. To Hobart.)

4601 Tasman Sea - New Zealand to S.E. Australia.

1695a Bass Strait - Eastern Portion. 1695b Bass Strait - Western Portion.

Aus. 423 Eddystone Point to Port Jackson. Aus. 201 Port Jackson - Sydney Harbour. Aus.202 Port Jackson - Sydney Harbour.

N.Z. 76 Western Approaches to the Foveaux Strait.

788 South Pacific - Western Sheet.

789 South Pacific - Eastern Sheet.

1373 S.E. PART OF Tierra Del Fuego. (Cape Horn).

2512 The Falkland Islands.

1614 Stanley Harbour and Approaches. 2550 Plans in East Falkland Island.

2536 Port William to Choiseul Sound.

The Long Way.

Two Against Cape Horn. - Hal Roth.

After 50,000 Miles - Hal Roth.

The Ultimate Challenge. - Barry Pickthall.

Round the World With Ridgway. - J. & M. - C. Ridgway.

Voyaging Under Sail. - Eric Hiscock.

Cruising Under Sail. - Eric Hiscock.

Come Aboard. - Eric Hiscock.

Single Handed Cruising and Sailing. - Frank Mulville.

The Self-Sufficient Sailor. - Lyn & Larry Pardey.

Survive the Savage Sea. - Dougal Robertson.

Survival at Sea. - Bernard Robin.

Heavy Weather Sailing. - K. Adlard Coles.

Ice Bird. - David Lewis.

Yachtsman's 8 - Language Dictionary. - Barbara Webb.

Boat Data Book. - Ian Nicolson.

Appendix II – Reading Books – "The Library"

Seven Pillars of Wisdom - T.E. Lawrence.
Slow Boats to China - Gavin Young.
Slow Boats Home - Gavin Young.
The Mystic Masseur/Miguel St./House for Mr.Biswas - V.S. Naipaul.
Mr. Stone and the Knights Companion /The Middle Passage - Naipaul.
The Old Patagonian Express - Paul Theroux.
The Great Railway Bazaar - Paul Theroux.
In Patagonia - Bruce Chatwin.
Erik The Red - Donald Ridler.
Schoonerman - Capt. Richard England.
Sailing Alone Around the World - Joshua Slocum.
The Pocket Oxford Dictionary
The Shipkiller - Justin Scott.
Adventures Under Sail - (Bill Tilman) - Libby Purves.
Tristan Da Cunha & The Roaring Fortties - A.B. Crawford.
God Is An Englishman - R.F. Delderfield.
For the Term of His Natural Life - Marcus Clarke.
Voyages - Capt. Cook.
A Voyage Round the World - Lord Anson.
Almayer's Folly/Tales of Unrest./Nostromo - Joseph Conrad.
Outcast of the Islands/Nigger of the Narcissus - Joseph Conrad.
Typoon/Falk./LordJim/The Shadow Line - Joseph Conrad.
Typee - Herman Melville.
The Sea-wolf - Jack London.
Voyage - Sterling Hayden.

Cruise of the Conrad - Alan Villiers.

Story Like the Wind/Flamingo Feather - Laurens Van Der Post.

The Hunter and the Whale - Laurens Van Der Post

The Riddle of the Sands - Erskine Childers.

Mutiny, Aboard the Bounty - R.M. Bowker.

Darwin and the Beagle - Alan Moorehead.

Trafalgar/Waterloo - David Howarth.

Six-volume "Life of Robert Burns" – James Barke.

Whisky Galore - Compton McKenzie.

The Sea for Breakfast - Lillian Beckwith.

The Cruel Sea/Three Corvettes/Master Mariner - N. Montsarrat.

Life and Death of St.Kilda - Tom Steel.

An Island to One's Own - Tom Neale.

Road to Elizabeth - John Ridgway.

Alone Against the Atlantic - Frank Page.

To Beat the Clippers - Alec Beilby.

The Sea Poems - John Masefield.

Appendix III – Miscellaneous

MUSIC
About 100 cassettes on board.
From Beatles to Bach to Brubeck, Mozart to Mendelssohn, Bagpipes to Baroque.
Favourites? - Handel, Mozart, Bach, Beethoven.
Beatles, Wings, Barbara Streisand.
John Williams, Julian Bream, Manas De Plata.

CAMERAS
Barbara's Cosina for slides.
My years-old Halina for prints.

TYPEWRITER
All the original manuscript for this book was hammered out on my Smith-Corona manual. It did a good job and survived many bangs and thumps. It had "Non-slip" feet which were a boon at sea. I used 4 ribbons.

Appendix IV – Suppliers of Equipment and Services

Design.	Alan Pape, Looe,Cornwall.
Construction	Oceancraft, Wadebridge, Cornwall.
Blasting & Painting	Cornwall Metal Treatments, Penwithick.
Fitting Out.	Mark Gamble Yachts, Ilminster, S'set.
Launching.	Brighton Marina Boatyard.
Sail Design.	Alan Boswell, Bosham, W. Sussex.
Sail Making.	W.G. Lucas, Old Portsmouth, Hants.
Sail Battens.	Norman Harper, Upper Quay, Fareharn.
Masts, Design & Constr.	Richard Mason, Cannon Rd, Bristol Docks
Jury Rig Spars.	David Hunt, Needlespar, Warsash.
Jury Rig Jib.	Jacknell's Sails, Wroxham, Norfolk.
Self Steering Equipment	Levanter Vane Gears, Colchester, Essex
Wind Generator.	L.V. Motors, Letchworth, Herts.
Paint.	Blake's Paints, Gosport, Hants.
Rope.	Jimmy Green Marine, Beer, Devon.
Insulation.	Aqua-Insulation, Fareham, Hants.
Plumbing	Acorn Fittings.
Zinc Anodes.	M.G. Duff.
Propellor, Stern Gear.	Teignbridge Engineering, Teignbridge
Bilge Pumps.	Henderson Mk. V./Jabsco.
Engine.	Perkins/Golden Arrow Marine, Newhaven
Rudder Hangings.	"Joe the Welder" Chard, Somerset.
Deck Hatches.	Canpa/Beaulieu Boat Jumble.
Decklight Prisms.	Davey & Co, London.
Deck Fittings.	Davey & Co, Beaulieu Boat Jumble.

Steering Equipment.	Whitlock Marine Steering.
Viewdome.	Goiot, France.
C.Q.R Anchor	Simpson-Lawrence, Glasgow.
Anchor Winch.	S-L/Aladdins Cave, Bursledon.
Anchor Chain.	Belsize Shipyard, Southampton.
Batteries.	Lucas/"B.K." of Plymouth.
Navigation Lights.	Aqua-Signal/Telesonic, London.
Radar Reflector.	Firdell Blipper 300.
Compass Swinging.	Roger Muir, Chandler's Ford, Hants.
Radio Receiver.	South Midlands Comms. Southampton.
Radio Transceiver.	Icom/Preston Electronics, Brighton Marina.
Lokata R.D.F.	LokatalPreston Electronics.
Compasses.	HenryBrowne./Munro-Sestrel-Barking.
Toilet.	Racan./Beaulieu Boat Jumble.
Echo-Sounder.	Seafarer 700./Telesonic, London.
Paraffin Cooker.	Taylor's 709/T. Foulkes, London.
Paraffin Lamps.	Tilley./ T. Foulkes, London.
Paraffin Lamps.	Fastnet./ T. Foulkes, London.
Thermal Clothing.	Damart, Bingley, Yorks.
Waterproofs.	Henri-Lloyd.
Nav. Watches.	Casio.
Sextant.	Davis Mk.25.
Cassette Player.	Saisho CX150.